C000078427

Making Sense
OF Proxy Wars

Related Titles from Potomac Books

Beating Goliath: Why Insurgencies Win
—Jeffrey Record

Asymmetrical Warfare: Today's Challenge to U.S. Military Power
—Roger W. Barnett

Chasing Ghosts: Unconventional Warfare in American History
—John J. Tierney Jr.

Also Edited by Michael A. Innes

Denial of Sanctuary: Understanding Terrorist Safe Havens (2007)

Bosnian Security after Dayton: New Perspectives (2006)

Making Sense
of Proxy Wars

States, Surrogates & the Use of Force

Edited by MICHAEL A. INNES

Foreword by WILLIAM C. BANKS

Potomac Books
Washington, D.C.

Chapter 2, "Missing Their Mark: The IRA's Proxy Bomb Campaign," by Mia Bloom and John Horgan, was originally published as an article with the same title in *Social Research* 75, no. 2 (Summer 2008): 579–614. Reprinted by permission.

A different version of chapter 6, "Multinational Corporations: Potential Proxies for Counterinsurgency?" by William Rosenau and Peter Chalk, was originally published as William Rosenau, Peter Chalk, Rennie McPherson, Austin Long, and Michelle Parker, *Corporations and Counterinsurgency*, OP-259 (Santa Monica, CA: Rand Corporation, 2009). Used by permission of the Rand Corporation.

Library of Congress Cataloging-in-Publication Data
Making sense of proxy wars : states, surrogates & the use of force / edited by Michael A. Innes ; foreword by William C. Banks.
    p. cm.
  Includes bibliographical references and index.
  ISBN 978-1-59797-230-7 (hardcover : alk. paper)
  ISBN 978-1-59797-586-5 (electronic)
    1. Terrorism—Case studies. 2. Counterinsurgency—Case studies. I. Innes, Michael A., 1969–
  HV6431.M3537 2012
  363.325—dc23

                                                              2012004496

Printed in the United States of America on acid-free paper that meets the American National Standards Institute Z39-48 Standard.

Potomac Books
22841 Quicksilver Drive
Dulles, Virginia 20166

First Edition

10 9 8 7 6 5 4 3 2 1

Contents

Transliteration Note

The chapters in this volume deal with culturally and historically diverse problems. After a decade of preoccupation with terrorism and insurgency of a certain kind, it is time to move beyond the alleged characteristics and dysfunctions of particular religious, ethnic, or other identity groups. The contemporary impetus for a book on armed proxies, of course, begins with the recent wars in Afghanistan, Iraq, Lebanon, and Somalia; its relevance is affirmed with the more recent revolutions across the Middle East and North Africa, in the world of media and state secrets, and in the ways human societies communicate and act. Such complexity, paradoxically, often begets in the writing of it inattention to cultural and linguistic detail, and any attempt at standardized transliteration from non-English-language sources is bound to disappoint and disatisfy. It is done here, relying where appropriate on the International Journal of Middle East Studies (IJMES) transliteration system, with all due respect for the richness of this book's subject.

Foreword

A persuasive argument may be made that the gravest threat facing nation-states today is not climate change, resource depletion, or catastrophic terrorist attacks but is instead an erosion of state sovereignty. Our world is vastly different from that facing the architects of the Treaty of Westphalia of 1648. The world that sovereign nation-states once dominated has been eclipsed by globalization and a resulting set of relationships between states and their citizens equivalent to that between a corporation and its consumers. To be sure, many good things have come from globalization: economic growth, greater sharing of consumer goods and more choices, digitization, and the spread of communications and other technologies at unprecedented rates. Yet the dominance of markets and private actors in global intercourse has made states ever more vulnerable to terrorist networks, international organized criminals, and surrogate armies, including proxies for sponsors ranging from other states to multinational corporations. As states reduce the size of their militaries, privatize an increasing array of security functions, and do little to reduce the vulnerability of their critical infrastructures to cyber and other forms of attack by private adversaries, they risk losing control. Governments may cede a growing swath of governing to a sordid range of non-state entities.

At the same time, the Western states that dominated the twentieth century increasingly find ways to attain their security objectives without putting their soldiers at risk—by outsourcing security to private security companies, by developing long-range and unpiloted weaponry, and by acquiescing in distant battles waged by proxies of uncertain allegiance that follow decidedly non-humanitarian tactics. The early twenty-first century's wars in Iraq and Afghanistan are illustrative of the new battlefields, where tribal militias turned back an al-Qaʻida-based insurgency in the Sunni Triangle; the Northern Alliance tribes of Uzbeks, Tajiks, and Hazaras drove the Taliban out of Afghanistan; and drone aircraft target insurgents and terrorists in Afghanistan and Pakistan, with no physical risk to those pilots operating the drones with joysticks in suburban Virginia. As the ongoing counterinsurgency operation in Afghanistan demonstrates, private forces are difficult to control, may have interests and allegiances at odds with the state, and engage in criminal activities and inhumane tactics that compromise the objectives of the states involved.

Unwittingly, even the most powerful states are seeing their influence wane and their control over previously secure domains diminish. The chapters in this incisive and important book, *Making Sense of Proxy Wars*, edited by Michael A. Innes, illustrate the wide-ranging parameters of the phenomenon of proxies. The authors show that our traditional categories of state sponsorship of terrorist activities, for example, are outmoded and fail to capture the fluid and more nuanced relationship between sovereign states and terrorists, insurgents, and other proxies. Indeed, proxies have matured in recent decades, and their relationships with states are now as often driven by hard bargains or ephemeral mercenary objectives as by traditional conceptions of sponsorship. These groups run the ideological and religious gamut, and many rely on drug dealing and other criminal enterprises to sustain their activities without direct state support.

Following the end of the Cold War, Western militaries downsized, and their hardened veterans found ready and often lucrative employment in a vast array of contract agencies and private security companies. As this book's contributing authors show, today's proxies serve a variety of masters, and they pursue a wide range of agendas. Many, such as peacekeeping and support operations conducted on behalf of international security organizations, surely have net positive impacts on humanity. Others, such as the private military and security companies (PMSCs), provide contract support to state militaries on the battlefield and in support environments. As has been often illustrated in recent years, however, contractors providing defensive security or support may deviate from their script and engage in offensive military operations. These proxies may also complicate humanitarian relief missions by creating an obstructionist barrier between those directly providing the aid and the people intended to receive it.

Evidence shows that some states and certain nongovernmental organizations and scholars have begun to awaken to the potential both for growing abuses by proxies in this arena and for the slippage of state control over the battlefield. The obvious control mechanism—state or international regulation—has been implemented to some degree, but with uncertain outcomes and tentative steps so far. Accountability of states for their proxies is, of course, of central importance to ensure sovereign control and to rein in excesses. Yet so much of the proxy work occurs in covert or at least invisible environments where attribution is hard to fix. Control devices include required adherence to international humanitarian law, human rights law, or other legal standards; contract terms that require parliamentary or legislative oversight and audits of proxy activities; and vetting mechanisms to review the backgrounds of the proxies' employees. For the most part, however, the PMSCs that operate transnationally escape effective domestic regulation—domestic laws generally do not reach across sovereign borders—and achieving consensus on effective international regulation has been and is likely to remain elusive. Simply too many competing agendas come into play.

Making Sense of Proxy Wars will enrich the corpus of thoughtful analysis and critique that should awaken the nations of the world to the importance of regulating proxies. Sadly, now, and at least in the near term, the grievous harm that proxies have inflicted on civilians in conflict zones will force a reckoning between states and proxies. The momentum for establishing better protections of human rights in conflict zones is growing, and the states and multinational and nongovernmental organizations that cooperate to reduce the human suffering in conflict will necessarily address the growing role and unprecedented discretion of proxy actors in these zones. Whether through better contracting arrangements, new forms of incentives, the creation of an accreditation scheme, or the involvement of international courts or arbiters, control over proxies may be the states' most vexing security challenge of the twenty-first century.

William C. Banks, *Board of Advisers Distinguished Professor, Syracuse University College of Law; director, Institute for National Security and Counterterrorism, Syracuse University; and professor of public administration, Maxwell School of Citizenship and Public Affairs, Syracuse University*

Preface

In the lead chapter to this book, historian Jeffrey M. Bale charges that the relationship between states and ostensible surrogates is "one of the most contentious and misunderstood issues surrounding modern terrorism." More, "Cold War–era themes"—typically, the substance of East-West rivalry—"were disseminated primarily for partisan political, if not explicitly propagandistic, purposes and often rested on incomplete, unverifiable, contaminated, spurious, or even manufactured evidence." Observations from Bale's in-depth review of the problem can readily be applied to the range of subjects covered in this book. Indeed, as he notes, misunderstanding has endured and migrated: "Similar sorts of themes have not only survived the end of the Cold War but also have either been updated and reprised or assumed new, politically convenient guises in today's post–Cold War, multipolar international environment." Subsequent chapters by Mia Bloom and John Horgan, Brian Glyn Williams, Antonio Giustozzi, Kevin A. O'Brien, and William Rosenau and Peter Chalk support Bale's assertions and illustrate a fuller—though by no means comprehensive—range of surrogate forces at work in modern conflict.

Since the end of the Cold War, the use and role of armed proxies have featured only sporadically as a serious subject of either academic or public inquiry. Those studying armed proxies have tended to fixate on terrorism. In that Cold War formulation, proxies were little more than third-party tools of statecraft without any agency, intent, or, indeed, interests visibly separable from those of a well-resourced state sponsor. The standard view that followed in the 1990s was that the end of the U.S.-Soviet rivalry also ended the resource pipeline that enabled terrorist and insurgent organizations, forcing them to look to criminal activity to survive and precipitating the growth of dangerously independent and well-resourced militants, mercenaries, and warlords. Since September 2001, however, events have conspired to force serious consideration of modern war's complications and, with them, the heterogeneous character and interests of proxy actors.

In a 2007 report of the Potomac Institute, a Washington, D.C., think tank, defense analyst Frank Hoffman wrote of the "hybrid threats" that "incorporate a full range of different modes of warfare including conventional capabilities, irregular tactics and formations, terrorist acts including indiscriminate violence and coercion, and criminal disorder." Significantly, Hoffman writes, hybrid wars "can be conducted by both states and a variety of non-state actors."[1] Attributing equal measures of agency, intent, and interest to both state and non-state actors is an important departure from earlier perspectives, which tended to characterize non-state actors as passively subordinate to the controlling authority of an outside party. But surrogacy and subordination, while related characteristics, are also clearly different issues. Surrogate forces, as the contributors to this volume illustrate, are more than passive players. They have their own interests and act to satisfy them. Moreover, they represent larger processes of substitution and intermediacy that need to be monitored and understood over the long term and in their many guises.

Contemporary problems, of course, include the legacies of the anti-Soviet jihad in Afghanistan; extended blowback from various long-term U.S. policies abroad; the growth of privatized military force and security; and a generally increased reliance on armed intermediaries of all kinds. From subcontracting national interests to attacking substitute targets (civilians) to establishing third-party interveners and umbrella alliances that offer surrogate sums greater than their constituent parts—all the potential degrees and displays of surrogacy are dizzying. Stretching our understanding of what constitutes surrogate forces is essential, given the complexification of conflict. Discussions of proxy warfare have traditionally been bogged down in conspiracy theories and scandals of one kind or another, a sorry state that has muddied already murky waters. A healthy disaggregation of the subject should and must reveal more of the state of international relations.

One argument, many years in the making now, suggests the growing capabilities and influence of non-state actors are clear indicators of the erosion of the Westphalian state. I would argue, instead, that a fundamental symbiosis between state and non-state actors underpins proxy warfare, and one need not be a critique of the other. Rather, understanding various forms of the sponsor-proxy relationship can provide a better understanding of their respective interests and of the role of intermediacy in international relations. Private military and security contractors, private corporations taking on roles formerly the exclusive purview of states, and local militias in Iraq and Afghanistan all serve forces that, in turn, act on behalf of both the host and intervening states. This vicarious experience has come to dominate how wars are being fought. It behooves us to understand more about the subject.

It is worth noting, too, that advances in modern military technologies have opened up the discussion to include the field of robotics, communications, and computing. This development is a qualitative departure from the state versus non-state debate. Strikingly, the use of remotely piloted drone aircraft for intelligence, surveillance, and reconnaissance and for targeted killings in Lebanon, Iraq, Afghanistan, and Pakistan has come to symbolize how current wars are conducted. Armed conflict is now, and has always been, a technologically mediated enterprise.[2] Machines can now act on our behalf but not autonomously. And in online environments, such as Second Life, participants' avatars—that is, graphic representations of their corporeal selves—carry out what appear to be virtual expressions of real militant sentiments.[3]

Such phenomena expand our understanding of violence and war, reduce direct human engagement on real fields of battle, and lower the direct risks to at least some of war's human participants. Indeed, the prospect of autonomous military robots dominating some future battle space (or autonomous digital avatars wreaking havoc on the Web) raises the moral stakes. It forces us to consider whether such capabilities will make it easier to go to war, whether the machines will be sufficiently sensitive to the nuances of hybrid environments where combatants and noncombatants freely intermingle, and whether the apparent one-sidedness of such resources, too, will generate adverse publicity for their users.[4]

While the implications and consequences of surrogate warfare are being served up in daily doses of current affairs, big-budget Hollywood movies such as *Surrogates*, *Gamer*, and director James Cameron's *Avatar* suggest a mainstream appetite for increasingly explicit themes of remote control behavior, biological substitution, and vicarious violence. It remains to be seen whether a cultural chord has been struck or whether it is a cathartic genre. What is clear is that, at some level, a fusion of virtual and tactile realities is fundamental to the vicarious experience of proxy warfare. In debating the role of armed proxies, determining whose interests are being served— the equally fundamental issue in trying to decipher their actions—will become increasingly difficult to answer as remote battlefield participation via drones and mechanoid substitutes for flesh and bone combat potentially disconnect us from the material costs and consequences of war.

Terrorists as State "Proxies"

Separating Fact from Fiction

JEFFREY M. BALE

[State-sponsored terrorism is] the most important component of the international terrorism problem.
    —R. JAMES WOOLSEY[1]

A terrorist organization requires more than money and guns . . . indispensable services [such as logistics and secure facilities] could only come from states.
    —MICHAEL A. LEDEEN[2]

Today, state sponsorship of terrorism continues unabated.
    —BRUCE HOFFMAN[3]

In today's world, the main threat to many states . . . no longer comes from other states. Instead, it comes from small [terrorist] groups and other organizations which are not states.
    —MARTIN VAN CREVELD[4]

Despite the Western view (and specifically the American view) that without state-sponsorship there will be no terrorism, reality proves otherwise.
    —GHADA HASHEM TALHAMI[5]

One of the most contentious and misunderstood issues surrounding modern terrorism is the extent to which diverse nation-states have been involved in using violence-prone extremist groups as surrogates or proxies. This theme was particularly salient during the Cold War, especially from the late 1970s to the mid-1980s, when governments on either side of the

Iron Curtain repeatedly accused each other of sponsoring or supporting terrorism and, indeed, often of secretly directing or controlling the actions of ostensibly autonomous terrorist groups. Despite the fact that these Cold War–era themes were disseminated primarily for partisan political, if not explicitly propagandistic, purposes and often rested on incomplete, unverifiable, contaminated, spurious, or even manufactured evidence, similar sorts of themes have not only survived the end of the Cold War but also have either been updated and reprised or assumed new, politically convenient guises in today's post–Cold War, multipolar international environment.

The purpose of this chapter is threefold: to subject current efforts to claim that "rogue" regimes are the primary drivers of contemporary Islamist terrorism—and thus to portray Islamist terrorists as being effectively the "proxies" of states—to critical scrutiny; to highlight some illustrative aspects of the actual history of state interactions with terrorist groups; and finally to develop a new categorization scheme for better identifying and distinguishing between different levels of state involvement in terrorism.[6] Although the aim herein is simply to present a scholarly analysis of what has always been a very fluid, dynamic, and complex pattern of state interaction with extremist groups, the conclusions have clear policy implications. After all, if Western democratic nations and their allies genuinely wish to lessen the present and future threat of jihadist (and other forms of) terrorism, they must understand the real sources of that threat and the actual objectives of the groups involved rather than uncritically adopting or cynically peddling a host of politically convenient but often spurious explanatory paradigms that are bound, if accepted at face value, to lead to the continued adoption of misguided and counterproductive policies.

Factors Promoting State-Centric Perspectives on Terrorism

Before turning to the main topic, however, it is necessary to discuss some factors that have led policymakers, scholars, and journalists to adopt a state-centric perspective regarding terrorism. Perhaps the most mundane but influential of these factors has to do with certain disciplinary biases associated with the field of political science, in particular those that have for decades underlain its international relations (IR) subfield. The primary premise in much of that subfield, especially its "realist" schools, is that the key actors in the international system are nation-states, a focus that was largely warranted in earlier decades given the overwhelming prominence, power, and influence of states in the international arena. Starting from such a state-centric premise, it is hardly surprising that so many IR scholars would emphasize the importance and preeminent role of nation-states, that they would focus on developing theoretical models and research method-ologies designed to explain the behavior of states in the "anarchic" interna-tional system, and that they would consequently overlook or at least minimize the role of non-state actors, including extremist groups and ter-rorist organizations.[7] There is no doubt that state-centric biases have per-sisted up to the present day, both within IR and in other subfields of political science, including comparative politics and even political theory. This is in spite of the fact that (1) the rise of the nation-state was a relatively recent phenomenon in historical terms, and (2) these long-standing disciplinary biases, theoretical preferences, and favored interpretations in the IR subfield have increasingly been subjected to criticism by both older and younger generations of scholars—especially those among the latter who are con-cerned, e.g., with the study of international organizations such as the United Nations, regional supra-state quasi-governments such as the European Union, nongovernmental lobbying organizations such as Amnesty Inter-national, or subnational groups of various types.

The practical result is that the overwhelming majority of scholars and aca-demicians—apart from those in the interdisciplinary field of terrorism studies, historians of revolutionary and counterrevolutionary groups, security specialists who focus on covert operations or counterinsurgency, and some "social move-ment" theorists in sociology—have never seriously studied extremist milieus or terrorist organizations.[8] For that very reason, they generally find it difficult, if not impossible, to understand the nature, ideologies, motivations, and objec-tives of such groups, to adopt appropriate methodologies for studying them, or to assess their importance and role in international affairs accurately, even within the narrower context of national or international security studies. Given these entrenched state-centric approaches and prejudices, it is hardly surprising that so many political scientists, and the pundits and policymakers they have influenced, have overemphasized the role that states have played in sponsoring terrorism.

A second, but far less excusable, factor that has contributed to the exaggeration of the role of states in fostering terrorism is the prevalence of political biases, whether pro-government or antiestablishment, in the terrorism field. Many terrorism specialists tend to be conservatives, Cold War liberals, or realists who have all too often adopted the self-serving perspectives of their own governments concerning the origin and nature of terrorism. As a result they have generally assumed a priori that Western governments are the innocent victims of terrorism and mistakenly portrayed modern terrorism as either an exclusively non-state, insurgent phenomenon or, paradoxically, as one that is really being "sponsored" behind the scenes by hostile enemy states, even when particular terrorist actions appear to have been carried out independently by small groups of political extremists.[9] Alas, these distorted and rather contradictory perspectives can themselves be traced in large part to the pernicious cumulative impact of disinformation and propaganda disseminated by what some left-leaning analysts have labeled as the "terrorism industry," a supposed coterie of co-opted terrorism experts and organizations that, consciously or not, have promoted the interests of hawkish factions in various Western intelligence agencies.[10] A good deal has already been written about some of these individuals and the network of research centers and funding institutions with which they have been associated, but the essential point is that they have collectively promoted one of the most politically influential interpretations of contemporary terrorism, one that depicts hostile enemy regimes—previously communist regimes but nowadays rogue Middle Eastern regimes—and their alleged non-state surrogates as the primary disseminators of terrorism.

In response to this one-sided and at times simplistic establishment literature on terrorism, an increasing number of left-wing or nonconformist academics and journalists have presented an alternative but no less Manichaean picture. In their view, right-wing governments and para-state apparatuses, with the backing of the United States and other Western nations, have been the main perpetrators of terrorism during the past sixty years.[11] Some have explicitly contrasted the "retail" terrorism carried out by insurgent left-wing groups with the "wholesale" terrorism carried out by authoritarian right-wing regimes.[12] Although they justifiably call attention to the prevalence and importance of right-wing state and non-state terrorism, topics that were systematically neglected by most terrorism specialists during the Cold War, these antiestablishment analysts have in effect only succeeded in reproducing and inverting mainstream biases by portraying Western democracies and allied third world regimes, rather than hostile states and non-state actors, as the principal terrorist villains.[13]

In other words, there has long been a perverse sort of symmetry observable in the extant literature on terrorism, a symmetry rooted in political partisanship. In pursuit of their respective political agendas, both the establishment and antiestablishment terrorism analysts have consistently displayed similar degrees of blindness, albeit in different eyes, by exaggerating the role of state sponsorship of terrorism. With rare exceptions, neither faction has made a serious effort to assess the evidence presented by the other. Their approach has been either to ignore one another entirely or to accuse each other of serving as conduits for intelligence-generated propaganda themes, which has unfortunately been true more often than one might think. They then stop, as if they had already proved their point, without actually examining and evaluating the substantive arguments or the evidence marshaled by their political opponents.[14] Given this polemical context, it is hardly surprising that diverse parties with vested interests have uncritically accepted or cynically exploited so many problematic and misleading claims concerning state-sponsored terrorism or the alleged role of terrorists as proxies.

The Mythology: Autonomous Terrorists as the Simple Agents of Nation-States

This toxic combination of built-in disciplinary biases within academia and blatant partisanship in the subfield of terrorism studies (which has often reflected, if not actually emanated from, state-sponsored propaganda or disinformation initiatives) has served only to obfuscate the fluid, dynamic, and highly complex nature of the interaction between nation-states and terrorist groups in recent decades. Indeed, it has resulted in the establishment of a mythology based on the notion that non-state terrorist groups are essentially the simple agents—or at least the proxies (i.e., confederates who can be relied upon to act on the sponsors' behalf) or surrogates (i.e., substitutes who can facilitate the maintenance of "plausible deniability")—of states. In creating this mythology, its proponents have failed to make a crucial analytical distinction between autonomous extremist groups with their own ideological and operational agendas that may decide, usually temporarily and often reluctantly, to collaborate with states, and pseudo-independent terrorist organizations that are secretly created and controlled by states and therefore tend to function as their genuine agents. It is patently obvious that these two types of relationships are fundamentally different, especially regarding the amount of de facto control that a state will likely be able to exercise over a non-state group. Yet the conspiratorial alarmists have often sought, for no valid reason, to deny this distinction. For example, Roberta Goren has written that "the sponsor state must have certain political or strategic goals in mind which may or may not be identical to those of the terrorist group. *In either case it can be said that the group is being used as a proxy*" (italics added).[15]

One of the most straightforward formulations of the theory of state sponsorship of terrorism is provided in Ray S. Cline and Yonah Alexander's book *Terrorism as State-Sponsored Covert Warfare*. Therein the term "terrorism" was defined—in contradistinction to the many official definitions that restrict the term to violence by non-state actors—as "the deliberate employment of violence or the threat of use of violence *by sovereign states or subnational groups encouraged or assisted by sovereign states* to attain strategic and political objectives by acts in violation of law" (italics added).[16] In short, for these authors and many others, terrorism was virtually inconceivable in the absence of state involvement on some level. However, a number of contrasting and competing versions of this mythology exist. Two of these have special salience because they seemed superficially plausible in a bipolar Cold War context in which both superpowers tended to view all localized conflicts as mere "fronts" in the larger global struggle against their main enemy.[17]

The most common mythology about terrorism during the Cold War era, at least in the West, is that the Soviet Komitet Gosudarstvennoy Bezopasnosti (KGB, Committee for State Security) and its client secret services in Eastern Europe and the third world were secretly and systematically directing the activities of ostensibly autonomous left-wing and ethno-nationalist terrorist groups, not only in Europe but also in various other parts of the world.[18] This theme was widely disseminated, especially during Ronald Reagan's administration, even though it assumed diverse forms ranging from alarmist and conspiratorial versions to relatively restrained and nuanced versions. Inveterate Cold Warriors who supported the rollback rather than the containment of communism, neoconservatives, and other foreign policy hawks who were ideologically predisposed to see the sinister hidden hand of the Soviet Union and its allies behind virtually every threatening development in the world, including international terrorism, promoted most of the overly simplistic and conspiratorial versions of this theme.[19] A few emblematic quotes should suffice to illustrate this one-dimensional perspective. According to Hans Josef Horchem, an official of the West German Bundesamt für Verfassungsschutz (BfV, Office for the Protection of the Constitution), the "KGB is engineering international terrorism."[20] For Cline and Alexander, Moscow served as the "nerve center" of the "international infrastructure of terrorism."[21] For journalist Claire Sterling, a diverse array of violent non-state groups—ethno-nationalist, religious, anti-colonial, criminal, and leftist—all came to "see themselves as elite battalions in a worldwide Army of Communist Combat."[22] Hence from this perspective, terrorists of all kinds, perhaps even ostensibly right-wing terrorists such as the Turkish would-be papal assassin Mehmet Ali Ağca, were effectively considered agents of the Soviet Union or its allied states.

Although the Soviet KGB was viewed as the chief "puppet master" behind international terrorism, in cases where the Soviets themselves were not secretly sponsoring or controlling terrorist groups, they allegedly relied on their client regimes in Eastern Europe, the Middle East, Latin America, and Asia to do so, mainly by contracting out these tasks to the secret services of East Germany, Czechoslovakia, Hungary, Bulgaria, Cuba, North Korea, Libya, Syria, or Iraq.[23] Many of these intersecting theories about supposed Soviet, communist, and rogue state sponsorship of different types of terrorism neatly converged in the case of the plot to kill the pope, according to which the KGB, with the help of the Bulgarian secret service, the Iranians, and the Turkish mafia, purportedly sponsored the 1980 assassination attempt against Pope John Paul II.[24]

In addition to viewing the world through unabashed ideological filters, the proponents of these theories—many of whom were former intelligence and military officers—tended to rely heavily on anonymous government insiders, inaccessible documents, or unreliable defectors as their primary sources of information, which they supplemented with unconfirmed and often sensationalistic media reports, without consulting other available sources to verify the accuracy of that information.[25] Indeed, a strong circumstantial case can be made that the authors of these reports, whether intentionally or unwittingly, were serving as conduits for propaganda or disinformation that hard-line factions within the Western intelligence community had generated. Hence it is not surprising that their methods and conclusions were criticized, sometimes harshly, both by more circumspect academicians and by serving or former intelligence officers associated with more moderate rival factions.[26]

However that may be, it is undeniable that during the Cold War the KGB and other Eastern Bloc secret services provided extensive tangible assistance—above all, funding, weaponry, hands-on training, and sometimes even operational direction—to a vast array of dictatorial client regimes and brutal self-proclaimed "national liberation" movements in various parts of the third world.[27] They did so for the same reason that Western secret services supported similarly unsavory anticommunist regimes and insurgents: they viewed these indigenous local struggles as fronts in the global conflict between the two superpowers. Many of those Soviet-backed guerrilla movements (and, for that matter, states) did in fact employ terrorism as one of their tactics. Nevertheless, since terrorism was often not their primary tactic, much less their sole tactic, they cannot be legitimately referred to as terrorist movements per se. It is only on the basis of such a misleading and unwarranted conflation between insurgents in general and terrorists in the strict sense that the proponents of the "KGB-sponsored terrorism" thesis have been able to buttress their exaggerated claims.

On the other side of the Iron Curtain, pro-Soviet secret services, a worldwide network of communist "fellow travelers," and Western left-wing activists promoted a parallel but diametrically opposed mythology. In this version, the U.S. Central Intelligence Agency (CIA) and other Western secret services were the primary sponsors of terrorism in the world, in particular the terrorism carried out by right-wing regimes and paramilitary groups.[28] However, the idea that American intelligence agencies were secretly orchestrating and directing all the counterrevolutionary terrorism against the world's progressive forces was as much of a propagandistic, conspiratorial fantasy as the notion that the Soviets were controlling international terrorism. This claim was based upon most of the same false premises concerning the alleged omnipresence and omnipotence of secret service puppet masters (in this case the CIA and its affiliates) and the supposed pliability of all the entities that received some sort of assistance from those services. An illuminating example of this unsophisticated, reductionist perspective was the notion that Operación Cóndor—a mid-1970s agreement between the secret services of authoritarian southern cone regimes in Argentina, Bolivia, Brazil, Chile, Paraguay, and Uruguay to wage a collaborative, continent-wide covert war against communist subversives—was a scheme that the CIA hatched and directed.[29] So sinister was this agency that it was even purportedly able, operating behind the scenes, to direct "pseudo-leftist" terrorist groups.[30] Moreover, according to pro-Soviet sources, the CIA itself sponsored the attempted assassination of the pope in order to implicate Bulgaria and the Soviet Bloc and thereby sabotage détente.[31]

Ironically, there is more reliable documentary evidence, at least in the public domain, about the covert support offered by Western democracies to authoritarian client regimes and civilian paramilitary groups that have engaged in terrorism, though this may well be an artifact of the greater openness and accessibility of information in free societies. Although some have conveniently attributed all such claims to communist and left-wing disinformation given that Soviet operatives and their "useful idiots" in fact systematically disseminated these themes, there is no doubt that the United States actively or tacitly supported numerous anticommunist regimes and right-wing vigilante groups that engaged in acts of terrorism against real and imagined subversives.[32] One may note, as examples, the brutal campaigns of state terrorism that the U.S.-backed juntas and affiliated death squads in El Salvador and Guatemala carried out; the antidemocratic violence perpetrated by some components of the clandestine "stay-behind" networks, which the secret services of North Atlantic Treaty Organization (NATO) members established in various European countries to resist a possible Soviet invasion; and the logistical if not operational support that American intelligence provided to anticommunist "freedom fighters" who regularly resorted to terrorism, such as right-wing Cuban exiles from the organizations Alpha 66 and Omega 7, contra elements from the Fuerza Democrática Nicaragüense (FDN, Nicaraguan Democratic Force), and select groups of fanatical Afghan mujahidin.[33]

Sadly, many of these partisan left-wing claims about Western state-sponsored terrorism were subsequently confirmed after various repressive military regimes collapsed, especially in cases where their archives were opened or when former members of their security forces began offering firsthand accounts of their past misdeeds.[34] Indeed, if one honestly applied the same loose criteria that are used nowadays to determine which rogue countries should be added to the U.S. State Department's list of state sponsors of terrorism, many Western client regimes during the Cold War would easily fit those criteria. Still, it would be absurd to claim that the CIA was—to appropriate the colorful phrase that foreign policy analyst Michael Ledeen applied to hostile regimes—the "terror master" behind such states and organizations.

Despite this long, sordid history of Cold War–era exaggerations and distortions, similar mythologies about state sponsorship of terrorism are still being peddled, most recently in connection with jihadist terrorism. Once again, there are two competing variants of this mythology.

One claims that various anti-American rogue regimes, in many cases the very same villainous states that were earlier identified as Soviet clients, are the principal sponsors of Islamist terrorism.[35] American neoconservatives and Israeli hard-liners have peddled this theme tirelessly. It is Ledeen who has perhaps expressed it most succinctly: "Western intelligence sources have long been reluctant to accept the fact that *modern Islamic terrorism is above all else a weapon used by hostile nation states against their enemies in the Middle East and in the West*" (italics added).[36] Similarly, for foreign policy analyst David Wurmser, the war against terrorism was "an epic struggle between a whole category of nations . . . the seven state sponsors of terror and us."[37] Basically, their argument is that states making up the so-called axis of evil and other renegade regimes are the principal sponsors of terrorism, including Sunni jihadist terrorism, in the Muslim world, and that without their support these particular forms of terrorism would not constitute a major security threat.[38] Different proponents of this distorted notion, while uncritically accepting that all the regimes on the State Department's list are actually sponsors of terrorism, have tended to focus their attention primarily on one or more of these renegade states—namely, Iran, Syria, or Saddam Hussein's Iraq.[39] Other hawks, with far more justification, have laid the blame for supporting global Sunni terrorism primarily on nominal U.S. allies such as Saudi Arabia and Pakistan.[40]

The second version is that the United States itself has been a principal sponsor of Islamist extremism and jihadist terrorism. The more restrained versions of this theory emphasize the pre-9/11 support that Western secret services provided to diverse Islamist movements, ranging from the Jami'iyyat al-Ikhwan al-Muslimin (Society of the Muslim Brothers, or Muslim Brotherhood) in Egypt and Syria to the jihadist opponents of Muammar al-Qaddafi's regime and, through the intermediary of the Pakistani Inter-Services Intelligence (ISI) directorate, local and Arab mujahidin in Afghanistan, claims for all of which there is some actual evidence.[41] The more alarmist, conspiratorial, and speculative versions argue that the CIA and other U.S. intelligence services have been secretly directing or manipulating Islamists and even some jihadist terrorists all along as part of a calculated strategy to weaken America's geopolitical rivals, obtain control of oil pipelines, or justify launching "imperialist" military interventions abroad.[42] Indeed, some of the many delusional 9/11 conspiracy theories suggest that the United States either ordered its jihadist "allies" to carry out the attacks or duped them into doing so.[43]

The Norm: Autonomous Terrorists as Willing Periodic Collaborators or Unwitting Occasional Instruments of the Secret Services of Nation-States

What, then, is the normal nature of the interrelationship between complicit nation-states and terrorist groups? The earlier criticisms of various conspiratorial mythologies about state sponsorship should not be misconstrued as a denial that numerous states, both hostile and friendly, have provided encouragement as well as tangible logistical or even operational aid to non-state terrorist groups. Regime components have indeed frequently offered diverse types of assistance to particular terrorist groups in their efforts to penetrate, manipulate, or exploit them instrumentally. Yet this support does not mean, as many have implied, that those states are actually controlling or directing terrorist organizations or that the latter normally function as the de facto agents of states. That is because such mythologies are based upon two naive beliefs (or duplicitous claims)—that states and terrorist groups both invariably benefit when they collaborate with one another, and that insurgent terrorism of various types develops into a serious threat only when there is state sponsorship. Both of these notions are mistaken for two reasons. First, such collaboration almost always creates difficulties and involves risks, often serious ones, for both parties. Second, several terrorist groups, such as Sendero Luminoso (Shining Path) in Peru or Oumu Shinrikyo (Aum Supreme Truth) in Japan, have gravely threatened their own or other societies without any significant state sponsorship.

In fact, most extremist political and religious groups in the world, including those that have relied primarily on terrorism to achieve their goals, have been relatively small, autonomous, sectarian organizations that emerged organically within particular historical and cultural contexts and were established independently in response to specific political circumstances. Moreover, the majority of those that had recourse to violence initially carried out acts of terrorism without having received any significant support from nation-states, depended largely on their own resources to support and sustain their activities, and managed to maintain a considerable degree of ideological, organizational, and operational autonomy even if at some point they opted to forge relationships, overt or covert, with particular regimes. This is clear from the historical record.

Moreover, apart from not being substantiated by the available evidence, these mythologies about the omnipresence of state sponsorship and non-state actors functioning as mere "agents" of states all rest on numerous unstated assumptions that are severely problematic if not manifestly false. The first is that extremist organizations, including those that rely on terrorism as a technique, are stable, disciplined, and internally united. After all, for states to control extremist groups effectively, the members of those groups would have to accept, more or less passively, the decisions made by their leaders who had opted to establish collaborative relationships with those states.[44] In actuality, a fluid, dynamic, and kaleidoscopic process of organizational fission and fusion characterizes all extremist milieus, since the organizations within those milieus are themselves typically divided into factions and riven by sometimes bitter internal conflicts deriving from personality clashes; disputes over doctrinal, strategic, or tactical matters; and social, if not cultural, ethnic, or national, distinctions.[45] In short, extremist milieus are rarely if ever in a condition of stasis, and extremist groups are often volatile and unstable, making them exceedingly difficult to manage, much less control. This description is even truer of today's diffuse, horizontal, and "franchised" jihadist terrorist networks than it was of the more centralized and hierarchical organizations during the Cold War.

Second, states are not monolithic organizations either. Even authoritarian regimes and those with totalitarian pretensions are often internally divided and factionalized, if not effectively polycentric.[46] In practice, this means that it is not always clear whether secret service collaboration with extremist and terrorist groups has been undertaken in response to the direct orders of national political leaders, by one or more of those services acting collectively, or on the initiative of officers on behalf of particular factions within those services.[47] Generally, such services are functionally specialized, structurally compartmentalized, and operate clandestinely on a need-to-know basis. Hence it may well be a mistake to assume a priori that such secretive initiatives are invariably authorized by the leaders of particular countries rather than by some of their underlings without official sanction.[48]

Third, these theories attribute almost preternatural powers to nation-states and their security agencies in terms of their ability to manipulate and control terrorist groups or their actions covertly. In practice, then, the most alarmist and reductionist of these portrayals of state-sponsored terrorism resemble "conspiracy theories" in the pejorative sense of that term.[49] This conspiratorial approach is precisely the problem, since the kind of omniscience, omnipresence, and omnipotence that conspiracy theorists attribute to alleged cabals of secret plotters, including the so-called terror masters, does not accurately depict the complicated, variegated nature of actual covert and clandestine politics. In the real world, the apparatuses that initiate covert operations are composed of inherently flawed individuals who, along with everyone else, are prone to commit errors of judgment and other blunders. Moreover, they not only have to cope with the formidable problem of unforeseen consequences, but also have to contend with numerous other more or less powerful groups that are likewise operating secretly, broader social forces that are difficult if not impossible to control, and deep-rooted structural and cultural constraints that place limits on how much they are able to affect the course of events.[50]

Fourth, these depictions ascribe far too much passivity or docility to members of extremist political and religious groups, whose members tend—almost by definition—to be fanatical true believers in their respective causes.[51] Whatever their specific doctrinal tenets, extremist ideologies are generally characterized by Manichaeanism (a sharp division of the world into good and evil), monism, authoritarianism or totalitarianism, collectivism, and a penchant for demonizing designated enemies. None of these characteristics of ideological extremism is conducive to the establishment of fraternal coexistence with persons or organizations that do not share their own perceptions and goals. Moreover, the people who are attracted to such radical doctrines tend to be deeply suspicious of anyone outside their own organizations and ideological milieus, making sustained collaboration with states and other non-state groups problematic and fraught with potential friction. Finally, the often egomaniacal or paranoid leaders of extremist groups tend to be hostile to perceived rivals and obsessed with preserving their own autonomy and influence, which causes them to distrust and resent outsiders, even those with whom they may be temporarily cooperating. These factors all militate against them willingly acting as the pliant, long-term agents of other, more powerful entities that do not fully share their own radical agendas.

This does not mean, of course, that terrorists never collaborate with states that do not share their own ideologies. They have often done so, albeit usually on the realist grounds that "the enemy of my (principal) enemy is my (temporary) friend." Indeed, resource-poor extremists are likely to accept tangible support from many different quarters—the more the merrier, since variety helps to lessen their dependence on any one sponsor—in order to pursue their objectives or resist common enemies. It does mean, however, that they are likely to be very suspicious and wary of the states that offer them support, since such support invariably comes with certain strings attached, and that they will assiduously strive to maintain their own autonomy, all the more so if the regimes in question do not share their particular worldviews or long-term goals. For their part, states are willing to collaborate with violence-prone extremists for a multiplicity of reasons, ranging from ideological solidarity to supporting coreligionists or co-ethnics to geopolitical realpolitik, although in this context ideological factors are arguably less important to states than to extremist groups.[52]

Despite these important qualifications, it is undeniable that the secret services of various states have often sought to infiltrate, manipulate, and instrumentally exploit autonomous extremist and terrorist groups for their own purposes. Some of these efforts may be regarded as basically legitimate (such as gathering information and attempting to prevent such groups from carrying out acts of violence), whereas others could be viewed as illegitimate (such as acting as agents provocateurs by encouraging or manipulating those groups into carrying out acts of violence). It is also true that many terrorist groups have at times tried to obtain tangible support and material aid from states. Although the historical record is replete with examples of these intertwined phenomena, a brief examination of three high-profile cases should make it abundantly clear that the clandestine relations between states and terrorist groups, when and where they have existed, are generally far more complicated and volatile than any of the discussed mythologies would suggest. However, it should be emphasized that evidentiary lacunae in the available sources necessarily make all conclusions about these complex matters tentative and provisional, and that the unanticipated appearance of reliable new information could drastically alter our present understanding.

If one considers the interaction between the terrorist Rote Armee Fraktion (RAF, Red Army Faction) and the East German Ministerium für Staatssicherheit (MfS, Ministry for State Security, better known as the Stasi), it quickly becomes clear that the more simplistic, alarmist interpretations of their relationship are problematic. Proponents of the Soviet terror network thesis had long claimed that Eastern Bloc secret services were secretly sponsoring European left-wing terrorist organizations, and these claims were partially confirmed when information from the MfS archives, former Stasi officers, and ex-terrorists surfaced after the Soviet and East German regimes collapsed. Nevertheless, not much can be said with certainty about the links between the Stasi and West German terrorists. First, in the late 1960s and 1970s some wanted West German terrorists had established contacts with the Stasi and thence had been provided with false documents and allowed to travel freely in the East (despite being kept under surveillance), usually when on their way to training camps in the Middle East.[53] Second, in the late 1970s and early 1980s, under the aegis of the new Hauptabteilung (Main Department) XXII: Terrorabwehr (Defense against Terrorism), ten members of the RAF and other German terrorist groups, most of whom were disillusioned terrorist "mistakes" or "dropouts," were brought to East Germany and allowed to assume new identities, lives, and jobs (in Operativer Vorgang [OV] "Stern II" [Operational Case "Star II"]).[54] Third, and perhaps most seriously, between 1980 and 1982 Stasi officers in a lodge near Briesen (in OV "Stern I") provided a few select members of the RAF's second generation, including its command level, with actual hands-on weapons and explosives training; in some cases, these individuals apparently carried out bomb and rocket attacks against American military officers in West Germany.[55] Finally, other West German terrorists affiliated with Ilich Ramírez Sánchez, "Carlos the Jackal," or with rival Palestinian factions also periodically took refuge in or transited through East Germany.[56]

However, the fact remains that the MfS always seemed to have had an ambiguous and rather strained relationship with RAF members. On the one hand, its leaders felt some romantic solidarity and sympathy for their supposedly misguided anti-imperialist comrades who shared the same class enemies or perhaps viewed them as potential auxiliaries if war should break out between the two Germanys; therefore, they offered them support. On the other hand, they distrusted the RAF so much that they characterized its members as potential enemies of the state in secret documents, kept them under constant surveillance, refused to collaborate in certain adventurist RAF schemes, and systematically exploited both the "new citizens" and visiting terrorists to gather intelligence on extremist milieus and vulnerabilities in the West.[57] In short, although there is no doubt that the Eastern Bloc secret services did periodically provide certain so-called fighting communist cells in Western Europe with logistical aid of various types, the role of those services in actually fomenting, much less directing, left-wing terrorism has frequently been exaggerated.[58]

Another example of conspiratorial alarmism regarding state sponsorship concerns the Munazzamat al-Tahrir al-Filastiniyya (PLO, Palestine Liberation

Organization). The proponents of the thesis that the KGB was secretly masterminding international terrorism paid particular attention to the PLO, which allegedly "became the chief and central agency for dispensing terror and death, for supplying fighters, arms, money, training, orders and advice to customers of every shade of political and ideological coloration who were eager or willing to destroy, terrify and kill."[59] Indeed, for writer Jillian Becker, the power for which the PLO "acted as agent in its mission of global partisan warfare was the Soviet Union."[60] This formulation grossly oversimplifies and mischaracterizes the real nature of the relationship among the Soviets, their clients, and the terrorist components of the Palestinian resistance movement, a relationship that was far more convoluted.

The first point to emphasize is that the PLO is an umbrella organization that the Arab League originally created in 1964 and that has long encompassed a wide variety of groups and factions, ranging from Islamic nationalists (and even some Islamists) to secular nationalists and Marxists. Such a disparate, fractious coalition has always proved to be extraordinarily difficult to manage and control, and it held together only for so long owing to the political skills of Yasir Arafat, the organizational predominance of his own Fatah group, and the collective support for the "Palestine liberation first" policy. Not surprisingly, this "lack of unity within the organization [made] it difficult for the Soviets to control its movements or even influence its policies."[61] Second, the centrist stance, flexible policies, and sometimes moderate approaches that Arafat and his loyalists in Fatah adopted periodically led other key components within the PLO to challenge Arafat's authority (for example, through the formation of the Rejection Front) or caused radical splinter groups to break away from the PLO.[62] Third, Arafat always sought to obtain tangible and intangible support from a diverse array of nation-states, not only to augment his resources but also to avoid becoming overly dependent upon any single state supporter. Over the years the PLO had received extensive support from, among others, Egypt, Saudi Arabia, other Gulf states, and Algeria as well as Libya, Syria, Iraq, China, the Soviet Bloc, and, more recently, several European countries, the United States, and Israel.[63] Fourth, since Arafat and his cronies shrewdly invested money that they had siphoned off from state-supplied funds or had earned from various licit and illicit business activities and thereby became very wealthy, they were able to maintain considerable operational independence for the PLO.[64]

More importantly, a documented history of distrust and friction, both public and private, existed between Arafat's organization and the Soviet Union, so much so that the latter periodically sought to moderate the PLO's goal of destroying Israel and to restrain Fatah and other Palestinian factions from launching terrorist actions outside Israel or against civilians.[65] Indeed, according to Professor Galia Golan, "Palestinian terrorism was generally— though not always—perceived by the Soviets as counterproductive."[66] However, this is by no means the entire story, because the Soviets seem to have pursued a two-track strategy with certain Palestinian groups. For example, hard-core Palestinian rejectionists and radicals, especially Marxist factions such as Jurj Habash's Jabha al-Sha'biyya li-Tahrir Filastin (Popular Front for the Liberation of Palestine, PFLP), openly criticized the Soviets for their pusillanimity and for not supporting their terrorist acts, and in return the Soviets publicly characterized them as extremists and adventurers.[67] At the same time, the KGB apparently recruited Wadi' Haddad, a leader of the PFLP's military wing, as an agent (code-named NATSIONALIST), and through him they sought to manipulate the PFLP covertly. In some cases, moreover, the Soviets not only provided advanced weapons to the PFLP but reportedly also instigated certain terrorist attacks carried out by Haddad and his operatives.[68] Nevertheless, even though the Soviet Union sold considerable amounts of military armaments to Fatah, provided paramilitary training to select Palestinian fighters at camps inside the Soviet Bloc, and apparently even covertly facilitated certain Palestinian terrorist attacks, it would be absurd to characterize the PLO as a whole, or even entire radical factions within it, as little more than the terrorist agents, surrogates, or proxies of the KGB.

If these two claims regarding state sponsorship involving relatively well-known cases are problematic, one is entitled to be even more skeptical of recent allegations that anti-Western jihadist groups are effectively the proxies of rogue regimes such as Saddam Hussein's Iraq. Indeed, in the period leading to the invasion of Iraq in 2003, many of the very same hawks who had earlier promoted theories about Soviet sponsorship of terrorism began insisting that the Iraqi, Syrian, and Iranian regimes were sponsoring contemporary jihadist terrorism. There is no doubt at all that the revolutionary Iranian regime has provided tangible logistical and operational assistance and even partial direction to Shi'i terrorist groups such as Hizballah and the militias affiliated with their Iraqi clients. Furthermore, Iraq, Syria, and Iran have all actively supported various Palestinian "rejectionist" groups, both nationalist and Sunni Islamist.[69] However, many neoconservatives also ostentatiously claimed that Hussein—together with Syria and Iran—had become one of the terror masters behind global Sunni jihadist networks such as al-Qa'ida. Although these alarmists were correct to note that ideological incompatibility would not necessarily prevent such disparate partners from warily cooperating, since both states and non-state actors at times forge at least temporary alliances against dangerous common enemies, in this case the available evidence does not support their more hyperbolic claims.[70]

Only a few points can be made with some confidence about alleged Iraqi relations with al-Qa'ida. First, in early 1996, in connection with Sudanese leader Hasan al-Turabi's efforts to forge a united Sunni-Shi'i jihadist front against the West, a senior Iraqi intelligence officer named Faruq al-Hijazi met with Osama bin Laden in Khartoum.[71] Second, on a few other occasions Iraqi intelligence officers were reportedly contacted by individuals linked to al-Qa'ida, but they either rebuffed their approaches or briefly exploited them to gather information. Third, in 1998 bin Laden sent an emissary named Abu Hafs al-Mawritani to Iraq. Abu Hafs was to ask Saddam Hussein to provide al-Qa'ida operatives with operational training, including in the use of chemical and biological agents, but the Iraqi leader refused to meet with Abu Hafs and ordered him to leave the country.[72] Fourth, after December 2001 numerous al-Qa'ida "associates" fleeing Afghanistan used Iraq, especially the Kurdish-controlled areas in the north, as a "safe haven and transit area," or as an operational base, though there is no evidence that Hussein's regime was complicit in this activity (though it may well have been acquiescent).[73] Fifth, in the summer of 2002, Abu Mus'ab al-Zarqawi and a dozen other al-Qa'ida-linked extremists who were collaborating with the Kurdish jihadist group Ansar al-Islam (Partisans of Islam) spent some time in Baghdad (apparently, in certain cases, to get medical treatment).[74] It is possible but by no means certain that Hussein provided covert support to Ansar, which had connections to al-Qa'ida, in order to make trouble for his secular Kurdish opponents.[75] It is also true, of course, that after the U.S. invasion commenced, elements of the Ba'thist underground formed insurgent coalitions with local Islamists and arriving foreign fighters.

None of this information demonstrates—unless one has a conspiratorial mind-set, an overactive imagination, or a political agenda to promote—that the secular Iraqi regime was a terror master controlling al-Qa'ida; that bin Laden was a proxy of the Ba'thist regime, his oft-declared enemy; or, even more fancifully, that Saddam Hussein secretly sponsored the 1993 World Trade Center bombing, the 1995 Oklahoma City bombing, or the 9/11 attacks.[76] Indeed, a June 2002 CIA report concluded that "in contrast to the traditional patron-client relationship Iraq enjoys with secular Palestinian groups, the ties between Saddam and bin Laden appear much like those between rival intelligence services, with each trying to exploit the other for its own benefit."[77] Furthermore, according to former CIA director George Tenet, the agency's "intelligence did not show any Iraqi authority, direction, or control over any of the many specific terrorist attacks carried out by al-Qa'ida."[78] Other U.S. government agencies and officials, as well as outside researchers, have reached similarly skeptical conclusions concerning such a proxy or operational relationship between al-Qa'ida and Iraq.[79]

If one compares these exaggerated claims about the sponsorship of jihadist terrorism by enemy regimes—excluding, perhaps, Iran—with the evidence documenting the involvement of friendly regimes such as Pakistan or Saudi Arabia in sponsoring, supporting, facilitating, or enabling this sort of terrorism, the contrast is glaring. Indeed, as Professor Daniel Byman rightly notes, "Pakistan is probably today's most active [state] sponsor of terrorism."[80] There is no doubt at all that Pakistan's powerful ISI has played a vitally important and sustained role in arming, training, supplying, and even providing operational direction to numerous radical anti-Western jihadist groups, including leading factions of the Taliban, Gulbuddin Hekmatyar's Hizb-i Islami (Islamic Party), Abdul Rasul Sayyaf's Ittihad-i Islami Bara-yi Azadi-yi Afghanistan (Islamic Union for the Freedom of Afghanistan), and Jalaluddin Haqqani's mujahidin network in Afghanistan, as well as Fazlur Rahman Khalil's Harkat-ul Mujahidin (Mujahidin Movement), Hafiz Muhammad Sayyid's Lashkar-i Tayyiba (Army of the Pure), Maulana Masood Azhar's Jaysh-i Muhammad (Army of Muhammad), and Bakht Zamin's al-Badr Mujahidin in Pakistan and Kashmir, to name only the most prominent.[81] Many of these same groups also developed close links with al-Qaʻida, indicating that a collusive albeit complicated three-way relationship has long existed among pro-Islamist factions within the ISI, South Asian jihadist organizations, and members of bin Laden's leadership directorate.[82] Such documented links have recently been further confirmed both by the indications that ISI officers were apparently directly involved in training the Lashkar jihadists who carried out the November 2008 terrorist attacks on Mumbai, India, and by the discovery that bin Laden had been living undisturbed for several years in a large compound in Abbottabad, right under the noses of the Pakistani military. The latter revelation has understandably given rise to suspicions that the degree of ISI complicity with al-Qaʻida was even greater than was previously thought.[83] However, even these ISI-backed jihadist terrorist groups should not necessarily be viewed as the docile proxies of that agency, since most of them have continued to pursue their own extremist agendas and have at times viciously turned on their supposed sponsors or "handlers."[84]

Yet despite its intimate, decades-long involvement in supporting jihadist terrorists, for geopolitical reasons Pakistan has never been labeled as a rogue regime or been added to the official U.S. list of state sponsors of terrorism, just as American-backed regimes that directly sponsored and perpetrated terrorism during the Cold War were conveniently never accused of being terrorist sponsors. Moreover, since the United States and Saudi Arabia have themselves provided extensive logistical and material support to the very same jihadist groups in Afghanistan—usually (but not always) indirectly using the ISI as an intermediary—they too were complicit in the facilitation or sponsorship of jihadist terrorism, which in both cases was later redirected, in textbook examples of intelligence "blowback," against them.[85] Indeed, given the intermittent covert support, dating back to the 1950s, that the U.S. and British secret services provided to Islamists against their mutual Cold War enemies, the State Department should have included the United States and its major ally as sponsors of jihadist terrorism once it began publishing its official annual list of state sponsors of terrorism—if it had fairly applied the same loaded, imprecise criteria that it now uses for designating enemy states.[86]

The Exceptions: Secret Service Creations,
Covert Penetration, and "Guns for Hire"

However that may be, in three types of circumstances one can legitimately refer to terrorist groups as agents or proxies of states. The first is when the secret services of particular regimes intentionally create pseudo-independent terrorist groups that remain under those services' direct control. Some examples are the Syrian-controlled Palestinian terrorist group al-Saʻiqa (The Thunderbolt) and its Iraqi-controlled counterpart, the Jabha al-Tahrir al-ʻArabiyya (Arab Liberation Front).[87] Other examples are the innumerable "death squads," or paramilitary groups normally consisting of both off-duty members of the security forces and civilian vigilantes, that have functioned as the terrorist auxiliaries of authoritarian regimes in such places as Sukarno's Indonesia, apartheid-era South Africa, the Philippines under Ferdinand Marcos, Spain before and after Francisco Franco, and various countries in sub-Saharan Africa and Latin America.[88] Using such groups to carry out various "dirty" covert jobs made it easier, at least for a time, for the state security forces to "plausibly deny" that they were perpetrators of terrorism.

In the second case, the regime's security agencies manage to penetrate a bona fide extremist or terrorist group and gradually assume control from within by maneuvering their own operatives or agents into key positions. When this process is making headway, the entire organization or factions within it may sometimes come under the effective control of the state and can therefore evolve into its de facto tool or agent. Since these types of covert operations are especially sensitive, it is often hard to obtain reliable evidence about them. Nevertheless, some of them have eventually come to light. Perhaps the best-documented example of this sort of manipulation is the case of Evno Azev, an agent of the tsarist Okhrana who became a member of the central committee of the Partiya Sotsialistov-Revolutsionerov (Socialist-Revolutionary Party) and the head of its notorious terrorist apparatus, the Boevaia Organizatsiia (Combat Organization).[89] In these contexts, agents provocateurs working secretly for regimes can often be found actively instigating violence.[90]

Here is an ideal point to digress briefly and discuss "false flag" operations. In these maneuvers, particular states or non-state groups (which are often either knowingly colluding with or unwittingly being manipulated by elements of certain secret services) secretly carry out terrorist actions that are then falsely attributed to groups from different extremist milieus.[91] One particularly illuminating and well-documented example of this phenomenon was the so-called strategy of tension in Italy, a series of provocations and terrorist massacres carried out in the late 1960s and early 1970s by neo-fascist radicals, operating more or less in collusion with hard-line factions within various security services, massacres that were often subsequently made to appear as if they were of anarchist or Marxist provenance.[92] Several other cases have also come to light, such as in the 1980s when elements from the secret services and neo-fascist groups in Belgium initiated a mini-strategy of tension, the so-called Mad Killers of Brabant Wallonia affair.[93]

Generally, three techniques are employed to initiate false flag terrorist operations. The simplest and least effective method is merely to claim publicly, in the wake of a terrorist attack, that someone other than the real perpetrators carried it out. The second method involves creating a bogus radical group, staffed by security personnel or complicit civilian extremists from a rival or opposing milieu, and then using it as a "cover" to launch terrorist attacks. Examples of this technique include the British Army–controlled pseudo–Mau Mau "counter-gangs" that systematically perpetrated terrorist attacks in Kenya, the Portuguese secret police's establishment of phony "national liberation" movements that engaged in terrorism in Mozambique and elsewhere in Africa, and an Israeli special operations unit, Unit 131, that set off bombs in Cairo and then attributed them to anti-Western Egyptians.[94] The third and most sophisticated method involves surreptitiously placing regime agents inside a bona fide extremist organization and thence inducing it, from within, to carry out terrorist attacks that can then be used as a pretext to discredit or destroy the infiltrated and manipulated group. Examples include the bombing of an Air France office in Lisbon by al-Da'wa al-Masih (The Call of Jesus Christ), a Libyan-backed terrorist group under the secret direction of a French intelligence officer, and several successful attempts by European neo-fascist militants, in collaboration with various secret services, to infiltrate certain far left groups and use them as a cover to carry out acts of terrorism.[95] If the testimony of former Algerian military and intelligence officers can be believed, the Algerian security forces apparently used all three techniques against the

Jama'at al-Islamiyya al-Muslaha/Groupe Islamique Armée (GIA, Armed Islamic Group) during the "dirty war" they waged against exceptionally brutal jihadist terrorist organizations.[96]

Returning to the main narrative, the third type of genuine proxy situation develops when certain extremist groups, or factions thereof, gradually lose their ideological purity over time and increasingly begin to act on the basis of vulgar materialistic motives, specifically by hiring themselves out to the highest bidder as contract killers or contract terrorists. This development certainly occurred in the case of the Abu Nidal Organization, with elements of the Nihon Sekigun (Japanese Red Army), and apparently also with various ad hoc groups operating under the command of Carlos the Jackal.[97] Once corrupted ideologically and morally, these types of groups tend to shift their "business" from one state "client" to another, having effectively become mercenaries with no real loyalty to any particular cause or paymaster. Needless to say, in such cases both the "guns for hire" and their employers are using each other instrumentally.

Levels of State Involvement in Terrorism:
A New Categorization Scheme

One of the reasons why misinformation and disinformation have become so prevalent in discussions concerning the relationships between nation-states and terrorist organizations is because the term "state sponsorship" is itself overly vague. At present, it is often applied casually and imprecisely to completely different levels of state interactions with non-state actors, ranging from providing rhetorical support and encouragement, at one pole, to engaging in hands-on logistical or operational activities, at the other. Indeed, the phrase "state sponsor" in relation to terrorism could conceivably signify virtually any type of interrelationship—however trivial, exploratory, or episodic it may be—which only serves to facilitate its partisan and propagandistic usage. Sadly, most existing attempts to categorize different levels of state involvement in terrorism have failed to capture all of its complex historical manifestations.

For that reason, it is important to present a more granular and sophisticated scheme to distinguish conceptually between varying levels of state involvement in terrorism. The first key distinction that must be made is between direct state terrorism and indirect state terrorism. Direct state terrorism is terrorism carried out, more or less overtly, by members of the state's security forces. An example of direct state terrorism would be the terrorist and, indeed, genocidal actions that the Cambodian secret police or military units of the Khmer Rouge waged against "reactionary" and "counterrevolutionary" segments of their own population. In contrast, indirect state terrorism is initiated secretly by the security forces in an indirect and deceptive manner by using intermediaries, usually civilian paramilitary groups, to carry out actions on behalf of a state. Those intermediaries can be willing participants, coerced individuals, or manipulated dupes, but whatever the specifics, their employment is normally designed to enable the state to launch especially sensitive or "dirty" operations while maintaining plausible deniability. This conceptual distinction between direct and indirect state terrorism is fundamental, even though in practice it is sometimes blurred when serving members of the security forces participate undercover in the actions carried out by ostensibly civilian organizations.

However, it is necessary to subdivide the category of indirect state terrorism further to more accurately reflect the different levels of state involvement with, or at the expense of, non-state groups. One can identify at least seven distinct levels of such participation, ranging from the most to the least active forms of engagement:

1. State-directed terrorism—elements of the state's security forces actually guide, supervise, or control the terrorist actions of their intermediaries.

2. State-sponsored terrorism—elements of the security forces provide hands-on operational assistance for acts of terrorism carried out by their intermediaries.

3. State-supported terrorism—elements of the security forces provide logistical support (training, specialized equipment, weapons, fi - nances, false documents, safe houses, cover), but not operational direction or assistance, to facilitate acts of terrorism carried out by their intermediaries.

4. State-manipulated terrorism—elements of the security forces use informants, agents in place, infiltrators, or agents provocateurs to

    manipulate their intermediaries into carrying out acts of terrorism covertly, without the latters' knowledge or consent.

5. State-encouraged terrorism—elements of the security forces incite their intermediaries to carry out acts of terrorism against mutual enemies.

6. State-exploited terrorism—elements of the security forces knowingly attribute terrorist actions to false perpetrators, usually declared enemies, either to protect their intermediaries or to discredit the political opposition.

7. State-sanctioned terrorism—elements of the security forces simply ignore or fail to punish acts of terrorism that civilian vigilante groups independently launch against targets that are perceived to be enemies by the state.

Note, however, that these distinct subcategories are not necessarily mutually exclusive. Elements of a given state's security forces have often engaged in several of these activities simultaneously.

It should be obvious that devising a more nuanced scheme that better reflects the fluidity, dynamism, and complexity of the actual relations between states and non-state paramilitary groups is preferable to using a single generic phrase—"state sponsorship"—that encompasses all potential levels of state involvement and therefore serves to obfuscate or obliterate vitally important distinctions. It really does matter, after all, if a state is actively helping terrorist groups plan and carry out operations or if it is simply supporting those operations rhetorically. These distinctions are all the more important when one government's security policies in relation to other states are directly affected by a reference to a generic category whose criteria are so vague and open-ended that they can easily be applied in an imprecise and wholly partisan fashion.

Conclusion

At this point, it should be clear that the clandestine relationships between components of the security services of various nation-states and extremist groups relying on the operational technique of terrorism do not generally conform to the simplistic notion that the former control the latter or that the latter are simple agents of the former. This concept was severely problematic even during the heyday of the Cold War, and at present it has arguably become increasingly outmoded and even less applicable.

In reality, these types of relationships are best characterized as double-edged swords inasmuch as they have normally been complicated, fluid, deceptive, risky, fractious, troublesome, and potentially dangerous for both parties. After all, the parties involved are usually struggling behind the scenes to exploit and manipulate each other. Terrorist groups are trying to finagle tangible assistance from states while retaining their organizational and operational independence, whereas states are seeking to penetrate, exploit, and use, if not actually control, terrorist groups for their own instrumental purposes. Often the security agencies have the upper hand in clandestine interactions with less powerful extremist groups, especially in their own countries when they covertly "assist" violence-prone radicals.[98] However, when security agencies are sponsoring terrorist organizations operating in more distant regions, the latter are often able to retain considerable autonomy. As such, in practice violent extremists often manage to con regime elements into giving them much-needed resources even as they stubbornly persist in pursuing their own radical, idiosyncratic agendas and goals, which may or may not conform, even in the short term, to the political interests of their state benefactors. Indeed, ideological fanatics of all stripes have sometimes explicitly violated prior agreements by using those state-supplied resources to carry out acts of terrorism that their would-be handlers have not sanctioned and that may well have been directly contrary to their so-called sponsors' intentions.

In assessing whether a given terrorist group is really an agent, proxy, or surrogate of a given nation-state, which implies that the group has lost some or all of the independence it may have once possessed, the key question is this: is the group now promoting political agendas or attacking particular targets that it would otherwise not have promoted or attacked if it were not receiving support of some type from a state? If the answer to this question is yes, then those terms may be at least partially applicable. However, if the group has not changed its overall objectives or its targeting priorities and if it is essentially still operating as it had previously and would presumably have kept doing so in the absence of state support, labeling the group as a proxy makes little sense. A subsidiary question that should be asked is this: is a given terrorist group now employing weapons or operational techniques that it would not otherwise have adopted had it not been receiving support of some type from a state? In this case, even if the group was using new weapons or techniques provided by a given state, it would be more accurate to characterize that group as the "beneficiary of state aid" rather than as an actual proxy of that state—unless, of course, in exchange for that aid, the group also shifted its objectives or targeting priorities to conform to those of its alleged sponsor.

In short, it is necessary to devise new policies that more accurately reflect the real, ever-shifting nature of the interactions between states and terrorist groups. After all, implementing security policies that are based on misperceptions or false allegations of state sponsorship only inhibits the U.S. government's ability to confront "really existing" terrorism and is liable to unnecessarily increase friction between the United States and designated terrorist sponsors. One possible step in this process would be to eliminate the blatantly partisan official list of state sponsors of terrorism, as it is unlikely that the vague criteria used to determine a state's inclusion on the list will ever be applied impartially—that is, applied to U.S. enemies and allies alike.[99] This action will hopefully make it more difficult in the future for vested political interests, both inside and outside of the government, to make bogus charges concerning state sponsorship of terrorism or to characterize terrorist groups falsely as the simple proxies of states. A second crucial step, however, would be to adopt a more nuanced, precise, and accurate concept that better reflects the multiple varieties and levels of state involvement in terrorism. It is crucially important to de-polemicize the entire subject of state sponsorship so that the real underlying phenomena—widespread but usually only semi-effective state efforts to manipulate and exploit terrorists—can be confronted in more effective ways and ultimately countered.

At the same time, it is even more necessary to recognize that the state-centric paradigm concerning terrorism is itself problematic, although admittedly not yet completely obsolete. The real terrorist threat to the world's security in the twenty-first century will likely emanate less from the clients of rogue states and more from a motley, disparate array of non-state entities:

left- and right-wing political radicals, religious extremists—including Islamist jihadists, Christian militias in the United States, Jewish fundamentalists in Israel, Hindu nationalists, and apocalyptic millenarian cult-type groups like Aum Supreme Truth—eco-radicals, ethnic gangs, drug cartels, and organized criminal groups. Most of these groups will be operating independently of de facto state authority or control.[100] Under these circumstances, the ideologies and objectives of such nongovernmental and often antistate groups need to be much better understood.

If, however, Western governments persist in maintaining the illusion that jihadist terrorist networks are essentially functioning as the surrogates of certain hostile enemy regimes, they will naturally conclude that the solution to winning the war on terrorism is simply to overthrow those alleged terror masters. Alas, this view not only represents an egregious distortion of the real situation, especially in relation to Sunni jihadist groups with a global agenda, but one that has already encouraged the adoption of counterproductive policies and the initiation of ill-advised military interventions that have significantly damaged the interests and international stature of the United States and its allies.

2

Missing Their Mark
The IRA's Proxy Bomb Campaign

MIA BLOOM AND JOHN HORGAN

An earlier version of this chapter was published as Mia Bloom and John Horgan, "Missing Their Mark: The IRA's Proxy Bomb Campaign," Social Research 75, no. 2 (Summer 2008): 579–614. Reprinted by permission. The work presented in this paper was supported (in part) by the Office of Naval Research under Grants #N00014-10-1-0915 and #N00014-09-1-1123. Any opinions expressed in whole or in part are those of the authors and do not represent those, nor reflect the official policy, of the Office of Naval Research, Department of the Army, or U.S. Department of Defense. The authors would like to thank Max Taylor, Jim Cusack, John Morrison, Jay Parker, Michael Freeman, and Andrew Kydd for comments on earlier drafts.

Suicide car bombs have become a commonplace and virtually daily event in conflicts such as the war in Iraq or Afghanistan. When an attack occurs, we make assumptions about the intent and motivation of the driver and the organization that sent him (and, increasingly, her). When such attacks occur in an Islamic context, we presume that the act is a deliberate *Istishhadi* (martyrdom) operation. This chapter challenges the basic assumptions about how the concept of martyrdom has been employed in the literature until now. Using the little-known case of the proxy bomb campaign of the Irish Republican Army (IRA) in Northern Ireland in 1990, we demonstrate how complex these operations are in reality.

A plausible assumption for most observers of terrorist movements is that such groupings, given their tendency to operate outside societal norms, are relatively immune to the vicissitudes and pressures of public opinion. In fact, most terrorist movements, like political parties, ultimately seek power and perceive themselves as the future leaders of their respective community. This case is especially true when the conflict in question relates to ethno-religious and territorial disputes. Consistent with Mao Zedong's theory that "guerrillas must live among the people as a fish moves through the sea," terrorists operate within certain parameters of the public and, for reasons explored in this chapter, are both cognizant of and susceptible to how members of their ethnic-religious community, rival groups, and international public opinion perceive them.

This sensitivity to public support occasionally means that when the terrorists engage in tactics that are perceived to be more radical or violent than that which their publics have become used to tolerating, the movement risks the consequences of backlash. It thus would seem to follow that terrorists may be circumscribed not only in the kinds of strategies they can pursue but also in the immediate tactical methods they can deploy. The main problem to date with analyses of terrorist incidents has been that we often take the event at face value and work backward to determine motivation and intention when, in fact, the reality might be quite different. The terms "suicide bomb" and "martyrdom operation" get thrown around far too easily to encompass many behaviors that may not in fact be voluntary.

This chapter challenges the way martyrdom is and has been constructed, and it forces us to examine terrorist events without preconceived notions. It is important to note that when we witness an event that on the surface appears to be an instance of martyrdom, the reality might be far more complex. Part of the problem has been the current inductive logic associated with the study of terrorism in which attacks are a given and experts will engage in a psychological autopsy to trace the perpetrators' intentions and motives after the fact. If the terrorists are religious, we assume that their act was one of self-sacrifice for a religious cause; however, this inference is not always the case. We argue that we need to question the intent of the action rather than assume that the event is automatically an act of martyrdom. Although attacks in Kabul or Baghdad may appear to be deliberate jihadi operations by the Taliban or by al-Qa'ida in Iraq, respectively, our investigation has determined that a portion of such attacks are the product of coercion and not martyrdom in the traditional sense; however, casual observers may understand them to be martyrdom operations.

The use of martyrs represents a strategic choice that can either mobilize large numbers of recruits and invigorate the support base of a community or enrage the rank and file to such an extent that it undermines the group's very credibility. The example of the IRA provides an interesting case in point. Although the IRA embraced many different concepts of martyrdom and linked them to the historical struggle against the British, it used the term "martyrdom" itself selectively. Martyrdom and self-sacrifice encompassed high-risk missions, including hunger strikes in which the strikers knew with certainty at what point they would die. Yet the IRA never used the term "suicide" and also refrained from using suicide car bombers (although it did use coerced car bombers). Rather than consider the proxy bomb a footnote in the history of the IRA, we argue that public support might circumscribe what terrorist organizations can and cannot do. Clearly, the nationalist community supported the self-sacrifice of the hunger strikers but rejected the notion of killing oneself deliberately or of allowing the organization to coerce one into doing it.

Although the IRA and its predecessors in Irish Republican militarism wholly embraced the broad concept of martyrdom—as perhaps best illustrated through the series of hunger strikes in which ten Republicans died in 1981—the IRA never engaged in martyrdom operations with the aim of physically attacking its enemies at the same time. However, in a series of notorious events in 1990, the IRA came close. Sometimes referred to as the human bomb campaign, these events are more commonly known as the IRA's proxy bombs. The operations involved the kidnapping at gunpoint of several Catholic civilians (not members of the IRA) who were subsequently coerced to drive vehicle-borne improvised explosive devices (VBIEDs) into military targets. In some cases the victim's family was held at gunpoint until the operation was completed. Public opinion against the IRA, even from within the broader Republican community, was so negative that the IRA quickly discontinued using the tactic.

Even though the reasons behind both the execution and discontinuation of the proxy bomb campaign are still poorly understood, the IRA is one of the few historical cases we have in which the use of human bombs (albeit of one particular type here) failed in a strategic sense owing to the limits of public sensibilities and a lack of tolerance for targeting civilians in this manner. The IRA campaign is the preeminent example of how a car bombing might be a coerced attack in which the driver has very little say or choice in the mission. Significantly, the use of coerced bombers has spread from Ireland to Colombia, Iraq, and Afghanistan and requires us to alter our assumptions regarding martyrdom and self-sacrifice.

Proxy bombing as a tactic suggests the extent to which the population is willing to support this use of violence against civilians. In the cases of Iraq or Afghanistan, it might signal a difficulty in mobilizing members of the population to volunteer for such actions. But Ireland's example teaches us that coercing individuals (as we have seen in Saudi Arabia, Iraq, and Afghanistan) might in fact drive a wedge between the organization and the very public it purports to represent. Proxy bombing may be, in fact, the last-ditch effort of a group losing popular support, or it might be the very incident that causes the group to lose support once and for all.

The Shift to Coercion

The term "proxy bomb" refers to the vehicle-borne delivery of an explosive with the distinct feature that the driver has been coerced into participating. In some cases, the coerced driver of the bomb has time to escape before it detonates, particularly when an accompanying terrorist unit operates the bomb through remote control. In other cases, however, the coerced drivers are blown up as part of the operation. As we have noted, the proxy bomb is perhaps most often associated with Irish Republican terrorism in Northern Ireland, but the tactic has since spread.

In Northern Ireland the delivery of terrorist bombs by proxy had a long history. The first scholarly reference to the proxy bomb was in 1970 in the *Irish University Review*.[1] As the IRA routinely began to kidnap civilians to drive bombs toward predetermined locations, the tactic caused increasing consternation and revulsion, perhaps characterized nowhere more effectively than in Benedict Kiely's 1977 novella *Proxopera*. In Kiely's fictional account, Latin teacher Mr. Binchey is forced to drive a proxy bomb to the local town. As he drives he speaks for the author: "Not even the Mafia thought of the proxy bomb, operation proxy, *proxopera* for gallant Irish patriots fighting imaginary empires by murdering the neighbors."[2] That such revulsion stood out in communities that for so long ran the risk of becoming immune to the surprise and shock of ever-evolving terrorist tactics (by both sides) is a testament to how abhorrent they considered the proxy bombs. Over the next two decades the phenomenon of proxy bombing proliferated and metamorphosed, culminating in a series of coordinated attacks in October 1990 that simultaneously would signal both the apex and the soon demise of the tactic.

Although the phenomenon of proxy bombs has received scant attention in contemporary literature, examples of coerced martyrdom abound throughout the history of terrorism and have been increasing in recent years. The concept of coercion becomes critical when we closely consider the nature of what we might term the "proxiness" of the bomb carrier; that is, it is possible to consider a bomber or bomb carrier as situated along a continuum between being fully conscious of the bomb he or she is carrying and willing to die in the process, being conscious of the bomb but carrying it against one's will (the cases under examination here), and being completely oblivious their involvement in a terrorist operation (sometimes associated with cases of a distant observer remotely detonating the bomb). These distinctions challenge the characterization of these events as martyrdom operations by negating the assumption that people necessarily volunteer to engage in such acts of violence. Surprisingly, these issues have escaped analysis to date. Although international relations theorists have long considered the coercive effect of bombing campaigns,[3] the theoretical literature does not assess whether individuals can likewise be coerced into bombing. The misleading analytical assumption of voluntariness has acquired more relevance and urgency in recent years with the dramatic increase in car bomb attacks (notably in Iraq and Afghanistan) by what appears to be an unending flow of voluntary recruits.

Historically, we have some interesting starting points. The investigations into the explosion of Pan Am Flight 103 over Lockerbie, Scotland, in 1988 have alleged that a proxy might have been the culprit. BBC News correspondent Christopher Wain has suggested that a "mule"—someone who knew he or she was smuggling something but thought it might be drugs or diamonds—may have unknowingly carried the explosive device on board.[4] Wain further draws a parallel with a previous case of Jordanian terrorist Nezar al-Hindawi, who duped his pregnant Irish girlfriend, Anne Marie Murphy, into carrying a suitcase bomb on board an El Al flight from London to Tel Aviv on April 17, 1986, without her knowledge.[5] Similarly, in the Middle East numerous proxy attacks have occurred in which the operative was unwilling or was unaware of the bomb's presence. Although we might assume that every car bomb attack in the Middle East involves operatives willing to die for the cause, the reality is far more complicated.

According to *Der Spiegel*, in Saudi Arabia in 2004, terrorists using remote-controlled detonators blew up cars and their passengers because the former supposedly "lacked confidence in their suicide bombing candidates." The same article notes that in Algeria, after a series of attacks in April 2007, local police described finding "a remote detonation device in one of the vehicles that exploded." Algerian interior minister Yazid Zerhouni alleged that the drivers "were blown up, along with the cars, without their knowledge."[6] News reports and interviews with military personnel have made similar claims regarding the dramatic increase of VBIEDs in Iraq. U.S. military personnel preempted several operatives found handcuffed to the steering wheel, possibly to prevent a last-minute defection or because of coercion. According to one interview, the driver was aware that he might be carrying contraband, but he did not know that he had "volunteered" for a martyrdom operation. The truck bomb was wired to explode using a remote-controlled signal that he did not control.[7]

Furthermore, two female psychiatric patients were used as proxies for bombings in and near Baghdad in 2008. Their handlers blew the women up using remote-controlled detonators through converted mobile phones. According to a U.S. Navy commander, Scott Rye, "There have been one or two incidents involving the mentally impaired in recent years. But this is the first time we have seen mentally impaired suicide bombers—women who were incapable of understanding what they were being used for."[8] If these reports are accurate, it would appear that al-Qa'ida in Iraq found a new way to overcome the collective action problem, but there are significant challenges for the way in which we unquestionably assume all the actors involved were volunteers.

The Irish Republican Army

As a result of tactical shifts over the first ten years of the IRA's campaign, the IRA proxy bomb underwent several incarnations. J. Bowyer Bell wrote that "the new bombs were elegant, dangerous, and allow persistence rather than promise escalation. Much the same is the case with other [IRA] initiatives like letter bombs, car bombs, trap-bombs, proxy bombs, bombs from fertilizer or courtesy of Libyan Semtex but never a device or a target that transforms the struggle."[9]

For a number of years, the IRA's modus operandi followed a typical pattern: A member of an IRA active service unit (ASU, the basic IRA cell unit) drove the car bomb to the target location and set it to detonate after several minutes. During this time the driver, and anyone else in the vicinity, could move clear of the blast. In the years that followed the IRA's resurgence in Northern Ireland, the tactic involved carjacking "clean" vehicles for the operations. In some examples, an ASU held the owners hostage and forced civilians to ferry the bombs against their will. In both cases, they allowed a time lag, often twenty minutes, because as a rule, such attacks were aimed at causing damage rather than taking life. These attacks thus resulted in few fatalities overall.

A tactical change in the early 1980s involved kidnapping civilians for use in these operations. Rather than use ASU members and risk having the British security forces capture them, the IRA sent a man with a bomb while his family was held hostage to ensure his obedience. Only after the civilian followed instructions and deployed the vehicle to detonate the target would the IRA release his family. In 1990, however, the IRA shifted tactics yet again, marking a fundamental change in the character of its operations: although civilians were again targeted to deliver the bombs, and their families were held hostage, this time the driver did not have the opportunity to escape.

Indeed, one interesting point here is that aside from the issue of risking capture in operations in which the driver escaped prior to detonation, it is significant that IRA ASU members were unwilling to drive car bombs to the actual point of detonation and kill themselves in the process. Although the IRA certainly never had any problems attracting and recruiting young men and women willing to risk their lives or their capture, finding one willing to drive a VBIED into a British military target appeared (at least on the surface) to have been more challenging. This complex question deserves careful consideration, but clearly a puzzle exists given that to the vast majority of IRA activists and supporters, the basic notion of "martyr for the cause" was widely accepted, implicitly if not explicitly.

As Sean O'Callaghan, the former head of the IRA's Southern Command, describes in his memoir, *The Informer*, the IRA did not reject the notion of martyrdom for the cause; instead, the organization embraced the willingness to sacrifice oneself. "The IRA is an organization that produces people prepared to starve themselves to death, people prepared to spend large parts of their lives in prison. In short, it produces people who are prepared to inflict death, pain and suffering on themselves as well as on others in pursuit of a cause."[10] After all, members of the IRA willingly took on high-risk missions in which their chances of survival were slim, and if they did survive, the promise of a brutal interrogation and lasting imprisonment were guaranteed. Most well known, perhaps, are the dramatic accounts of the hunger strikers, replete with the knowledge that they could expect death after fourteen days without liquids. Throughout the history of Irish Republicanism, volunteers willingly affirmed the notion of martyrdom, and for the leadership it long formed a powerful image for both local recruitment and international propaganda. Well before the hunger strikers' era, during Oliver Cromwell's time, Catholic priests knowingly sacrificed their lives for their religious beliefs. Perhaps best celebrated in Irish Republicanism was the doomed 1916 Easter Rising, from which militant Irish Republicans would forever draw inspiration and which would later be synonymous with the "blood sacrifice" of Irish rebels throughout the ages.[11]

This legacy of martyrdom linked the Fenian Brotherhood struggles of the late nineteenth century to the uprisings of 1916–1919 to Bobby Sands and the hunger strikers in the early 1980s. The historical resonance of these events greatly benefited the IRA and its political arm, Sinn Féin, as it transitioned to electoral politics. In the aftermath of the hunger strikes, support for the IRA exploded. "The IRA no longer had to harken back constantly to 1916 or 1919 to reaffirm the legitimacy of their struggle. The hunger strikers provided them a whole new iconography of martyrs to exploit."[12]

Detailed in the memoir of former IRA intelligence officer Eamon Collins, martyrdom linked religion and nationalism in a profoundly important fashion:

In my mind, [Padraig] Pearse and [James] Connolly were all linked together. They were martyrs for our Catholic faith, the true religion: religion and politics fused together by the blood of the martyrs. I was prepared to be a martyr, to die for this true Catholic faith. I felt those heroes of 1916 were like the priests who died for us at Cromwellian hands. I felt my mother must be right; the struggle for our faith was not yet over.[13]

In sum, although IRA activists viewed themselves as would-be martyrs, it would appear that either the individual members of the ASUs were unwilling to become human bombs or the leadership was unwilling to approve the execution of such operations against the British. They took this stance despite the fact that such operations would represent a logical next step in the evolution of their terror tactics. The IRA had used car bombs successfully since December 1971 and employed timed devices since the 1980s. In the 1990 proxy bomb attacks, the IRA used several familiar elements in an unprecedented combination.[14] The 1990 attacks marked the first time that the civilian proxies were not given a chance to escape before the bombs detonated. In addition, it is significant that the civilian proxies were Catholics, from the community where the IRA traditionally drew its support (though at times grudgingly). As Bell explains, prior to these attacks, the IRA tended to kidnap "off-duty policemen, informers, soldiers on leave, strikebreakers and suspected Protestant vigilantes."[15] Now the IRA combined the use of a VBIED with the coercion of Catholic civilians. This tactic at once reflected both a lack of resonance for violence against civilians in the nationalist and Republican communities with what could well be perceived as the IRA's refusal to sacrifice its own members. It instantly made the IRA appear callous and cowardly.

The Historical Background

To put these developments into a broader context, it is worth considering aspects of the development of IRA bombings and the organization's attitude toward military and civilian casualties. Although the car bomb was not invented in Northern Ireland, it soon became associated with the Anglo-Irish conflict with alarming frequency and to devastating effect. The IRA would soon perfect its originally crude devices and introduce chemicals into the bombs, which would burn longer and hotter and wreak greater damage than simple explosives. In Ed Moloney's *A Secret History of the IRA*, the author details how the Irish car bomb came into existence:

> The car bomb was discovered entirely by accident, but its deployment by the Belfast IRA was not. The chain of events began in December 1971 when Jack McCabe, the IRA's quartermaster, was fatally injured when an experimental fertilizer-based mix known as the "black stuff" exploded as he was blending it with a shovel in his garage in Dublin. Although General Headquarters warned that McCabe's car bomb mix was too dangerous to handle, it did fit perfectly within the new strategy of provoking a counter reaction from the British. So the idea was to pair the "black stuff" with a car, a fuse and a timer and dump it in downtown Belfast.[16]

According to Sean O'Callaghan, Seamus Twomey, a senior member of the IRA, invented the car bomb in 1972 and revolutionized IRA operations.[17] Soon afterward, in March, he sent a unit driving two cars packed with explosives into the center of Belfast.[18]

Using increasingly professional means, the IRA detonated thousands of bombs that were built from chemicals or stolen or imported explosives and included ever more sophisticated timing devices. Bell explains, "As long as a bomb would be used, it was best if it was planted on some important or symbolic objective. And even if the targets were soft—hotels—best that a more complex or compelling rationale be devised such as the destruction of the tourist industry or facilities used by the British Army."[19] Ed Moloney writes, "At the height of the bombing, the center of Belfast resembled a city under artillery fire; clouds of suffocating smoke enveloped buildings as one explosion followed another."[20] In time, rubble marred the centers of most northern towns, and barbwire and troops protected hotels across the region.

The Provisional IRA Belfast Brigade's enthusiasm for car bombs was nowhere more evident than on July 21, 1972, when the IRA left twenty-two ammonium nitrate and fuel oil (ANFO) car bombs and concealed gelignite charges on the periphery of the city center, with detonations timed to follow consecutively at five-minute intervals. That infamous day became known as "Bloody Friday." Moloney describes the potential for carnage that the new car bombs offered: "Then we knew we were onto something, and it took off from there."[21] The car bomb allowed the Provisional IRA (aka the Provos) to strike at British targets and reduce the likelihood of volunteers' accidental deaths. "The sheer size of the devices," Moloney observed, "greatly increased the risk of civilian deaths in careless or bungled operations."[22]

The IRA often provided warnings, although at times warnings were not given or were given too late. Massive civilian casualties resulted when the bombs exploded prematurely or crowds were too close to the explosions, and many innocent civilians and members of the security forces alike suffered significantly during the campaign. According to IRA insiders, as early as 1972 a consensus existed on the IRA's tactical priorities and limitations, a consensus rarely discussed but one that was understood. Civilians were not appropriate targets except under special and specific circumstances. Although this tacit agreement may have been a constraint on the kinds of operations available to them, it reflected an understanding of the importance of the civilian community's support. According to Collins, "[I would say that] the IRA fought with one hand tied behind its back: in general it did not carry out the indiscriminate campaign of all out war, which it would have been capable of fighting."[23]

O'Callaghan echoed this sensitivity to civilian targets: "We carried out a number of successful operations that summer, bombing attacks in Omagh and Cookstown, mainly aimed at government buildings, police or army barracks, and financial institutions. I was anxious that there should be no civilian casualties and put a lot of planning into the detail of them. Thankfully it paid off and no civilians were injured."[24]According to Collins, civilians were off-limits.[25] He alleges that the IRA was extremely sensitive to public reactions to its targeting. To this extent, there was a virtual hierarchy of acceptable targets in which civilians were generally unacceptable except under the most extreme circumstances.

More often than not, tactical innovations in Britain followed from successful testing in Northern Ireland. Mortars (used in the attack on Downing Street in 1991), proxy bombs (used in Whitehall when a taxi was commandeered and used to plant the bombs), and hoax calls following a real bomb (used to disrupt the Tube system) were all examples of tactics first used in the north and then "imported" to Britain. Large quantities of explosives caused simultaneous London bombings at the Baltic Exchange and at the Staples Corner interchange on the M1. Typifying the IRA at its most deadly, this strategy is echoed today in many of the tactics associated with al-Qa'ida.

In 1973, the IRA used car bombs against both military and civilian targets initially in Northern Ireland and in London, where volunteers often preferred softer targets—for example, the Tower of London, Harrods department store, and a variety of elegant clubs and fashionable restaurants—and rarely worried about civilian targets. Although standard operating procedures dictated that the IRA would usually call in a warning ahead of time, such calls did not always protect the innocent, especially if the bomb detonated prematurely or if the authorities mixed up locations because phone warnings became garbled. The IRA would frequently attempt to displace responsibility for civilian casualties and blame the police and emergency services for not acting fast enough to the messages that often panicky ASU members had left. The telephoned warnings often hurt more than they helped as a result. Within the organization considerable finger-pointing took place when an operation went bad and civilians were killed. According to Sean O'Callaghan,

> The half hour warning was worse than useless in an area filled with Christmas shoppers [i.e., the Knightsbridge attack]. Eight people were killed. . . . Such were the shock and anger both in the UK and in the Irish republic that the IRA was reluctant to take responsibility: suggestions were leaked to the media saying that the bombing had not been authorized by the IRA leadership. These were untrue. The subsequent inquiry within the IRA found that specific permission had been given to bomb Harrods, which was seen as a symbol of the British establishment. However the leadership knew that civilian casualties on that scale did not advance their cause, and privately criticized the lack of planning and foresight by the bombers.[26]

According to Eamon Collins, errors and mishaps arose from a variety of sources, including the IRA's own incompetence. Referring to a 1984 bombing in which seventy-one people were injured, Collins explained that the IRA had accidentally "attacked the Catholic population. . . . He [Hardbap, an IRA colleague of Collins's] had used . . . volunteers from out of town who did not know the area. They had got the streets mixed up and had abandoned the bomb in a panic, unable to phone in a warning until it was too late for the police to clear the area."[27]

From Collins's perspective as a core IRA intelligence officer in Newry, County Down, the public's willingness to forgive civilian casualties steadily declined as a result of the atrocities of Bloody Friday and the excesses on the British mainland typified by the no-warning pub bombings in 1974 in Woolwich and Guildford and, later on, at Harrods. Accordingly, civilian casualties hurt the IRA's public image at home and abroad and eroded the public support that the IRA recognized was crucial to its continued survival and development. Killing innocents did nothing to advance its cause, as Collins pointed out:

> [It was] the community upon whose support the IRA depended. . . . Without the community we were irrelevant. We carried the guns and planted the bombs, but the community fed us, hid us, opened their homes to us, turned a blind eye to our operations, even though that community support had dwindled over the years. Part of me wanted the community to say: We need you, as you need us.[28]

The sensitivity to public support and its reaction to operations circumscribed what the IRA could and could not do. Why did the IRA never produce a suicide bomber? One answer is found in the cultural context in which the IRA operated at the time. Given the overtly Catholic character of the community the IRA claimed to represent, as well as the broader historical influences the IRA drew on for its legitimacy, the issue of suicide posed immense difficulty. The use of suicide as part of the IRA's operations would certainly have been frowned upon and led to a considerable risk of alienation from the population.

Another reason for the lack of suicide bombers might relate to something more straightforward, that is, the success to date of the IRA's bombers. Throughout the IRA's campaign of violence, there was rarely a target that the IRA could not successfully penetrate. The movement planted bombs in a Brighton hotel in an attempt to assassinate Prime Minister Margaret Thatcher in 1984 and fired mortar bombs toward Prime Minister John Major's cabinet at 10 Downing Street in 1994. In 1979 an IRA splinter group, the Irish National Liberation Army, successfully planted a bomb underneath the car of Member of Parliament Airey Neave. These and numerous other examples lend strength to the argument that the IRA may not have needed to use suicide bombers. According to Sageman, terrorist organizations will use suicide terrorism when they are unable to achieve their goals using other methods.[29] It is rarely a strategy of first resort and relies significantly on the approval or rejection of the larger community that the terrorists purport to represent.

The IRA did not appear to have had any such difficulty in attacking high-value targets using more conventional means. This observation is consistent with the fact that as the British Army hardened checkpoint security, the IRA altered its tactics to shake the British Army from its complacency. However, the proxy operations soon proved that this tactical innovation was more costly than it was worth.

Setting aside the reasons for using proxy bombs as a tactical innovation, the reasons for its discontinuation appear clear. In the wake of the proxy bomb operations, extensive public pressure eventually forced the IRA to adjust its tactics accordingly. It meant essentially that if the group engaged in violence beyond what its public was willing to tolerate, it could alienate the people's support. Donatella Della Porta describes how terrorist organizations can inadvertently make themselves obsolete by engaging in activities that isolate the group, make recruitment problematic, and alienate group members to such an extent that they cease to provide a viable alternative to the opposing government.[30]

Nevertheless, groups are often willing to sacrifice members of their own population and engage in tactics that potentially alienate them from their base of support. Children have been used as both human shields and leverage to force parents to carry out missions. Tony Geraghty wrote,

> The most vivid example of the coarsening spirit during the Republican
> blitz of the late 1980s and early 1990s was the IRA's habit of taking

children as hostages, so as to force the owner of the car or lorry—usually the child's father—to drive a bomb to its target as a proxy "volunteer." Unlike Muslim fundamentalists, IRA volunteers were not prepared to be used as human bombs, though the effectiveness of this form of attack could not have been lost on them.[31]

The Proxy Bomb Attacks of 1990

In the autumn of 1990 a senior member of the Provisional IRA Army Council, nicknamed Spike, who was responsible for multiple atrocities in Northern Ireland, devised a plan for a unique type of proxy bomb operation.[32] The plan was to kidnap a civilian, hold his or her family hostage, and force the kidnapped person to bring the explosives to a target. Rather than allow the driver to escape prior to detonation, an accompanying ASU, who would closely follow behind the bomb-laden vehicle, would detonate the driver.

The IRA's targeting "ideology" had shifted the meaning of who might be considered a legitimate target. Previously, the IRA had taken steps to distinguish between civilians and military personnel and police officers, but increasing antipathy toward collaborators and informers meant that Irish Catholics could be targeted under specific circumstances. Although this dynamic had existed for some time (even dating back to the early days of the Troubles, from 1969 to 1994), in 1985 the IRA officially declared that those people working for the security forces were "legitimate targets." As a result, the IRA killed fifteen people, including owners, managers, and workers in building companies and other firms, between 1985 and 1990. The IRA statement continued, "Those involved in such work should desist or be prepared to suffer the consequences."[33] It is clear that this statement eventually paved the way for the human bomb operations.

On October 24, 1990, the IRA executed simultaneous car bomb attacks (timed within six minutes of each other) 150 miles apart against British checkpoints at Londonderry (Derry) and Newry. A failed attack at Omagh also took place.[34]

Patrick "Patsy" Gillespie, a forty-two-year-old kitchen hand who worked at a British Army base, was forced to drive a car loaded with a thousand-pound bomb into the Coshquin checkpoint outside Londonderry, Northern

Ireland's second-largest city. Five soldiers died in the bombing, and another five military personnel were seriously injured. John McEvoy, sixty-five years of age and a cancer survivor, was also forced to drive a car bomb to the army checkpoint at Cloghogue. The explosion killed Cyril Smith, a Royal Irish Ranger, as he tried to drag McEvoy out of the vehicle and to safety. McEvoy died seven months after the attack (of cancer), but his family described him as having "never got over what happened that night in October."[35]

In the third attack, Gerry Kelly escaped unhurt when the IRA coerced him to drive his bomb to Lisanelly Army Base, Omagh, in a caravanette (motor home) loaded with two hundred pounds of explosives. IRA men had strapped him into the seat and followed in a car behind him to the Sherwood Foresters military base (they had assured him that the explosives were attached to a forty-minute timer).[36] According to Kelly, "They said: 'don't try anything stupid as we will have a rifle trained on you.' They were driving behind me. I drove through the gate and shouted 'bomb, bomb' and managed to struggle free. Everything was going through my head that this was my last moment."[37]

The two bombs that successfully detonated caused the highest one-day death toll of soldiers in Northern Ireland in more than two years. The attacks resulted in unprecedented outrage in both the Protestant and Catholic communities among Unionists and Nationalists alike.[38]

The IRA had attacked vehicle checkpoints in the past, using weapons that ranged from rifles to mortars, and they had called in hoax bomb attacks against both of the targeted checkpoints in the twelve months prior to the attack. The dry runs may well have been crucial for the bombers, who timed the three attacks within minutes of each other though the targets ranged 150 miles apart. An earlier incident in Newry also appears to have been a dry run for the 1990 attack. The IRA forced a local man to drive his car to the Newry checkpoint after they told him that a package on the passenger seat was a bomb. The man alerted soldiers at the checkpoint after jumping out of his vehicle. Also, in 1989, in what was believed to have been another dry run, the IRA forced a man to drive a bomb to the High Court in Belfast.[39]

According to interviews that John Horgan conducted, the main objective of the proxy bomb operations was to send British forces a clear and unambiguous message: the IRA had fundamentally altered its tactics. The effect, in the words of a former IRA bomber, was to "shake the Brits out of their complacency," for with previous proxy bombs the checkpoint personnel had had time to evacuate the area.[40] For other analysts, the proxy bombs simply represented revenge. The IRA was eager to strike at British security troops after the Special Air Service (SAS) had shot dead several top IRA gunmen near Loughgall in County Armagh.

A further view alleges that the IRA's "message" was a response to the British technological innovations.[41] The British Army and the Royal Ulster Constabulary had been reasonably efficient—once they determined IRA patterns of activity and standard operating procedures—at methodically working out effective countermeasures. As a result of the hoax attacks, the British undertook a major review of checkpoint security. The British had hardened many of the checkpoints to be immune to timer-controlled vehicle bombs. To combat the efficacy of the IRA's devices, the British established radio-free zones where signals were routinely jammed. According to Collins,

> There was a problem with radio-controlled bombs—problems with the signals penetrating the army's protective radio wave shield which surrounded every police station, army base, and military vehicle and blocked signals between sophisticated radio devices. . . . Once an IRA radio bomb had failed to detonate, the army could retrieve the weapon and identify the radio code on the receiver, thus neutralizing all bombs using the same signal. . . . [It] could take a year to find a new signal.[42]

There was speculation that the IRA had triggered the bombs using a radio signal instead of using timed devices. The IRA had discovered a wavelength that the sophisticated electronic countermeasures set up around the Londonderry and Newry checkpoints as a protection from radio-detonated bombs had not intercepted.[43] This tactical shift represented a departure from previous modus operandi in that the attack took place at close quarters, involved large numbers of terrorists, and was aimed at an installation that had previously been regarded as practically impregnable. One could argue that the coordinated, three-pronged nature of the attack was intended to show that the IRA's military and tactical setbacks in the province had not blunted the overall efficacy of its mobility and ability to shock. Contrary to views expressed in Horgan's interviews, the IRA's official statements affirmed that the proxy tactic was merely a response to changing British military tactics and the hardening of checkpoint defenses. According to Sinn Féin's official newspaper, *An Phoblacht* (Republican News),

> Throughout the late 1980s the British engaged in a massive programme of refortification at their military bases throughout the six counties and the building of more and even bigger spy posts along the border. Meanwhile the IRA mounted a highly successful campaign against civilian collaborators who, for colossal sums of money, were assisting in the strengthening of crown forces bases. Next, the British attention focused on a campaign of blowing up bridges and roads along the border while massively increasing the strength of permanent border crossings. With the IRA continuing to hit on many fronts and embarking on a policy of forcing collaborators to drive bombs into heavily fortified positions, something had to give, hence the latest deployment of troops.[44]

The old proxy bombs, detonated at a distance, had given British authorities sufficient time to evacuate the premises. It also gave the army's ammunition technical officer time to disarm the bomb. During interrogations of IRA suspects, former IRA members alleged that the British harangued and mocked them about the futility of their tactics.[45]

In all three of the 1990 bombing cases, the IRA asserted that the coerced men worked for the British security forces. Perhaps obviously, but far from pretending that the men had volunteered for the operation, the IRA portrayed the three Catholic civilians as collaborators and traitors. The IRA subsequently went to great lengths to emphasize—and, indeed, exaggerate—the victims' relationship with the British authorities and their work in the arms industry (or construction work for Henry Brothers, which did work for the security forces) whether or not the victims had. Significantly, the IRA had used Patsy Gillespie in a proxy bomb operation four years earlier, forcing him to drive a bomb to an army checkpoint. Republicans had designated Gillespie a "collaborator" and "legitimate target" owing to his work at the Fort George army barracks as a kitchen hand. Likewise, John McEvoy, the victim of the Newry attack, owned a gasoline station, and in the IRA's eyes, his crime was that he served members of the security forces.[46]

In contrast to several earlier (unclaimed) bombings in which civilians were killed, the IRA actually claimed responsibility for the 1990 attacks immediately after the operation. In a statement to the Press Association in Belfast, the IRA stated, "This morning's military operation again devastates the myth of containment. . . . Until the British Government end their futile war in Ireland, attacks such as this morning's will continue."[47] The IRA even admitted to forcing the drivers to conduct the operations after another proxy bombing a few months later when members kidnapped Ken North, his wife, and their son, Peter. The attackers almost broke Peter North's legs and then placed him in a van with a bomb containing more than a thousand pounds of explosives. Forced to drive to a checkpoint, North was able to jump from the van and shout a warning. The detonator went off, but the bomb failed to explode.

Reactions and Responses

Though the IRA stopped using proxy bombs, a pressing question remains: why? According to Horgan's interviewees, the IRA's main purpose in engaging in the proxy bomb operations was to shift tactics dramatically and to teach the British security forces a lesson they would not soon forget. Despite knowing that the public reaction would be extremely negative, some IRA members made the argument that "it will be worth it." What was unlikely, however, was that the IRA could have predicted the extent of that negativity, and apparently the tide of public revulsion was enough to force the IRA to abandon the tactic altogether after only a handful of incidents.[48] Adding to the undercurrent of despair surrounding the incidents, the British government's attempt to hold political talks aimed at ending London's eighteen years of direct rule was on the verge of collapse. The IRA's new tactic had damaged mixed working-class neighborhoods and united many Catholics and Protestants in outrage.[49]

A resident of the Buncara checkpoint area repeatedly cited in the press reflected the typical reaction of many locals. "Everybody was in tears. I've never seen a community so moved. There wasn't a dry eye." Sobbing as she spoke out against the IRA, she added, "Mrs. Thatcher ought to send in the SAS and clear them (the IRA) out once and for all. . . . I don't mind saying it, today I'm ashamed to be Irish."[50]

Whatever the precise reasons for the apparent discontinuation of the tactic, the proxy operation was a public relations disaster for the IRA. Reactions across the Irish political spectrum were uniformly negative and condemned the operation outright. The British secretary of state for Northern Ireland, Peter Brooke, officially stated,

> They have sunk to new levels of depravity by using people whose families have been held hostage as human bombs. It is hard to imagine anything more evil than tying a man into his car laden with explosives and then forcing him to drive to where the bomb was detonated. Horrible as these murders have been, they have not advanced the cause of those who perpetrated them by a single millimeter. Indeed, they have set it back still further.[51]

The moderate and predominantly Catholic Social Democratic and Labor Party (SDLP) leader John Hume said, "The anger at this particular atrocity is far deeper than anything I have seen in this city since 1972 when a local youth who had joined the Army was shot while visiting his family. The one word that is on everybody's lips is the word 'coward.'

"Let me repeat it. I hope you're listening, you cowards, using a human being in the way you did."[52]

Former SDLP member Seamus Mallon, then also a member of Parliament, said the Catholic community in particular would condemn the use of such proxies. Speaking at the scene of the Newry attack, he observed, "To use a 65-year-old man to do the IRA's dirty work is the essence of cowardice. . . . I think there will be great anxiety about the use of proxy bombs in this way because it means that every single person who owns a car in the north of Ireland is vulnerable, every single person can be used in that way."[53]

In fact, other Republicans offered little to no support for these new tactics. According to one former member of the IRA, staunchly pro-IRA Republican supporters complained to IRA members that the proxy bomb operations made the IRA "look like those fanatics in the Middle East."[54]

Newspaper headlines screamed both disbelief and revulsion, and the Catholic clergy also voiced its opposition.

In contrast to the sometimes ambiguous proclamations from mullahs and sheikhs that often accompany Islamic martyrdom operations in the Middle East and South Asia, the Catholic Church was far from ambiguous in its condemnation of the proxy attacks. Throughout the Irish Troubles, the role of the Catholic Church and its members was poorly understood. Although the Catholic Church officially did not promote Republican ideals, many of its members often tacitly supported the goals of a united independent Ireland. More extreme examples are easily found, however. Certain sympathetic clergymen blessed ASU members before their operations or at times provided shelter to ASU personnel. Both Sean O'Callaghan and Eamon Collins provide numerous examples of clerical collusion.

> The IRA regularly used this house for meetings, for the induction of recruits and as a general safe house and base in the area. The priest was an active IRA sympathizer with influence at the highest levels of the republican movement. He was as good as regarded as a senior IRA activist . . . : "That was a good job" he would say. . . . As the four of us entered the [safe] house the senior priest insisted on blessing us with holy water from the little font inside the door. It was something he always did.[55]

However, on the occasion of the 1990 attacks, the church uniformly spoke out against them. The city of Londonderry, once the IRA heartland, turned its back on the men whom its Catholic bishop, Dr. Edward Daly, described as "Satan's followers." In one of the most powerful condemnations ever made of the terrorists and their supporters, Daly stood by Gillespie's coffin and described the IRA as "those who try to justify the unjustifiable."[56] In the poor Catholic neighborhoods where Republican support was the strongest, Patsy Gillespie's death sparked a backlash against the IRA.[57]

The consensus at the time was that the IRA Army Council had seriously misjudged the mood and tolerance of even its own supporters. What Home Secretary Reginald Maulding once famously described as Northern Ireland's "acceptable level of violence" had been fundamentally breached.

A psychological barrier had been crossed, and the IRA was going to pay for it. Amazingly, actually a few more proxy attacks occurred before the tactic was abandoned altogether. But the exact combination of targets, locations, and victims proved elusive, and the IRA struggled to find the right combination that might prove acceptable to its public. Perhaps assuming that their use of Catholic drivers had caused the negative public reaction, the IRA tried to construct another proxy bomb operation—this time with a Protestant man—in 1991. On February 3, the IRA forced Tommy Wallace to drive a five-hundred-pound proxy bomb from Tobermore to the Ulster Defence Regiment Army Center on Station Road, Magherafelt, while they held his wife hostage in another car.[58] Wallace escaped and shouted a warning before the improvised device exploded, damaging part of the base and fifty surrounding houses. Wallace had also worked for the construction firm Henry Brothers, a company that the IRA chronically targeted (and murdered three of its employees) because the firm did construction work for the security forces.[59]

In addition, occasionally the IRA used hoax proxy bombs deliberately to disrupt everyday life and create a false sense of security until the time when the next proxy driver would deliver "the real thing." As Horgan's interviewees argued, the strategic logic of the proxy bomb—and the psychological security the IRA derived from the operations even though they were low in number—meant from the IRA's perspective that the British security forces were disabused of the belief that the IRA would not "attempt the unimaginable."[60] According to one interviewee, despite the backlash, the proxy bomb operations of 1990 managed to achieve the limited objective of shaking the British "out of their complacency." Later, a series of false proxy bombs, in which the IRA claimed cars were filled with explosives, subsequently closed off Belfast's city center for hours, and in December 1992, a series of bomb warnings in Belfast and Lisburn caused widespread economic disruption.[61]

It is probable that the lack of resonance for proxy bombs within the broader Republican family eventually convinced the IRA to abandon their use altogether. Within the first few months of 1991, the IRA shifted tactics and its focus back to the British mainland, bombing railway stations in London and British military hospitals. If they used proxies, they did so on the mainland rather than in Northern Ireland. But the key characteristic of the 1990 attacks was forgone: the IRA reverted to its previous policy and allowed the driver to escape after he (or she) delivered the explosive. Even once the tactic was exported to London—this time using taxi drivers held at gunpoint—the driver was not destroyed along with his vehicle.

The IRA had not launched an attack on Britain since December 1983, when six people died and ninety-one were injured in a car bomb attack on Harrods. The civilian deaths caused in this attack led to public outrage, exacerbated divisions within the Republican leadership, and caused a tactical rethink and switch in focus to military and political targets. Sinn Féin repeatedly emphasized that the IRA's campaign was against what it called military and establishment targets. A mini explosion in the West End, on St Alban's Street behind Piccadilly Circus, was the first example of the proxy bomb's use in London. The attack marked a new stage in the IRA's terror campaign, which included fourteen explosions in the first twenty-nine days of October 1993 to upset the tourist industry, and targeted Whitehall and Downing Street with some of the most audacious operations that the Provos ever conducted.[62]

Gerry Adams, president of Sinn Féin, urged the IRA to "think, then think again" before launching attacks against civilians.[63] For insiders like Sean O'Callaghan, the bombings were an indication that IRA hard-liners were interested in high-profile terror tactics, such as those used in the 1970s and 1980s.[64]

The IRA's attacks on Britain, typically, were intended to shift what was perceived as the British public's indifference to the daily realities of Northern Ireland. On November 15, 1993, the foiled plot to explode a one-ton bomb at Canary Wharf in London's Docklands (where, three years later, an explosion would herald the end of the IRA's 1994 cease-fire) succeeded in nudging a reaction from the business world. The Association of British Insurers announced the next day that its members would no longer routinely offer comprehensive cover against terrorist damage to businesses and buildings.[65]

An Phoblacht published an interview with an "IRA member" that outlined the apparent theory behind the IRA's broadening of its targets. The anonymous "volunteer" said that the IRA's tactic was to "chop and change guerrilla tactics": "We will spread the Crown Forces [the IRA's term for the security forces] into guarding as many areas as possible and stretch them to the utmost. We will nibble and bite at them from every angle. We will not allow them to set the agenda or choose the field of battle. . . . We will not let them contain the fighting."[66]

Impact

Six men were arrested in the Irish Republic for the 1990 proxy bomb attacks. All were accused of IRA membership, and one was charged with possessing arms and ammunition.[67] Two of the accused, Anthony Heaney and William McGuinness (brother of Martin McGuinness, currently the deputy first minister of Northern Ireland), were charged with membership in a proscribed organization as well as failing to account for their movements. In a Special Criminal Court in April 1992, both were acquitted of IRA membership charges, but in June they were convicted of offenses under section 52 of the penal code and sentenced to six months' imprisonment.[68]

Although suicide bombers may cause mostly fear, there can be no doubt that in Ireland, proxy bombs have caused mostly anger. Despite the IRA members' perception of having achieved the upper hand in the psychological warfare waged against the British Army, overall the proxy bomb tactic resulted in weakening the legitimacy of "armed struggle" in the eyes of Irish Republicans.[69] Indeed, that the tactic was largely discredited suggested that it may well have been a calculated gamble that certain figures in the Republican movement allowed to proceed in order to weaken the position of alleged IRA hawks, or those who favored armed action over electoral politics.[70] The logic of this approach is that the widespread public revulsion would have strengthened the position of the so-called doves in the Provisional IRA and, in particular, that of Gerry Adams, who was largely responsible for considering how the movement could effectively abandon violence and subsequently focus on electoral politics.

Another popular theory alleges British collusion in the attacks and the deliberate promotion of the tactic by Martin McGuinness, who was allegedly working as a double agent for the British MI6. This theory resurfaced in mid-2006 when Martin Ingram, a former operative with the covert Force Research Unit, publicly endorsed what he claimed was a transcript of a secretly recorded conversation between McGuinness and his handler in which the tactic is supposedly discussed. The British-Irish Human Rights Watch said, "This month [we] sent a confidential report to the Historical Enquiries Team on the three incidents that occurred 24th October 1990. . . . At least two security force agents were involved in these bombings, and allegations have been made that the 'human bomb' strategy was the brainchild of British Intelligence."[71] The human rights organization raised questions as to whether the Royal Ulster Constabulary (now known as the Police Service of Northern Ireland) and the army's Force Research Unit had prior intelligence about the bombings. McGuinness naturally denied the claim that he was an agent.

A broader issue here worth considering comes from the work of Andrew Kydd and Barbara Walter, who argue that acts of suicide terrorism function as a spoiler mechanism during possible peace processes.[72] Although proxy bombs are certainly not martyrdom operations as popularly conceived, the similarities between elements of proxy bombing and suicide terrorism are powerful and significant. Prior to the 1990 attacks, and despite dramatic attacks throughout the previous years, a relative calm and stability that is rarely acknowledged now had begun to creep tentatively into Northern Ireland. The region had enjoyed "a series of successes in persuading companies from the United States and elsewhere to build factories, offices, stores and a hotel" that had "given rise to a spirit of optimism among Roman Catholics and Protestants."[73]

Thus it is possible to argue that the choice to use human bombs was less a tactical innovation to overcome British target hardening, or even a retaliatory strike by Active Service Units, and more of a way to promote dissent within the Republican movement and spoil a possible peace process with Great Britain. The timing of some attacks would lend credibility to Kydd and Walter's argument that the orchestration of such campaigns is deliberate in order to negatively impact any progress on the peace front.

Yet another example of this spoiler dynamic occurred in April 1993. On April 24, the day before John Hume and Gerry Adams issued their first joint statement, the Provisional IRA forced two taxi drivers to ferry bombs to Downing Street and New Scotland Yard. The operation failed when both drivers managed to abandon their taxis and shout warnings. That same day, however, the IRA exploded a one-ton bomb in Bishopsgate, London, at the

National Westminster Tower, causing damages in excess of £1 billion. A critical article published in the *Guardian* argued that the "timing suggests that they may have hoped to disrupt yesterday's meeting of the Anglo-Irish Intergovernmental Conference, and generally to diminish the wasting hopes that the Northern Ireland Secretary, Peter Brooke, might succeed in his attempts to bring the parties, North and South, into talks about political development."[74] Rather than advance any progress toward peace, the proxy bombs prompted the British government to send additional troops into Northern Ireland for the first time since 1986.[75] It is well documented that the increased likelihood of peace negotiations encouraged splits and divisions in the IRA. The Real IRA splinter group formed in 1997 after the mainstream Republican movement signed the Mitchell Principles of peace and democracy (named for U.S. senator George Mitchell, who helped negotiate them).[76]

Interestingly, in the changing environment of Irish tactics and innovations, the use of the proxy bomb shifted from the IRA to the Ulster Defence Association. Former U.S. ambassador James W. Spain wrote, "In a return to the 'notorious proxy bombings' of a few years before, the Ulster Freedom Fighters (UFF) thugs compelled a Catholic cab driver to carry a bomb into a church which they then detonated by remote control, killing him and two others."[77] According to Spain, outside the church a Protestant crowd chanted, "Yabba Dabba Do, Any Fenian will do!"

British home secretary Kenneth Baker always claimed that the IRA had close connections with several other terrorist organizations worldwide, especially Arab groups.[78] This alleged connection among various terrorist groups might explain how proxy bombs have spread to conflicts beyond Northern Ireland. Though the human proxy bomb had been unpopular in Ireland, unsurprisingly it has caught on in conflicts as diverse as those in Iraq, Afghanistan, and Colombia.

Guerrillas from the Revolutionary Armed Forces of Colombia (Fuerzas Armadas Revolucionarias de Colombia [FARC]) first used a variety of proxy bombs to devastating effect in the 1990s. FARC employed diverse delivery mechanisms, including dog bombs and donkey bombs as well as booby-trapping victims' corpses to explode when the authorities attempted to investigate a crime scene. In January 2003, FARC guerrillas forced a civilian into becoming a proxy bomber in an attack on the Colombian security forces. This attack is set against a backdrop of long-standing collaboration between the IRA and FARC. In particular, FARC has long mirrored Irish Republican terrorist tactics. It began developing its own homemade mortars in 1998 with "many similarities in both design and operation systems" to the IRA mortars.[79] IRA booby-trap devices, which used flash units to detonate the explosives, were found in a FARC training camp. The devices were identical to what the IRA Active Service Units in Northern Ireland used and what the Republicans had originally developed to kill a suspected British Army undercover agent. The IRA-FARC links came to light in August 2001 when Colombian authorities at Bogotá airport arrested three well-known and prominent Republicans: James Monaghan, Martin McCauley, and Niall Connolly. Prosecutors alleged that the men had been training FARC rebels in the construction and use of explosive devices.

In Afghanistan, the Taliban have adopted proxy bomb techniques perfected in Ireland. As *Irish Independent* journalist Jim Cusack detailed, explosive devices and bombing techniques almost identical to the IRA's have reached Afghanistan through al-Qa'ida in Iraq, which learned its methods from Middle Eastern terror groups such as the PLO and Hizballah. They, in turn, had trained with the IRA in Southern Lebanon.[80]

After considerable success in Iraq, since 2006 several VBIEDs have been used in Afghanistan. In March 2007 a bomb was detonated outside Jalalabad next to a convoy of U.S. embassy officials, injuring five. In January 2006 another attack killed twenty-one civilians in Kandahar Province.

These attacks have been defined as suicide bombings, but more recently the North Atlantic Treaty Organization forces have discovered that, as in Ireland during the proxy bomb campaign, "the drivers are often forced to transport the bombs after their families have been held hostage. They are deceived into thinking they simply have to park the vehicle and leave it to detonate but, instead, the bomb is detonated by remote control by bombers following in another car."[81]

An increase in the use of proxy bombs mirrors the Irish experience. According to reports from Iraq, several failed suicide car bombers have been preempted, and U.S. forces found the drivers handcuffed to the steering wheels of their vehicles.[82] Truck drivers in Iraq were aware that they were

carrying weapons or illegal materials but did not know that they were suicide car bombers. According to terrorism specialist Marc Sageman, the
trucks bombs were detonated from a distance by cellular phones, which
were used to trigger the devices.[83] In one case, a taxi driver in Baghdad who
had left his vehicle briefly to buy coffee returned to discover a bomb under
the backseat.[84] If it had gone unnoticed, his case almost certainly would
have been viewed as an unwitting or perhaps "oblivious" proxy bomb.

In July 2008 the driver of a car at the Fourteen Ramadan Street checkpoint in western Baghdad jumped into the street shouting, "A mine is hidden in my car!" The man had been kidnapped a short time earlier, and only
while he was waiting at the checkpoint did he notice that the kidnappers
had hidden explosives under the seat of his car.

The same scenario was repeated at the same checkpoint two weeks later.
It is noteworthy that this checkpoint is the first point at which cars coming
from the Jamia neighborhood are required to stop for inspection. After the
U.S. troop surge in 2007, al-Qa'ida in Iraq fighters had been pushed into
Jamia. Their new strategy was to send their kidnapping victims, people who
had no idea they were carrying deadly cargo to attack American troops,
including people who allegedly had Down syndrome.[85]

Tentative Conclusions

Although the IRA appears to have responded to the public rejection of
human bombs, it continued to engage in escalating violence throughout the
1990s as peace negotiations developed. Its rejection of human proxies did
not signal a shift away from extreme forms of violence; rather, it signaled a
shift in the IRA's focus on and sensitivity to civilian targets. After a cease-fire
between August 1994 and February 1996, hopes were high that a new framework for peace was achievable, but as David McKittrick details, the 1996
Canary Wharf bombing all but extinguished that incarnation of the peace
process.[86] Part of the IRA's renewed campaign of violence (albeit without
using proxy bombers) was a reflection of what the Irish Republicans widely
perceived as a stalled peace process, a process that produced nothing for the
IRA. In an interview in An Phoblacht, a council hawk reportedly said, "There
wasn't even a glimmer of hope that Britain and the Unionist leaderships were

remotely engaged in positive engagement at this time. The IRA therefore couldn't persist in a sham [peace process] whose sole purpose had become the attainment of IRA surrender."[87]

Despite often dramatic setbacks, the Irish peace process continued to bear fruit. In the aftermath of the horrific Real IRA bombing of Omagh in August 1998, the IRA proxy bombs were relegated to a historical footnote. Undoubtedly the significance of the 1990 attacks and the subsequent shift in tactics because of public disapproval were echoed in the reactions to the Omagh bombing.

We do not know for certain what motivated the IRA to shift its tactics toward (and soon after, away from) using the proxy bombs of 1990. What we do know is that the proxy bomb campaign demonstrates the ultimate power of public opinion. Although terrorists might not be easily deterred, might respond to increased coercion with more violence, and might use their opposition's counterterror tactics to mobilize more recruits, the most powerful countermeasure tool of all may be the ways in which their community perceives them.

Fighting with a Double-Edged Sword?
Proxy Militias in Iraq, Afghanistan, Bosnia, and Chechnya

BRIAN GLYN WILLIAMS

You're faced with people put in power, and they obviously aren't going to want to give it up.

—LT. ERICK KUYLMAN, FIRST BATTALION, SIXTY-EIGHTH ARMOR
REGIMENT, ADHAMIYA, IRAQ

The use of proxy warriors is as old as warfare itself, even in Manichaean clashes of ideas and civilizations. The pagan Philistines used the soon-to-be-king David and his warriors to fight for them; the Persians hired Xenophon and his Greek mercenaries; the Romans hired Attila and his Huns. When the United States commenced its own war of ideas with the Soviet Union, American Cold Warriors continued this tradition and used Vietnamese Montagnards, Afghan mujahidin, and Nicaraguan contras to wage proxy war against the Communist "evil empire."

It is not surprising that a new generation of Americans has similarly chosen to make use of little-understood surrogate fighters, tribal proxies, and mercenary militias in their Manichaean war against the "evil doers." The most notable example of this practice has been in Iraq, where as many as 100,000 members of the much-touted *Sahwa* (Awakening) militias were hired to eradicate al-Qa'ida in Iraq from Sunni areas. In one of the most unexpected developments of the war, these proxy fighters helped transform the dreaded Sunni Triangle into a showcase for the success of Gen. David Petraeus's "surge" strategy.

In light of this remarkable success, this policy has recently been applied in Afghanistan, where local anti-Taliban militiamen known as *arbakai* (messengers) have similarly begun to be used in counterinsurgency activities.[1]

The Afghan strategy is built upon the stunning success of 2001's Operation Enduring Freedom, which was essentially a proxy war. The campaign saw the Afghan tribal force, comprising Uzbek, Tajik, and Hazara members of the Northern Alliance opposition, "eviscerate" the Taliban. These native fighters provided America with its "boots on the ground" (there were only 350 U.S. special operators in Afghanistan when the Taliban regime was destroyed) and helped mop up Taliban resistance in the cities and country-side with the Americans' close air support.

But as the cases of David and Attila clearly demonstrate, proxy forces do not always make the most reliable allies. Although David fought for the Philistine *serens* (commanders) against various Canaanite groups, he and his mercenaries ultimately turned on their masters and destroyed them. Attila similarly took funds from the East and West Roman Empires to keep other tribes of the steppes at bay, but then he turned on them and earned the title Scourge of God. Similarly, few issues are as contentious in Afghanistan today as the destabilizing role of America's Northern Alliance proxy warlord allies vis-à-vis the Hamid Karzai government.

Iraq is no exception to the rule. Although undoubtedly surrogate warriors have played a major role in some of the greatest successes of the war in Iraq, questions remain about the long-term implications for funding and training a massive force of predominantly Sunni gunmen (many of them ex-Ba'thists or insurgents) in a country that has come close to the brink of a full-blown sectarian war between Sunnis and Shi'a. These concerns are especially important now that the Sahwa Council's American paymasters have with-drawn as of December 2011.

Some fear that the United States has not thought out the long-term ramifications to the centralized (Shi'i-dominated) Iraqi state of arming of so many non-state (Sunni) actors. Many observers want to know whether the U.S. military is simply arming an untrustworthy element for an even-tual war with the U.S.-backed Shi'i government of Prime Minister Nouri al-Maliki. Will the surrounding Sunni states use this Sunni Awakening force to wage proxy war against Iranian-backed Shi'i groups, such as the Badr Organization's militias or Moqtada al-Sadr's Jaish al-Mahdi (Mahdi Army), in the future? Should this potentially dangerous policy be applied to Afghanistan before its ramifications for Iraq are fully understood? And most importantly, are there any historical precedents for such a policy that can provide insight into the possible long-term implications for this sort of proxy counterinsurgency strategy?

Although the West has been using surrogate fighters to wage counter-jihad in the Middle East ever since T. E. Lawrence (known as Lawrence of Arabia) armed the Arabs to fight against the Ottoman sultan-caliph, several case studies have relevance for studying the implications of America's proxy war in Iraq. Namely, one should review the Soviets' use of "Revolutionary Defense" militias during the anti-mujahidin Afghan war of the 1980s, the Serbs' use of Muslim proxy forces against Alija Izetbegovic's Muslim government in Bosnia in the mid-1990s, and the Russian Federation's use of Chechen militias in its wars with Chechen jihadi-secessionists from 1994 to the present. These historical precedents have similarities to the U.S. strategy in Iraq and can point to some of the short-term benefits and long-term pitfalls of using proxy fighters to wage counterinsurgencies in Afghanistan and greater Islamic Eurasia. History in effect can help predict possible outcomes of using proxy forces in the war in Iraq.

Before commencing this background study, however, this chapter will provide an overview of the recent developments in Iraq from the creation of the Anbar Awakening militias in the autumn of 2006 to the winter of 2012. This analysis will lay out the benefits and drawbacks of this unfolding strategy as they apply to Iraq and will demonstrate the urgency for studying the earlier precedents.

Anbar Awakens: Iraq's Sunni Tribes Turn on al-Qa'ida

In the summer of 2006 the war in Iraq was at a low point for Coalition forces. Although the leader of al-Qa'ida in Iraq (AQI) Ayman al-Zawahiri had been recently killed, his organization felt confident enough to declare the establishment of the Islamic State in Iraq. The headquarters for this new jihadi caliphate was to be Ramadi, the provincial capital of Anbar, Iraq's largest province and a hotbed of Sunni insurgent activity.

Al-Qa'ida could not have chosen a better base for its state-building project than Anbar Province. Inhabiting Anbar were the xenophobic Sunni tribes that had risen up against the U.S.-led Coalition when it overthrew Saddam

Hussein's Sunni-dominated regime. The Sunni tribesmen resented both the de-Ba'thification of the government and military and the rise of their Shi'i rivals. Anbar formed the western front of the Sunni Triangle, a deadly realm of improvised explosive devices (IEDs), sniper attacks, ambushes, and fanatical Sunni insurgent groups, such as the Islamic Army of Iraq, the 1920 Revolution Brigade, Ansar al-Sunna, and most deadly of all, al-Qa'ida in Iraq (or the Islamic State of Iraq). The province's Sunni tribes and insurgent groups protected AQI operatives because they were leading them in the struggle against the Americans, who had installed their Shi'a enemies in Baghdad.

Secure in the protection of their Sunni Arab allies, al-Qa'ida's leaders not only claimed leadership of the Sunni insurgency, they also launched a destabilizing jihad on Shi'a "snakes." AQI's war against the Shi'a soon surpassed its war against the U.S.-led Coalition in its brutality (ultimately, though, the Sunnis would lose this war, a point that will be addressed later).

Although many Americans grew despondent as the death toll from the Sunni insurgency increased, AQI's fortunes soared as its brutal online videos of beheadings, sniper attacks, and IED ambushes inspired hundreds of foreign jihadi volunteers to come to Iraq and fight. Al-Qa'ida warrior-terrorists openly flew their jihadi *al-Rayah* (banners) on the streets of Ramadi to proclaim their dominance. It seemed to many jihadis as if the dream of Abu Mus'ab al-Zarqawi was coming true. The country would descend into a chaos that would destroy U.S. president George W. Bush's vision for a democratic Iraq and allow the Sunni insurgents (led by AQI's new amir [commander], an Egyptian named Omar al-Masri) to carve out a state in north-central Iraq. From there the Salafi-jihadi caliphate would spread the holy war against "apostates" throughout the Middle East.

But for all of its outward signs of momentum, AQI made enemies in the very region considered to be the cradle of the Sunni insurgency. The problems began when the foreign-led AQI fighters began to offend the sensibilities of the prickly Sunni tribesmen in Anbar Province. Many of the AQI fighters were foreign Wahhabi-Salafis, takfiris (extremists who label other Muslims "non-Muslim" and fight them), or local converts to these puritanical Islamic sects. Problems arose when the AQI fighter-terrorists began to enforce their strict interpretation of Islam in an area traditionally known for its Sufi-mystical Islamic tradition and support of the secular, Ba'thist regime. Whereas some of the fundamentalists' new decrees were laughable (for example, women were banned from buying cucumbers because of their phallic shape), others, such as bans on cigarette smoking, participation in elections, and the use of Internet, infuriated many tribesmen.[2] One report from Fallujah—a city in Anbar Province where U.S. contractors were gruesomely executed, burned, and hung on a bridge in 2004—described the growing tension between AQI and locals as follows:

"People in Fallujah, known as the city of mosques, have chafed at the stern brand of Islam that the newcomers brought with them. The non-Iraqi Arabs berated women who did not cover themselves head-to-toe in black—very rare in Iraq—and violently opposed local customs rooted in the town's more mystical (Sufi) religious tradition." In one case in Fallujah, a Sufi man killed a Kuwaiti because he said he could not pray at the grave of an ancestor (a Sufi tradition that has been attacked by fundamentalists from the Gulf states as "un-Islamic").[3]

Local sheikhs also complained that the AQI thugs were bad for business and particularly for concrete production, which was a lucrative source of income for many tribal leaders. As the violence against those tribesmen whom AQI defined as spies and traitors increased, the economy of Anbar Province began to suffer. AQI also undermined one influential Anbar sheikh's smuggling to Syria, and he came to see AQI as a competitor. Other sheikhs wanted to partake in elections to increase their power against the Shi'a, but al-Qa'ida threatened them if they collaborated with the "infidel elections." One observer also noted that the Arab sheikhs also disliked the AQI outsiders marrying local women because it impinged on their sense of *ird* (honor).[4] Another bone of contention was AQI's jihad against the Shi'a. Several Anbar tribes included both Shi'i and Sunni branches, and they resented the AQI's killing of fellow tribesmen.

As these tensions simmered, AQI amirs began to undermine the power of influential Arab sheikhs from the Zoba and Dulaim confederations and even resorted to killing tribal heads who refused to submit to their rule. Tensions came to a head when AQI militants killed a sheikh whose followers had taken salaried jobs working with the Coalition. AQI's goals were clearly to intimidate other Anbar tribesmen from working with the Coalition and to seize power. To add insult to injury, AQI went against all tradition and committed the sacrilege of refusing to permit the grieving sheikh's family to bury his body for three days. AQI compounded matters when it blew up Arab tribesmen from the other tribes who lined up at police stations for desperately needed jobs.

But AQI's policies of intimidation, fighting with the Shi'a, and attempts to dominate the Sunni insurgency ultimately backfired. As businesses closed, children were prevented from going to school, defeated Sunnis were cleansed from Shi'i neighborhoods, and lawlessness increased, one tribal sheikh from a subbranch of Iraq's largest tribe, the Dulaim, decided that he had had enough. The leader, Abdul Satter Abu Risha, was head of the 160,000-member Abu Risha subtribe and had a personal grievance against AQI. As it transpired, AQI members had killed ten of his relatives, including four of his brothers. He had cause for a tribal vendetta, and Abu Risha, as he became known, decided to approach the Americans and offer to work with them to gain his revenge. In September 2006 he left his walled compound in Ramadi, walked to the nearby American base, and offered the services of his tribe to Col. Sean McFarland.

Abu Risha offered McFarland the service of hundreds if not thousands of Anbar tribesmen who knew the pulse of their communities. They knew which people were members of al-Qa'ida, where their weapons caches were hidden, where their safe houses were located, who smuggled them into the country, and who supplied them with food and shelter. If the United States helped the tribesmen clean AQI out of their neighborhoods, they would provide the Coalition forces with the intelligence and manpower to ensure AQI was destroyed.

Thrilled to have a prominent Anbar leader come over to their side, the Americans agreed to work with Abu Risha and several allied sheikhs. The agreement was that the Americans would not supply the sheikhs' followers with weapons (which would mean arming nongovernment actors, and besides, Iraq was awash in weapons), but they would provide the Iraqis with salaries of ten dollars a day, uniforms, supplies, and logistic support. By the fall of 2006 Abu Risha's bold stance had inspired other sheikhs, who began to join what became known as the *Sahwa al-Anbar*. In U.S. military speak, its members were originally called Critical Infrastructure Security Guards or Iraqi Security Volunteers. Thousands of Anbar tribesmen now offered their services to the Americans to help fight AQI. Many of them were disgruntled former insurgents, and others were simply unemployed tribesmen searching for a way to bring security to their neighborhoods and earn a salary. The Americans ended up paying the Anbar Awakening militiamen, whom they called CLCs (concerned local citizens), three hundred dollars a month to patrol their neighborhoods, run checkpoints, join them on joint patrols and raids, help them find IED, and, most importantly, wage proxy war against AQI.

One Anbar tribesman described his community's newfound resolve to challenge AQI as follows: "They [AQI terrorists] ask how I would feel if they kidnapped my wife and children and kill and rape them. But I am not worried about those bastards. I know they could kill me at any moment, but if we do not fight them we will all die anyway." Another claimed, "Al Qa'eda came here saying they would give freedom. But they killed the innocent people and made problems between the Sunni and Shia. They are liars and terrorists, not resistance fighters."[5]

By November 2006, Abu Risha and leaders similar to those interviewed in the preceding paragraph had fulfilled their promise to Colonel McFarland and had supplied hundreds of policemen to patrol Ramadi. While AQI fought back, ferociously killing many Awakening members in a targeted assassination campaign, more and more nationalist insurgents joined the Anbar Awakening Council. Many of them had been involved in "red-on-red" internecine violence with AQI and decided to throw in their lot with the lesser enemy, the Americans. For both the Americans and the Anbar tribesmen, the maxim "The enemy of my enemy is my friend" created the foundation for a working alliance.

By the summer of 2007 the U.S. military and its Anbar Awakening allies were gradually able to retake Ramadi, and U.S. casualties in the greater region dropped by more than 90 percent. Over forty major Anbar tribes came over to the CLCs' side, and Anbar gradually began to experience peace. One source called the American decision to wage a proxy war against AQI "perhaps the best thing to happen to the U.S. in Iraq since it invaded 4½ years ago."[6]

In September 2008 President Bush recognized the importance of this allied-mercenary fighting force and publicly met with Abu Risha during a brief visit to Iraq. Abu Risha, who showed up for the meeting in a gold embroidered dishdasha robe and with a well-coifed beard, played the role of an enlightened tribal ally. But in so doing, he may have inadvertently signed his death warrant. As he spoke of boldly spreading the Anbar model to other provinces, AQI decided to kill him.

Ten days after Bush's visit, AQI finally succeeded. Abu Risha was killed in a terrorist bomb attack that was meant to send a warning to other "traitors to the jihad." But Abu Risha's death only infuriated more leaders, who then publicly attended his funeral and vowed revenge on AQI. By the spring of 2008 the momentum had turned, and AQI was on the run. AQI had been largely driven out of Iraq's largest and most deadly province.

In the fall of 2008 Anbar was declared to be peaceful enough for the Americans to transfer its control to the Iraqi government. AQI had been thoroughly defeated in less than two years, thus providing the United States with its greatest victory in the counterinsurgency. Although the surge in U.S. troops in the spring and summer of 2007 certainly contributed to these developments, those troops on the ground understood that America's proxy fighters had largely won the war in Iraq's largest province (especially as the surge was focused primarily on securing Baghdad).

As the Anbar Awakening Council (also known as Anbar Salvation Council) helped bring peace and stability to the province, AQI transferred its headquarters to Diyala Province (northeast of Baghdad). Once again AQI brought chaos and bloodshed. In response to the mayhem (which included executions, forced marriages, robbery, and the enforcement of harsh Islamic law), local tribesmen in Diyala formed their own Diyala Salvation Council. This council united members of the Shamar, al-Jabbour, al-Zawba, Dulaim, Tamim, Bani Lam, and other tribes in a coordinated effort to resist AQI. Interestingly enough, local insurgent groups, including the 1920 Revolution Brigade and the Islamic Army in Iraq, also sent members to join the Diyala Salvation Council to fight their AQI rivals.

Frustrated in Diyala, AQI tried to establish its headquarters in other provinces as well, but this move only led to the birth of other CLC militias in those zones. By the spring of 2008 numerous groups, such as the Sons of Baghdad, the Guardians of Ghazaliya, the Amriya Freedom Fighters, the Baquba Guardians, the Hunters of Foreign Fighters, and the Knights in the Land of the Two Rivers had sprung up across Sunni-dominated areas of central Iraq. Anbar-style militias were found in Baghdad, Nineveh, Diyala, Babil, Tamim, and Saluhuddin Provinces, and their membership grew accordingly. In the beginning of 2008 their numbers were estimated to be at 50,000, but by the summer the number had soared to 100,000 members in more than 180 CLC militias. By this time AQI had fled north to Mosul, an area without a CLC presence, and there AQI is currently involved in occasional acts of terrorism.

In the process of chasing AQI out of the Sunni Triangle, Sunni neighborhoods throughout the region came under the de facto control of Sunni militiamen who were plainly identifiable at their checkpoints by their fluorescent vests or belts (similar to what American crossing guards wear) and light weapons. These men became responsible for keeping attacks on U.S. troops at bay and keeping AQI out of their neighborhoods.

But for all the undisputed success that CLCs have had in crushing al-Qa'ida and lowering U.S. and Iraqi Army casualties, some have questioned the long-term wisdom of funding and training former foes to act as a surrogate counterinsurgency force. Some voices have said that this subcontracting of the war to Sunni proxies has simply put the Sunni insurgency in suspended animation. Far from solving the problem, CNN correspondent Michael Ware, who has reported extensively from Iraq, claimed, "primarily it's been putting your enemy on your payroll—the Sunni insurgents and many members of al Qaeda. That's what's brought down the violence. This is your American militia, the counterbalance to the Iranian militias."[7]

This strategy of hiring former enemies (many of them secular Sunni nationalists from the 1920 Revolution Brigade) has many observers worried that the Americans may be inadvertently sponsoring a faction for future civil war. Not surprisingly, the voices that have been raised loudest in opposition to this policy are found in the Shi'a-dominated government of Prime Minister al-Maliki.

Many of these same Sunni fighters had attacked al-Maliki's government just a year earlier. Al-Maliki's officials wanted to know whether the Americans, who had devoted millions of dollars to arming surrogate fighters to wage jihad against the Soviets in the 1980s, were once again embarking on a short-sighted policy that would lead to a disastrous case of blowback. Were the Americans aware that they might be inadvertently planting the seeds for the destruction of the Iraqi central government in a Lebanese-style civil war? Were they aware that today's allies could be tomorrow's enemies?

The "Sons of Iraq": Short-Term Friend, Long-Term Foe?

By the summer of 2008 the United States had come to depend upon the various CLC militias, which it now dubbed Sons of Iraq, to keep AQI out of vast swaths of territory. Both partners in the alliance knew the United States needed the proxy solution to work in order to demonstrate back home the success of the troop surge. With this knowledge came a newfound assertiveness on the part of disenfranchised elements that had joined the Sons of Iraq. Many former insurgents began to demand a greater say in running the country. They wanted a political role that reflected their increasing importance in the counterinsurgency, and they wanted to be recognized as Provincial Police Units.

This situation posed considerable problems for al-Maliki since many of the Sunni militias were strongly anti-Shi'a (not all Sons of Iraq were Sunni, as about 20 percent of them were actually Shi'a and were usually found in mixed Sunni-Shi'a areas). When the Sons of Iraq demanded that they be brought into the regular (salaried) police and army, the al-Maliki government balked. It was most reluctant to integrate its former enemies into the police and military structures that kept it in power.

In theory, however, the al-Maliki government promised to assume responsibility for paying the salaries of the Sons of Iraq on October 1, 2008, and to find all 100,000 of them jobs. Twenty thousand of the members were to be integrated into the security forces, and 80,000 were promised civilian jobs.

But such policies have been hindered because the al-Maliki government itself harbors many elements that are deeply anti-Sunni and disinclined to work with their former foes.[8] While with the Center for a New American Security and briefed by the U.S. military on the issue, Colin Kahl wrote of Prime Minister al-Maliki, "He thinks they [the Sons of Iraq] are thugs; he thinks they're hooligans."[9]

Far from embracing the Sons of Iraq, in September 2008 the al-Maliki government issued an arrest warrant for 650 of them for various crimes. The al-Maliki government arrested various militia leaders on charges ranging from kidnapping to killing Shi'a.[10] Brig. Gen. Nassir al-Hiti, commander of the Iraqi Army's Muthanna Brigade, which patrols the Abu Ghraib area west of Baghdad, declared of the Sons of Iraq, "These people are like cancer, and we must remove them." Sheikh Jalaladeen al-Sagheer, a Shi'i member of Parliament, agreed and said, "The state cannot accept the Awakening. Their days are numbered."[11] Such actions have led Kahl to claim that the al-Maliki government is "trying to pick fights with them [the Sons of Iraq], hoping that they will start a fight so that he can then turn around and finish them."[12] Those who are reluctant to embrace the Sons of Iraq also ask why the Iraqi government has moved to seize Basra from Moqtada al-Sadr's militia while ceding control of parts of Baghdad and the Sunni heartland to Sunni militias. In response to such actions, Sunnis have spoken in dark terms about what might happen if this new "third force" (along with the Shi'i-dominated army and police) is not rewarded for its achievements in establishing security. The Arab newspaper *Asharq Alawsat* predicted, "Failure on behalf of the Americans or the Iraqi authorities to integrate these men into governmental posts in the future will lead to a loss of confidence in the government and it will give these elements a reason to rebel—and they will be better equipped to do so, especially since they now have arms."[13] One Sons of Iraq leader warned that if the government does not add them to payroll, "people will be absolutely angry. . . . If any one offers them money to plant bombs or attack Americans they might go back to the insurgency."[14]

For their part, U.S. commanders have tended to downplay the tension between their Shi'a and Sunni allies. They have talked in optimistic terms of shifting tens of thousands of Sons of Iraq into the Iraqi government (in essence undoing the efforts of demobilizing the Iraqi Army in 2003–2004). But thus far fewer than six thousand Sons of Iraq militiamen have actually received jobs in the government, army, or police.[15] Sunnis see this number as far too low and feel they are being deliberately excluded from the govern-ment security forces.

In response to this crackdown and lack of integration, Sons of Iraq militias engaged in widespread protests and left checkpoints. There were also gunfights between Sons of Iraq and Iraqi Shi'i security forces. Many of these ex-insurgent militiamen feel that they have been betrayed and that the Iraqi government, which thinks it no longer needs them, has used them. They have threatened to return to the insurgency if 20 percent of their forces are not brought into the government security apparatus as promised.

At times it seemed as if the only thing preventing the al-Maliki government from turning on the Awakening Council was the presence of U.S. military personnel who came to rely upon their Sunni allies to deter casualties. The Americans intervened on behalf of arrested Sons of Iraq personnel on several occasions and tried to push the government to integrate more of them. Many U.S. servicemen grew close to their former foes and saw them as key to winning the war against the real enemy, al-Qa'ida.

But not all Americans embraced the Sons of Iraq. And there is some truth to the al-Maliki government's accusations about their unreliability. Abu Risha himself is reported to have been a mafia-style bandit who gave aid sanctuary to al-Qa'ida fighters before clashing with them in a turf war. Coalition troops actually arrested him on more than one occasion before he joined them. One Iraqi source claimed of Abu Risha, "He has no loyalty to anybody or any ideology. He wants money and power, and will shake the hand of anybody who he thinks can get him money and power. But tomorrow, he can turn and cut off the same hand if somebody else offers him more."[16]

Coalition forces have arrested Sons of Iraq members for involvement in kidnapping, blackmailing, and engaging in insurgent activity. (The Coalition had retinal scans on file for easy identification to help prevent this sort of activity.) Armed clashes at joint checkpoints have taken place between Sons of Iraq and Shi'i government security forces. Many Sons of Iraq openly refer to the government as the "Iranian occupation." One Sunni who met with Sons of Iraq militiamen summed up the ambiguities about this movement as follows:

> These people proved that they are qualified to stand against the killers who are trying to conquer our society and take it back to the Dark Ages.
> But that does not mean that all of those fighters can be trusted. For sure they are infiltrated by bad persons who are trying to hide themselves inside the Awakening Councils.

For me, when I was there, I did not trust those fighters for a second because I believe that everything was motivated by money and personal interest. I challenge any one of those fighters to say they are fighting for the sake of Iraq. Can I ask where those groups were in 2003? When the door was open for all Iraqis and Sunnis to join the new security forces and there was not any presence of Shiite militias to assassinate them?

. . . Most of them say that the Americans will leave sooner or later, so it is better to stand against the hidden occupation [Iran].

. . . Maybe the pullback of the American forces will be the occasion when the Iraqi government witnesses a new surprise from the Awakening.[17]

Some U.S. troops who have served alongside the Sons of Iraq have also grown disillusioned with them. Lt. Eric Kuylman, who served alongside the Sons of Iraq in Adhamiya, for example, claimed, "What you have is essentially armed factions, like mini-gangs, that operate in certain territories. They have outlived, I think, their service."[18] Nir Rosen, a former fellow at New York University Center on Law and Security, told Congress in April 2008, "The Americans think they have purchased Sunni loyalty. But in fact it is the Sunnis who have bought the Americans by buying time to challenge the Shiite government."[19]

Clearly there is trouble on the horizon for the Sons of Iraq (especially because the Shi'i-dominated security forces have more than 440,000 members), and the question of their potential to wage war against the Shi'a is of paramount importance. It seems to many observers as if the Sons of Iraq, similar to Moqtada al-Sadr's Jaish al-Mahdi (Iraq's largest and most powerful militia), are simply biding their time for a power struggle with their sectarian rivals now that the Americans have withdrawn. With more than 100,000 members in control of vast swathes of territory in central Iraq, America's proxy allies are seemingly well placed to lead Iraq down the path that Bosnia, Lebanon, Somalia, and Afghanistan followed. As President al-Maliki moves against Sunni lawmakers to assume more power, there is an increasing chance that the disenfranchised Sons of Iraq will take to their arms to fight the Shi'i for control of post-U.S. Iraq.

But is there a historical basis for making such a pessimistic read on the Sons of Iraq and their potentially disruptive role in post-U.S. Iraq? What does history tell us about the political and military role of similar counter-jihadi proxies in other lands after their "infidel masters" left them behind?

The cases of post-Soviet Afghanistan, post-Serbian northern Bosnia, and post-Russian Chechnya provide several cautionary tales with applications for Iraq. These tales would seem to support the contention that the United States is indeed arming a faction that will be involved in a civil war, retribution, and abuse of power. Although none of these case studies is perfect, the parallels and precedents they offer are perhaps the best indicator of what the future holds for the Sons of Iraq in post-2011 Iraq.

Pro-Communist Militias in Afghanistan, 1981–1998

By the mid-1980s the Soviet Fortieth "Limited Contingent," an occupation force roughly the size of the pre-surge Coalition force in Iraq, found itself confronted with an increasingly deadly mujahidin insurgency. While the allied Communist government of Afghan president Najibullah controlled the cities, the insurgents were making considerable gains in the countryside. By this time fanatical foreign fighters were also adding a deadly edge to the insurgency as they would later do in Iraq. Meanwhile, as the Russians' death toll climbed, the Soviet High Command looked for alternative strategies.

At this time the Soviets hit upon the idea of training and equipping disenfranchised "Afghanistani" ethnic groups (i.e., ethnic minorities that were not members of the dominant Pashtun-Afghan ethnic group) and disgruntled Pashtun-Afghan tribes. These victimized ethnic groups and disgruntled Pashtun-Afghan tribesmen could then be employed in a counterinsurgency role. Most importantly, with their knowledge of the local terrain, customs, and languages, they could assist the Soviets in interdicting rebel supply routes, waging combat, and clearing and holding territory. They would be the perfect proxy response to the CIA's policy of waging surrogate war via the predominantly Pashtun and Tajik mujahidin.

The Afghan Communist leader, President Najibullah, knew all too well that most of Afghanistan's peoples identified themselves first and foremost on the basis of their *qaum* (tribe, clan, district, or ethnic group), and he helped the Soviets exploit inter-qaum rivalries. Najibullah's intelligence officers carefully canvassed the country's various tribes and ethnic groups and quickly found that many were eager to take up arms against mujahidin groups to settle vendettas. Among the Pashtuns, for example, Najibullah was able to hire such prominent tribes as the Jajis, Tanais, Andarabis, Shinwaris, Arghandabis, Mohmands, Wadir Safays, and Afridis to guard mountain passes and keep mujahidin *ashrars* (bandits) out of their territory.[20] In addition to these tribes, the Communists hired Pashtun warlords, such as the infamous Khano and his rival Allah Noor, in the southern province of Helmand.[21]

But the most effective of all the pro-Communist Pashtun militias was the Achakazai tribal force of Ismatullah Muslim. In 1983 Ismatullah, a mujahidin commander, fell out with the Pakistani Inter-Services Intelligence over his unwillingness to submit to one of the major mujahidin parties based in Peshawar. He subsequently defected with his tribe to the Communist government and offered to help it wage counter-jihad. The Afghan Communist government promptly made Ismatullah a general, and when he was not entertaining guests in his house in Kabul with prostitutes and alcohol, he and his men kept the road between the Pakistani border and the southern city of Kandahar free of mujahidin.[22]

When the mujahidin gained the momentum in the late 1980s, Ismatullah proved to be a fickle ally. He tried to go back over to the mujahidin on at least one occasion and tried killing President Najibullah in a shoot-out. Without Soviet help and distrusted by the mujahidin, Ismatullah was eventually defeated on the Pakistani-Afghan border and died in exile in 1991.

The Pashtun militias were known as *watanparasts* (roughly meaning homeland defenders), or arbakai (messengers), and were successful in pacifying numerous districts in the tribal regions along the Pakistani border. When the Afghan Communist government finally collapsed in 1992, many of them became robbers, warlords, and opium compradors. These *jang salars* (warlords) robbed the local people at checkpoints, fought turf wars, and helped create the conditions that led to the rise of a new fundamentalist force that destroyed both the Communist militia heads and their mujahidin opponents, the Taliban.

In the north, the Afghan Communists and their Soviet allies also hired a militia made of oppressed Ismaili-Shi'i Hazaras (a Mongol ethnic group that speaks Farsi-Dari) to guard the strategic Salang Pass. The Hazaras, who were led by a *pir* (holy man) named Sayed Mansur Naderi, were only too pleased to accept guns, uniforms, and ammunition from the Soviets to wage a proxy war against their historic oppressors, the Pashtuns (the Sunni mujahidin resistance was made up of six Pashtun groups and one Tajik group). But for all their outward commitment to defending the Communist revolution, Naderi and his people fought against all sides that threatened their autonomy. They later joined in the bloody infighting during the Afghan Civil War from 1992 to 1998 with the aim of carving out an autonomous zone. By 1998, however, the Taliban had overrun the Ismaili Hazara militia, as it had the Pashtun arbakai equivalents.

But the largest pro-Communist proxy militia in Afghanistan was that belonging to the ethnic Uzbek commander, Gen. Abdul Rashid "Dostum" (a nom de guerre meaning my friend).[23] As with the Ismaili Hazaras, the dominant Afghan-Pashtuns had horribly repressed the Turko-Mongol Uzbeks. The Uzbeks were only too happy to accept the opportunity to take up arms against their hereditary enemies in return for money and a modicum of autonomy.[24]

Dostum and his Uzbek militia originally were hired to protect oil wells in his native province of Jowzjan, which is located in the northern steppe region known as Turkistan. The Soviets also paid the Uzbeks of the so-called Revolutionary Defense Militias to maintain security on the northern sections of the *Doroga Zhizn* (Russian for the Road of Life, or the supply route from Soviet Uzbekistan to Kabul). By the mid-1980s Dostum and his horse-riding Jowzjani Militia had cleared the rebels out of their province, and its capital, Sheberghan, became known throughout Afghanistan as Little Moscow. The effect was in many ways similar to the Anbar Awakening, and northern Afghanistan was, in Russian terminology, "pacified."

During the author's time spent living with Dostum and interviewing the people of the north (2003 and 2005), numerous sources gave glowing accounts of the security benefits Dostum had gained for his people by working with the Soviets. While Pashtun and Tajik villages were bombarded in Soviet search and destroy missions, Mazar-i-Sharif, the Uzbek-dominated capital of the north, flourished. There, women could attend university, markets were filled with Soviet goods, refugees found sanctuary, and the disruptions of warfare were minimal.[25]

In a 2005 interview with the author, Dostum summed up his reasons for joining the Soviet version of the Anbar Awakening as follows:

> When the mujahidin came to burn our [gas] facilities we fought them off. I gathered hundreds of our Jowzjani lads and we began to defend Sheberghan from the mujahidin. I knew who the local [Uzbek, Turkmen, and Tajik] mujahidin were and began to lure them to our side. If they did not attack us, we didn't attack them. I also offered them better pay.
>
> I pointed out that we were all good Muslims, none of us were Communists. I told them that outsiders [here he was referring to Gulbuddin Hekmatyar's Pashtun fundamentalist faction] were just fighting for their own gains under the banner of jihad. The mujahidin were being controlled by the Pakistanis who did not care about us people of the north the way the [Communist] government did.
>
> We were being used like we always had. But now we had the chance to fight for ourselves. The government gave us everything we asked for, from ambulances for our troops to tanks and salaries.[26]

Having successfully brought peace to the north, the Soviets decided to use Dostum's ferocious Uzbek troops against fundamentalist Pashtun mujahidin elements in the southeast. Dostum's fighters appear to have taken to this task with such a relish that the local Pashtuns took to calling them *gilamjam* (carpet thieves). Dostum's Uzbek militia was thrown into the most ferocious combat in the south and earned a reputation for effectiveness. For example, when Pashtun government troops were suspected of turning a blind eye to Pashtun mujahidin infiltration in the Paghman district and Khost, Kandahar, and Nangarhar Provinces, the Uzbeks were used to flush them out.

Although Dostum and his militia, which eventually came to include as many as fifty thousand salaried fighters, became a mainstay for the Najibullah regime following the Soviet withdrawal in 1989, many Pashtun Communists distrusted the Uzbek *ghulams* (an ancient Persian word meaning slave warrior).

For these Communists, ethnicity began to trump allegiance to the Communist government. Pashtun critics warned that the central government had simply bought off tens of thousands of potential ethnic enemies, armed and equipped them, and granted them de facto autonomy in return for their support.

Most alarming, they pointed out that there were only fifty thousand men in the regular army and air force. When one included the estimated fifteen thousand pro-government tribal militias in other areas along with Dostum's fifty thousand fighters, these militias outnumbered the forces directly under Kabul's control.[27] Not surprising, the militias had begun to ask for greater political power and recognition of their accomplishments in suppressing the mujahidin insurgency in their areas.[28]

As Soviet funds dried up by 1992, the Pashtun Communists (as with al-Maliki's Shi'a) feared that their praetorian guards would turn against them. Many of them, including Pashtun defense minister Shahnawaz Tanai, openly came to see the war in ethnic terms. These voices sought to have Najibullah demobilize Dostum's Uzbek forces as soon as possible so they could work out an agreement with Pashtun mujahidin. Prominent Pashtun Communists such as Tanai reached out to Pashtun mujahidin as the war began to ethnicize.

Forewarned about his enemies' plan, Dostum seized the last shipment of arms from the Soviet Union and revolted against his Pashtun-Communist masters. Tanai's prediction thus became a self-fulfilling prophecy as the government's proxy militias turned their guns on Kabul. Within days the Communist government collapsed, and President Najibullah fled for his life to the United Nations compound in Kabul.

As the jihad devolved into an ethnic scramble for power and territory, Dostum allied himself with the famous Tajik mujahidin rebel leader, Ahmad Shah Massoud, known as the Lion of Panjsher. But Dostum let it be known that he and his Uzbek ghulams were not about to be disarmed and "put back in their place" now that the jihad was over.[29] This boded trouble for Dostum and his ghulams.

When the new Tajik-Pashtun-dominated mujahidin government refused to give Dostum's ex-Communist militia a role in the new dispensation, he took his troops back to the north. There he carved out a de facto autonomous mini-state around Mazar-i-Sharif.[30] Although Dostum tried to avoid the struggle for Kabul that ensued among the Hazaras, the Tajiks, and the Pashtun mujahidin, he was drawn into it when his realm in the north was attacked. With the help of the pro-Communist Ismaili Hazara militias of Sayed Mansur Naderi, he fought against both the Tajik Massoud and the Pashtun leader Hekmatyar.

On one occasion, however, Dostum allied himself with Hekmatyar and joined in a bombardment of Tajik-controlled Kabul. Thus the Soviets' Uzbek proxy force morphed into an ethnic militia that helped carve up the country and partake in the destruction of Kabul (although Dostum played a far lesser role in destroying Kabul than the Pashtun leader Hekmatyar, Tajik leader Massoud, or Hazara leader Abdul Ali Mazari). For this reason non-Uzbeks saw Dostum as a warlord and blamed him for some of the Afghan capital's destruction. In the end, Dostum was loyal to himself and his own ethnic constituency and not to his country or the central government, which he felt had used him.

But for all his faults, Dostum the secularist did continue to work for the interests of his former Russian masters after the Afghan Communist government fell. Dostum's autonomous enclave in the plains of Afghan Turkistan served as a defensive shield for post-Soviet Central Asia from 1992 until 1998. During this period Dostum helped the Russians keep foreign jihadis out of the civil war in Tajikistan and prevented the mujahidin and Taliban from threatening Russia's Central Asian underbelly. In return, the Russians continued to supply Dostum's Uzbek faction known as the Jumbesh with Scud missiles, tanks, spare parts, weapons, and funds until the Taliban finally defeated him in 1998.[31]

In the post-Communist context, anti-jihadi proxy militias thus had a mixed record at best. At their best they continued to fight for their Afghan Communist allies until the funds dried up and local ethnic interests began to supercede their ties to the central government. In Dostum's case he also continued to serve his Russian masters' strategic interests for six years after the fall of the Afghan Communist government in 1992. At their worst the militias devolved into plundering bands that helped fragment Afghanistan and transform it into patchwork of warlord principalities. The ex-Communist militias helped wreak the sort of havoc that led to the birth of the Taliban as a cleansing force intent on destroying both the mujahidin and the Communist militias. Clearly the Communists' devolution of power to various tribal armies proved to be an effective tactic when they were strong. But when they were weak, these militias reverted to their local ethnic roots and partook in the Afghan Civil War that left the Afghan capital in ruins and tens of thousands of Afghans dead.

Pro-Serbian Bosnian Militias, 1992–1995

When the self-proclaimed Republika Srbska (Serbian) forces began to clash with the Bosnian Muslim government of President Alija Izetbegovic in 1992, not all Bosniaks (Muslim Bosnians) were committed to the struggle. Tens of thousands of self-proclaimed "moderate pragmatist" Bosniaks living in the isolated Bosnian enclave of Velika Kladusa (northern Bosnia) opted not to fight. Accusing the Izetbegovic government of being fundamentalist, they rallied under their leader Fikret Abdic, or "Babo" (Father), and created Bosnian Territorial Defense Militias to defend their neutrality.

Similar to Dostum's Uzbeks, this group proved to be more secular than many of their countrymen were. One of Babo's followers claimed at the time, "We are not fanatics and criminals like those from the [Bosnian Army's] Fifth Corps. We all bow, go to mosque, and respect the Quran. But we do not need an Islamic state of Alija Izetbegovic. Whether my sister will wear a veil, is up to her to decide and not up to some stupid *effendi* [Muslim scholar]." Although the Bosnian government was not overtly fundamentalist, it allied itself with foreign fundamentalist fighters who formed the dreaded Kateebat ul-Mujahideen Brigade. The foreign Wahhabi-Salafis soon outlawed drinking, smoking, and dancing and began to enforce veils and shari'a Islamic law in areas where they fought. Such un-Bosnian activities infuriated many of the moderate, former Yugoslav Sufi Muslims who loved Josip Broz Tito, plum brandy, and soccer.

When the Bosnian government decided to use the Bosnian Fifth Corps and allied foreign mujahidin fighters to destroy Babo's mutinous Western Bosnian Autonomous Region, his followers fought back. Hundreds of members of the Bosnian Army's Fifth Corps were killed in this fighting. At this time Babo's small army of three brigades began to act as a pro-Serbian proxy force to prevent a Bosnian Army takeover. With Serbian funding and weapons, Babo's fighters were eventually able to pin down the Bosnian Fifth Corps in the Bihac enclave from 1993 to 1995. This containment allowed the Serbs to fight elsewhere. During one offensive known as Operation Spider, Babo's troops even fought alongside the Red Berets of the notorious Serbian ethnic cleanser Zeljko Raznatovic, or "Arkan."

But for all his efforts to paint himself as a moderate secularist who was fighting against fundamentalists in the Bosnian government, most saw Babo as an opportunist. One Western observer wrote, "He always sells his soul—or should I say weapons—to the richest devil."[32] As with Dostum and Abu Risha, who were similarly accused of being opportunists working for local economic interests, Babo also was defending a local production facility known as Agrokomerc. For this effort, his enemies in the Bosnian government called him a sellout and tried to crush his enclave for two years.

Babo, however, managed to maintain an oasis of stability in his enclave that was drastically different from the climate in the besieged Bosnian cities of central Bosnia. Similar to Dostum's headquarters at Sheberghan or to Anbar Province following the Anbar Awakening, Babo's capital at Velika Kladusa was spared the fighting that destroyed the Bosnian cities of Srebrenica, Sarajevo, Bana Luka, and Brcko. But this stability came at a high price, and Babo gained many enemies in the Bosnian Army.

The Muslim-on-Muslim violence between Babo's militia and the Bosnian government proved to be some of the most vicious of the war. The bloodshed portended greater violence to come should Babo's autonomous region fall. The reckoning was not long in coming. A U.S.-backed, joint Croatian–Bosnian government offensive, known as Operation Storm (1995), finally overran Babo's proxy forces. As many as fifty thousand of Abdic's followers, whom the Bosnian government labeled *murtadis* (apostates), fled for their lives when their enclave fell. As with the pro-U.S. Montagnards in Vietnam or the South Lebanese Army Christian militias that the Israelis used in southern Lebanon, Abdic's followers paid a heavy price for their "betrayal." Many were run to the ground and killed while Bosnian forces hunted down and captured the "traitors" in the thousands. Babo himself was eventually tried for treason and war crimes and sentenced to fifteen years in a Bosnian jail.

Without their Serbian allies and sponsors to protect them, the vast majority of Bosnians who had supported Babo were forced to flee to surrounding lands. Tens of thousands of them continued to live for years in refugee camps. Thus Babo's quixotic attempt to ally his forces with the Serbs resulted in short-term security gains for his people but ended in catastrophe when his Serbian partners were finally defeated. The moral of this story is that proxy fighters who put themselves on the line to defend foreign occupation regimes tend to face the risk of tremendous retribution from their enemies when the occupying force withdraws. This scenario has already been seen in the al-Maliki government's arrests of Sons of Iraq and al-Qa'ida's war of vengeance against these Anbar Awakening members, who have seen scores of their leaders killed in terrorist attacks. Osama bin Laden himself called for jihad against the Sons of Iraq, and in the fall of 2008 al-Qa'ida in Iraq's minister of war Abu Hamza al-Muhajir declared,

> I advise al-Sahwha (the Awakening) soldiers to repent to Allah, to be remorseful and return to righteousness. I am telling them, "Hey drunk [man], you will live sadly as a spy and you will die as an infidel, an apostate, and your son will inherit nothing but shame and disgrace. What will your grandchildren say about you? Be careful nobody points to them and says; 'Hey, children of a traitor.' And be careful that your son might spit on your grave when he experiences the humiliation that survives you. By God, we are certainly going to kill you, God willing, if you do not return to God. Therefore, you, the miserable, repent!"[33]

Pro-Russian Militias in Chechnya, 1999–Present

In 1996 the self-proclaimed Chechen Republic of Ichkeria achieved independence from the Russian Federation after a bloody two-year war. While most ex-Soviet Chechens dreamed of a stable, secular homeland, many foreign *vakhibity* (a catchall term for Wahhabi-Salafi volunteer jihadists) from abroad began to settle in their homeland in the following years. Although these foreign fighters had been useful during the war with the Russians, most average Chechens detested the jihadists' uncompromising fundamentalism. As in Bosnia, Afghanistan, and later Iraq, the foreign Salafis tried to ban smoking, drinking, and dancing of *zikirs* (Sufi chants or dances), and attempted to force women to use the veil. Khassan Baiev, a Chechen doctor, wrote a book titled *The Oath*, detailing the foreign fighters' arrival in his homeland. Baiev claimed, "These so-called Wahhabis were beginning to cause problems in Chechnya. They claimed our traditions contradicted the Quran . . . we did not like it when they told us our Islam was not true Islam."[34]

To make matters worse, the foreign extremists began to raid neighboring Russian territories, hoping to expel the Russian infidel from the Caucasus. These fighters, as with the foreigners in Iraq, Bosnia, and Afghanistan, dreamed of creating a caliphate-style jihadi state. Many Chechen moderates began to fight back during the interwar period from 1996 to 1999. The moderates did not want their lands turned into a fundamentalist caliphate any more than the Afghans or Bosniaks had before them or the Anbar tribesmen after them did.[35] After the foreign fighters joined with a local extremist commander named Shamil Basayev to invade the neighboring Russian republic of Dagestan in August 1999, the moderates held public rallies to disavow this dangerous provocation.

When the Russian Federation responded to this incursion by invading Chechnya in the fall of 1999, the moderate Chechen mufti (chief Islamic official) Ahmed Kadyrov chose to ally himself and his men with the Russians. Kadyrov's men and those of several other secular warlords (such as the Yamadiyev brothers) eventually fought alongside the Russians against the foreign extremists and Basayev's militants. As in Afghan Turkistan or Anbar Province, the pro-Russian proxy fighters proved useful in hunting down local and foreign extremists since they knew the lay of the land and clan traditions better than the Russian invaders did. As Russian losses mounted, they also turned to the so-called Kadyrovtsy militias to fight in Chechnya's mountainous terrain.

By 2004 this "Chechenization" policy had proved successful. The Russian Federation gradually regained control of Chechnya's capital and much of the countryside.

With Ahmed Kadyrov's death in May 2004 in a bombing, which was blamed on extremists, his son Ramzan Kadyrov took over as the "Chechen face" of the Russian occupation of Chechnya. Ramzan continued his father's policies and sent armed militias into the mountains to hunt rebels. These militias now operate under the auspices of the Russian Ministry of Internal

Affairs and are organized into road patrols, security services, and the Oil Regiment. Roughly five thousand men are in the Kadyrovtsy militia.

Ramzan Kadyrov, who has a pet lion and is known for his martial arts skills, also used his newfound power to force the Russians to provide desperately needed funds to rebuild the Chechen capital of Grozny. By 2007 Grozny had begun to rise from the ashes as the war-weary Chechens joined Kadyrov and took advantage of the wealth and security that his militia provided. Roads were paved, buildings that had been ruined in the war were demolished and new apartments built in their place, and new government facilities were built across a town that had previously been known as the Caucasian Hiroshima. As with Abu Risha, Dostum, and Babo, Ramzan Kadyrov showed his people that real benefits could be accrued by working with the foreign invader instead of waging jihad against them.

But drawbacks stemmed from the Russians' reliance upon the Kadyrovtsy militia to maintain the peace during the construction of civil society in Chechnya. Human rights activists claimed that Kadyrov's forces achieved their successes at a high cost. Families of suspected insurgents had their homes burned, even if they had disavowed their relatives' actions. Abductions of real or suspected insurgents were also common. Anna Politkovskaya, a Russian journalist who was slain in 2006, published a scathing attack on these militias in her last article. Among other accusations, she wrote:

> Members of these units are involved with the same kidnappings of people, they commit murders and torture, and in terms of brutality, for a long time already they've been compared to the "death squads" consisting of regular officers of the Russian special forces, but even so, those units' actions have a selective nature. They usually don't molest residents who don't resist them and the federal authorities.
>
> What do these units represent, what men are they made up of? The mass media, using feeds from governmental authorities, position their members as former fighters who, "having realized the hopelessness of continuing to resist", went over to the Russian side. This claim is far from the truth.[36]

Many of the members of the Kadyrov regiment were actually former criminals or insurgents who had blood on their hands and were simply out to increase their own power. One report stated,

> A significant number of members of these groups are people with criminal past. In some cases a whole detachment is made up of people who had committed criminal offence and economic crimes in the period between wars. Thus, the "kadyrovtsy" group in the village of Gikalovsky is under the command of Sultan Patsaev, who used to be a fighter in the Gelaev group. After the end of the first Chechen campaign he robbed oil wells and participated in kidnapping people for ransom.[37]

Other issues, such as election fraud, extortion, nepotism, and clan-related violence, arose as the Kadyrov clan used its power to kill or intimidate its enemies. In essence, Kadyrov turned his pro-Russian militia into a personal army, and it dominates the republic to this day.

But Kadyrov is not the only pro-Russian proxy warlord with his own militia operating in Chechnya. Another Chechen commander named Sulim Yamadayev and his brothers Dzhabrail, Badrudi, Isa, and Ruslan had previously fought for the Chechen secessionist government. But the Yamadayev militia had clashed with Islamist jihadis in Chechnya's second-largest town of Gudermes since the late 1990s. When the Russians invaded in 1999, the Yamadayev brothers were dismayed at the ad hoc alliance between the moderate Chechen government of President Aslan Mashkadov and the Islamists. As the Chechen war for national independence came to resemble a jihad, the strongly secular Yamadayev brothers went over to Moscow.

The Yamadayevs subsequently helped the Russians gain control of the area surrounding the city of Gudermes and helped them hunt rebels in the Vedeno mountain region. Unlike the Kadyrovtsy, the thousand-man Yamadayevtsy militia (known as the Vostok, or "East," Battalion) is under control of the Russian Foreign Military Intelligence and not the Ministry of Internal Affairs. The Russians actually used the Yamadayevs' Vostok Battalion in conjunction with the Forty-Second Motorized Rifle Division to invade the Georgian Republic of Ossetia in the summer of 2008.[38]

But for all the militia's usefulness both at home and abroad, the Yamadayev brothers were involved in numerous clashes with their rivals, the Kadyrovtsy militia. These conflicts led to the killing of three Yamadayev brothers and several widely reported shoot-outs with the Kadyrovtsy militia, which was later disbanded on the orders of Kadyrov himself, in a move to exert greater control over militias in his republic.

A third pro-Russian proxy force in Chechnya is made up of the Zapad (West) Battalion, otherwise known as the Kakievtsy Battalion. Said-Magomed Kakiev, who was against Chechnya's separation from Russia right from the beginning, heads the battalion. Its members have been involved in tit-for-tat killing and abductions of Chechens who supported independence or those who sought to bring in foreign Wahhabi customs. As with the other two pro-Russian militias, critics have accused the Zapad Battalion of human rights violations and criminality. They claim that it has helped turn Chechnya into a "warlordocracy."

The positive lesson from all three proxy militias would seem to be that the United States should encourage the moderate Sunni sheiks of Iraq to defend their Sufi traditions against those Wahhabi-Salafis who threaten them, just as the Russians have done in Chechnya. By presenting themselves as the defenders of Iraq's traditional moderate version of Islam, the U.S.-backed militias can win the support of wide portions of the Iraqi population.

But safeguards should be put in place at an early stage to make sure groups such as the Sons of Iraq do not "go rogue" as the Kadyrovtsy and other pro-Russian militias in Chechnya have. If not, U.S.-sponsored Sunni militias may devolve quickly into death squads that are more focused on settling scores with competing tribes or the Shi'a than on maintaining the struggle against al-Qa'ida in Iraq. Such armed non-state actors could wreak havoc in the Sunni Triangle in the long term if they feel that the central authorities are against them or do not have the power to control them. They may also act against the central state if they feel they can use their weapons and newfound clout to empower themselves without suffering negative consequences, as was the case in Chechnya or post-Communist Afghanistan.

Conclusions

As the Taliban insurgency gains traction in Afghanistan, many voices are calling for an Anbar-style approach to the insurgency that has gained de facto control of much of the Pasthun-dominated lands in Pakistan and Afghanistan. The Afghan government has already begun arming arbakai (local Pashtun) militias and the Pakistani government has been encouraging *lashkars* (tribal militias) in the Federally Administered Tribal Areas and North-West Frontier Province (now known as Khyber Pakhtunkhwa) to attack Taliban and al-Qa'ida militants in their midst.[39] In the fall of 2008 the Pakistani lashkars helped the Pakistani Army clear and hold territory during its offensives in the Bajaur Tribal Agency.

On December 30, 2008, the former U.S. ambassador to Afghanistan William Wood revealed plans to create a new tribal militia known as the Community Guard Program. Its objectives were to "strengthen local communities and local tribes in their ability to protect what they consider to be their traditional homes."[40] But the Karzai government disarmed arbakai in the northern province of Kunduz in the summer of 2011 after they were accused of robbery and levying "taxes" on local villagers. The new arbakai proxy policy nonetheless was slated to begin in Wardak Province south of Kabul and then spread to tribal zones on the frontier that have a history of forming local community defense militias: Paktia, Paktika, and Khost. The United States has also contemplated arming and equipping the Pakistani Frontier Constabulary, a loosely organized tribal force operating in the Pashtun areas of Pakistan, to act as a proxy counterinsurgent force.

The United States has thus been involved in farming out two wars to proxy forces and using local fighters to achieve successes against an elusive enemy in both Iraq and Afghanistan. But as the three previous case studies makes clear, fighting with proxies can have unintended consequences. In every case explored in this chapter, the external occupation force made rapid security gains using local surrogate fighters to wage war against extremist, die-hard elements in the enemies' ranks. But this progress always came at a subsequent price. That price took the form of civil war and lawlessness in post-Soviet Afghanistan, retribution in post-Serbian Bosnia, and a climate of impunity and banditry in Chechnya.

It can be surmised that Iraq will experience some variant of all three outcomes in the aftermath of the 2011 withdrawal. The conditions in Iraq have similarities with all three zones of conflict. Like post-Soviet Afghanistan, the Americans in Iraq have armed a disenfranchised minority that the central government distrusts; as in Bosnia, a campaign of retribution against this armed militia has already begun; and as in Chechnya, many criminal elements in the Sons of Iraq have indicated that they will wreak havoc should the central authority weaken.

The same dire ramifications would seem to hold true for Afghanistan, which has already experienced a civil war involving former Soviet surrogates, should such a proxy policy be implemented. All three episodes demonstrate that using proxies to fight counter-jihad is indeed a double-edged sword. Only by understanding the mistakes of the past can the United States and its Coalition allies prevent the troubles of previous short-term proxy solutions from being repeated in Iraq and Afghanistan with potentially devastating long-term consequences.

Auxiliary Irregular Forces in Afghanistan
1978-2008

ANTONIO GIUSTOZZI

Irregular armed forces have always been used in Afghanistan, in part because of the difficulty of paying for an army sufficiently large and in part because of the unsuitability of regular armed forces for much of the terrain. Even in the 1970s, on the eve of the long series of conflicts and civil wars whose end in 2009 was not yet in sight, some irregular formations were in existence. The government paid small border militias to secure the border. This arrangement amounted to little more than a residue of old patronage relationships going back to the 1919 war against the British. In total only two thousand men were part of these militias, which did not play a significant role from 1978 onward.[1] As the Afghan polity gradually stabilized, avoided conflict with its neighbors, and consolidated the monopoly of violence, the need for auxiliary irregulars diminished. However, all the gains made in state building up to 1978 started unraveling rapidly after the radical leftists gained power in April 1978 and blundered into a series of controversial and antagonistic policies. This chapter looks at how Afghan and foreign armies operating in Afghanistan have used irregular forces in auxiliary roles since 1978. With little knowledge of the terrain, foreign armies needed many more scouts and screening auxiliaries than their Afghan counterparts did. Afghan regular armies too, however, had to use auxiliary militias to penetrate and control the rugged countryside, where local knowledge of terrain and people was a decisive factor.

Auxiliary irregular forces (militias) are semi-trained or untrained armed groups, are under a loose chain of command from the political authorities, are deployed near home, have limited or no access to sophisticated weaponry and limited or no logistical capability, and hence are dependent on the logistical support of a regular army. Their advantages, particularly from the perspective of counterinsurgency, include local knowledge, easier recruitment (villagers do not like joining the regular armed forces, which are usually deployed away from home), quick mobilization, and sometimes remarkable fighting skills and motivation, as they might be fighting against local rivals. In short, militias can be mobilized cheaply, quickly, and in large numbers to hurt badly a specific enemy. As this chapter will show, however, their use also has significant drawbacks.

The 1980s and 1990s

The pro-Soviet regime of President (and party leader) Babrak Karmal gradually started to rely on militias more and more to solve the difficulty of recruiting for the regular army. The main militia organization (regional forces) was established in 1983, after some experimentation begun in 1980 and mainly at the hand of the Soviet Army. The aim was to use sectors of the rural population, which would otherwise have rejected service in the regular army, to exercise control over the countryside, to hamper the movement of rebel groups, and to recruit others. Not all the militias of the 1980s played the same role in the war. The regional forces were used as a battle force and needed a great deal of space in order to motivate them to fight. An elaborate framework was established to ensure that the militias did not acquire a patrimonial character. In practice, however, it was always the group leader who was appointed and received military ranks to turn his armed group into a company, a battalion, a regiment, or (later) a brigade, and even a division. Political work was expected to transform former "bandits" into real "soldiers of the Revolution." In some militias political work was actually carried out, but it was not done in most. Meanwhile, great efforts were made to recruit Hizb-i Demokratik-e Khalq (HDK, Communist Party) members among the rank and file, but in most units their influence remained negligible.[2] Their charismatic leadership was essential to maintain the character of these warlike organizations, and the government could not challenge them. The border militias were similar in nature and composition to the regional forces.

That former opposition fighters soon accounted for most of the regional forces, and border militias compounded the difficulty in exercising their control. By the end of 1989 and at the beginning of 1990, 100,000 former mujahidin had joined the various types of irregular armed formations, most of them in the regional forces.[3] At the outset, the militias were expected to deal mainly with controlling villages and rural roads and paths, taking over part of the duties of the police. Because of the regular forces' weaknesses, their military tasks gradually increased. From 1985–1986 onward, they were entrusted with recruitment in the countryside, and in fact it became one of their main tasks. Particularly after the Soviets' withdrawal, they were even requested to go beyond local defensive roles and to participate in fighting throughout the national territory. High salaries played a fundamental role in the rise of the regional and border militias: already in 1987 a militiaman received a salary twice as high as that of a regular soldier. In the drive to expand the militias, some provinces abandoned recruitment for the army and instead even offered an enrollment prize of 20,000 Afs (Afghanis) for those willing to join the militias. President Najibullah himself not only offered exemption from military service to the tribal youth who agreed to form local self-defense units but also declared his readiness to release from military service those already recruited. Furthermore, bonuses were available to militiamen for capturing deserters and so on. Other advantages offered to communities joining the militias included electricity and televisions in the villages. Offers of military hardware turned out to be particularly seductive to opposition military leaders. From 1988 and particularly from 1989, even heavy weapons and armored vehicles, including armored transports and tanks, were distributed in large quantities to trusted militias. Perhaps more importantly, military ranks were more and more generously distributed to former opposition commanders.

By this time militias and the government were clearly developing a symbiotic relationship. Although some militia groups deserted over the course of the war, the patronage relationship established with the government proved quite strong, as it was based mostly on mutual interest. Many opposition military leaders may have approached the government just as an expedient, but then they became dependent on its patronage. If Kabul's patronage policies had trapped the former opposition commanders, the contrary was also true: by the early 1990s the Kabul government was effectively dependent on its militias.[4]

Other militias proved much easier to control. Party militias such as the Revolution Defense Groups and the "Soldiers of the Revolution" played a modest role in the economy of the war, but they contributed to secure key installations—cooperatives, bridges, and so on—in the cities and in the countryside. Because their staffs were mostly or exclusively party members, they were loyal and disciplined. Some women's militias also existed, which in a few instances saw fighting and performed rather well; these were staffed by party activists and relatives of male members of the party, who all expected the worst should the opposition prevail. Apart from the tribal regiments, the most interesting type of irregular force used in the 1980s was the police. Although officers were professionally trained and regular troops fully staffed the mobile units, in the rural areas the police relied on untrained villagers to constitute the rank and file. These mixed forces proved reasonably disciplined and effective at controlling towns and villages in areas where the government had a reach. The desertion rate was much lower than in the army, because the villagers were serving in their own communities. Many such recruits were former mujahidin who had surrendered to the government. Although their combat capability was restricted to defending villages and their mobility was usually limited, they proved useful in holding hundreds of villages in areas such as northern Afghanistan, where the opposition was not too strong.[5]

From Kabul's standpoint, the massive reliance on the regional forces as a fighting force and more generally on militias created three problems. First it faced the risk of full-scale rebellions, made all the greater as many militia commanders developed peer-to-peer networks and even maintained contacts with the opposition parties. Although the patronage link to the government was quite solid, if the financial resources at Kabul's disposal were reduced, an explosive situation was bound to surface.

The second problem was that the higher priority given to the militias for recruitment further reduced the pool of available troops for the regular forces. Many, in fact, enrolled in the militias to avoid being recruited to the army. Making the problem worse, even city dwellers sometimes entered militias to avoid the draft. Najibullah himself even accused some regional units of sheltering deserters and draft dodgers and complained that others were not doing much to implement the draft. A vicious circle had been started, where expanding the militias led to the army being condemned to a perpetually weak role and, in turn, forced an ever greater recourse to militias. As a result the militias' leverage was ever stronger.

The third problem was the increasing autonomy and undisciplined behavior of many militias. The militias wanted the task of protecting the main roads, as it enabled them to raise much additional money through the "taxation" of drivers and travelers. The existence of a link between the militias and tax extortion along the roads is confirmed; all the most important militias were involved in it. Often militia commanders had sufficient leverage to choose relatively freely where to deploy their men. The growing autonomy of the militias was not merely financial. The 1989 law on local autonomy stipulated that criminals would be brought to the religious judges, who operated in areas outside government control, and when condemned, they would be delivered to government prisons. A military attorney followed the trials in the militia courts, but in fact the government accepted all verdicts without complaint. The National Security Court tried only those prisoners charged with political crimes. This system was clearly drifting toward some sort of feudalism. The government's encouragement of the "retribalization" of the local communities—that is, the rediscovery of tribal and ethnic links that had faded away, or had never been very important, to bolster their influence and legitimacy among the population—might have further strengthened the autonomization of the regional forces.[6]

The growing autonomy of the regional forces and border militias further reduced their inclination to behave in a disciplined way. Far from spending their energy on forming party organizations, reactivating schools, doing work useful to the population, and reopening agricultural cooperatives, as Najibullah had wished in January 1988, after the Soviets' withdrawal the militias of the regional and border forces produced a "wild west" atmosphere around the country. Their feuds caused dozens of wounds that had to be treated each month in only one Kabul hospital. It was widely reported that the government eschewed lodging any complaint with the militias. It is true that even regular army units indulged in various sorts of abuse, particularly in the first years of the conflict, but militias went beyond that indiscipline.

Regular officers acknowledged that militias were "beyond control" even in a town like Balkh, and visitors were warned to leave the town by 4 p.m. Unsurprisingly, the population was hostile to them. The growing arbitrariness of the militias' violence clearly damaged the reputation of the government, whose attempt to recover some legitimacy had cost huge efforts. It risked affecting its pacification policy, as the attraction of a peaceful life had been one of the main trumps in Kabul's hands. Economic activity, already in a bad shape, was further jeopardized.[7]

The Soviets' withdrawal in early 1989 further tilted the balance of power massively in the militias' favor. The government tried to balance their rising power by deploying some guard brigades in the north, where militias formed the great majority of the armed forces. Attempts were also made to force the militias to increase their discipline. A bill envisaging the introduction of military uniforms for the regional forces was examined in 1987, but it is not clear whether it was approved, as such troops still did not wear uniforms. In December 1989 the Supreme Army Command forcefully stated the need to take steps toward increasing discipline, with little impact. In 1990 Najibullah faced a crisis when he tried to speed up the process of incorporating the regional forces into the regular army, and he had to backtrack. In any case, transferring the regional forces to the regular forces was in itself no guarantee that a real change was in the making. Clearly the idea of exercising relatively strict monitoring, let alone direct control, over the tribal units was not realistic, given the vastness of the territory and the persistent weakness and ineffectiveness of the regular forces. If the scarcity of cadre and political officers was added, any effort at reducing the militia's autonomy was clearly bound to meet huge difficulties. Rather than shaping the militias according to the government's wishes, it would seem that the relatively small numbers of regular officers sprinkled around the militia ranks ended up being absorbed by them.[8]

As mentioned already, the militias' degree of success depended primarily on the charismatic leadership of their commanders. Charismatic leadership allowed some of them to appeal more successfully than others did to their fellow members of the emerging military class. Abdul Rashid Dostum excelled in this interaction. This influence proved difficult to reconcile with the long-term consolidation of state power; indeed, even after having been formally turned into regular army units, the largest militias played a key role in the collapse of the Afghan state in 1992.

The Soviet Army was relatively little involved with the militias. After taking a lead in convincing opposition groups to switch sides, the Soviets handed over the militias' recruitment and control to the Afghan authorities. Since operations on the ground were always combining a Soviet and Afghan presence, the Soviets had little need to maintain direct relations with the militias, which they mostly used directly as scouts.

After the collapse of the leftist regime—and arguably of the state itself—in 1992, there was little distinction between regular and irregular forces drawn from the parties that had formed the new government. Although initially at least two of the warring factions—Dostum's Jumbesh and Ahmad Shah Massoud's Jami'at—maintained a number of regular units, they gradually decayed into irregular forces because new levies were not trained, retaining professional officers and specialists became difficult, and the leadership generally lacked interest in a regular force. After all, regular forces had proved unsuitable to fight the war in Afghanistan's rugged landscape.

The Taliban regime, in power in Kabul from October 1996, did not have regular armed forces either. In its case, however, it was possible to distinguish between a mobile, full-time, and politically trusted militia, which could be deployed around the country as needed, and those local militias that were recruited from the ranks of the old mujahidin, which were bound to a particular province or district. The mobile and full-time militia, which the Taliban called an army, gradually showed signs of absorbing some trained staff and underwent minor training, although it never wore uniforms. Its discipline in the field compared favorably with that of most other militias, even if it fell short of a properly trained and staffed regular army. The auxiliary militias existed only in areas where the Taliban felt threatened, that is, in general the north and center of the country. The old mujahidin groups were either disarmed and then rearmed on a much smaller scale (their task was essentially local policing) or requested to hand over part of their weaponry. In general the auxiliary militias seem to have served the Taliban well. The only known example of an attempt to revolt was in Baghlan Province, where a former commander of Hizb-i Islami was arrested for having plotted to rebel. Only with the start of Operation Enduring Freedom did these auxiliary militias start defecting to their original factions, and quite a few of them were quite slow at that too, waiting until the Taliban's collapse appeared imminent.[9]

After 2001

Allied irregular forces played a key role in the Americans' strategy during Enduring Freedom. A combined Central Intelligence Agency–Special Operations forces effort was put in place to recruit, pay, advise, and provide with close air support the remnants of the anti-Taliban opposition inside Afghanistan.[10] A similar effort was established to mobilize selected anti-Taliban figures in Pakistan and convince them to cross the border and start fighting.[11] The most intense fighting occurred in northern Afghanistan and most notably around Mazar-i-Sharif, where General Dostum's revived forces fought with determination and, with the help of the U.S. Air Force, captured the key northern city. Some intense fighting also occurred around Herat, in parts of Hazarajat, and in the northeast, where the predominant attitude of the allies, however, was to spare their own forces and let U.S. airpower wreck havoc on the Taliban's ranks. These forces in any case could not be described as auxiliaries, given that U.S. troops on the ground were very few and could be counted in the tens more than in the hundreds of men; the Afghan irregulars bore the brunt of the fighting.

After the Taliban regime collapsed, the Americans' presence on the ground started building. By the end of 2001, thirteen hundred U.S. troops were in Afghanistan, and their number increased to nine thousand the following year.[12] They were mainly tasked to hunt down remnants of the Taliban in the eastern and southeastern parts of the country. In this task, given the absence at that time of a regular Afghan army or of a capable police force, they had to rely extensively on auxiliary forces recruited ad hoc from among the militias that had been mobilized or strengthened to fight the Taliban. Most of those militias by then had been integrated under the supervision of the Afghan Ministry of Defense (MOD) and were not supposed to leave their barracks, but in practice many militia commanders neither strictly maintained discipline nor brought all their men under MOD supervision.[13]

Unsurprisingly, in the search for auxiliary irregulars the Americans privileged commanders with whom they had good relations. In the east they were Haji Zaman, Haji Zahir, and Hazrat Ali, who belonged to different factions and were personal rivals. After Operation Anaconda (2002) was botched and several wanted al-Qa'ida figures were believed to have slipped through, Commanders Zaman and Ali accused each other of being responsible for the failure. Attributing responsibility proved impossible in those circumstances, a fact that highlighted a limitation of occasionally renting auxiliary irregulars and letting them operate without close supervision. In particular, the wisdom of recruiting three bitter rivals to fight side by side is questionable. In the ensuing power struggle in Nangarhar Province, Hazrat Ali, who for a number of years shared with Haji Zahir the privilege of cooperating with the Americans in Nangarhar and Laghman, rapidly marginalized Haji Zaman. Zahir's men were incorporated into the Afghan Border Police and Ali's into the police and the MOD militias. The latter, however, maintained unofficial militias after his MOD militias were disbanded. Ali's militias continued to cooperate closely with the Americans in chasing insurgents, even if their role gradually declined as the Americans increasingly had the option of relying on other forces, including the police, the Afghan National Army (ANA), and permanent auxiliary forces called the Afghan Security Forces (ASF) and Afghan Security Guards (ASG). Both Zahir's and Ali's men in the police forces also cooperated closely with the Americans, often in practice serving as irregular auxiliaries.

By 2007, however, the commanders' role as the Americans' main proxies in Nangarhar had declined after the appointment of a governor who also cultivated friendly relations with the Americans. Gul Agha Shirzai, one of the strongmen Washington had armed to fight the Taliban in 2001 in Kandahar, was determined to turn Nangarhar into a new personal stronghold. In 2007 he co-opted a group of tribal elders to organize a lashkar (tribal militia) and chase the Taliban from the Tora Bora Mountains.[14]

In the southeast, another region of Afghanistan where the Americans had a significant military presence, they could not count on any local strongman as a source of auxiliary irregulars for their operations. Badshah Khan Zadran, who had received American assistance in 2001 to fight the Taliban, compromised his relationship with the Americans with his involvement in violent factional fighting around the town of Gardez in January 2002. American Special Forces were caught in the cross fire and were less than impressed with his temperament. The Americans occasionally cooperated with Badshah Khan afterward for some time, mainly for information, but they never used his men as auxiliaries.[15]

Without reliable strongmen, the Americans opted to work with former officers of the pro-Soviet government of the 1980s. The Twenty-Fifth Division in Khost was unique among the militias under MOD supervision because some former officers and businessmen—not strongmen and existing militia commanders—had formed it as a local initiative. The Americans used it effectively to contain insurgents looking to infiltrate the border. The unit was better disciplined and tactically more effective than were the untrained militias commonly found south of the Hindu Kush. Despite the growing availability of ANA troops from 2005 onward, the Americans decided to keep the unit de facto operational after officially disbanding all MOD militias in 2004–2005. A Provincial Security Force was set up and staffed with mostly Twenty-Fifth Division members. At this point the force was on the American paybook and was therefore an auxiliary unit of the American armed forces.[16]

In southern Afghanistan the American presence until 2008 was limited to small contingents, mostly of Special Forces, that occasionally cooperated with local pro-government militias and government security forces. There is no record of any cooperation with Mullah Naqibullah's militia, which secured the Arghandab and Khakrez districts of Kandahar from the Taliban, except that his men staffed much of the local police and as such were cooperating closely with the Americans and Canadians. It is also not clear whether militias linked to engineer Mohammed Ibrahim Spinzada (deputy of the National Security Council) in Farah Province actively cooperated with the foreign troops. Particularly in Uruzgan the Special Forces maintained a relatively close relationship with the militias of Jan Mohammad, a strongman allied to President Hamid Karzai and a governor of the province until the end of 2005. Among Jan Mohammad's lieutenants, his nephew Matiullah was the most active, having his men in the police force and his own unofficial militia, estimated at a thousand men. From 2006 Jan Mohammad refused to cooperate with the foreign troops, in protest of the Dutch forces' lobbying to have him sacked as governor, but Matiullah's men continued to fight alongside the Special Forces and on their own.[17]

The militiamen loyal to Jan Mohammad and his lieutenants would accompany the Special Forces or cooperate with them; therefore, they could be described as ad hoc irregulars, similar to Hazrat Ali's men in Nangarhar. In both places the assessment of this cooperation leads to controversial results. Although the cooperation was by all accounts close and friendly (more so in Nangarhar), the irregulars continued to pursue their own local rivalries and enlisted U.S. support against the local enemies, regardless of whether these engagements were linked to the insurgents. Evidence suggests that this attitude and the Americans' inclination to blindly trust their irregulars' advice might have pushed substantial numbers of individuals and communities into the hands of the Taliban, at least in Uruzgan. In Nangarhar, Hizb-i Islami mostly confronted Hazrat Ali's men, perhaps contributing to the growing shift toward armed opposition to government and foreign troops among that party's members. The Dutch troops in Uruzgan avoided any contact with Jan Mohammad and his allies, instead relying on the elders' and community leaders' militias, which were less effective in pursuing the Taliban but valuable in defending specific communities and towns.[18]

In Helmand from 2006 onward the British troops maintained a rather ambiguous relationship with numerous militias linked to the former governor, Sher Mohammad Akhundzada, and encouraged President Karzai to sack him before deploying to the province. Sher Mohammad adopted a hands-off approach similar to Jan Mohammad's in Uruzgan, but a number of his militia commanders kept fighting the Taliban alongside British troops. Although the British generally avoided a direct relationship with these militias, at least as long as they had an unofficial status, they accepted their participation in joint operations. The British experimented and formed their own militias of former Taliban around Girishk in 2007, but the local National Directorate of Security (NDS) actively sabotaged the plan. Of five small militia commanders deployed around the town, two were arrested. Two more were assassinated, and some locals believe that the NDS was a more likely culprit than the Taliban was for their murders. The fifth one fled.[19]

These strongmen's militias proved the most effective militarily against the insurgents, for whom they usually felt a genuine hatred. They proved more capable in pursuing or repulsing the Taliban than the police and even most ANA units were. For example, with the Dutch, Rozi Khan's militia in

Chora (Uruzgan Province) played an important role in taking the district from the Taliban in 2007. In June 2007 a similar militia proved crucial in repelling a Taliban attack on Tarin Kot and in limiting Dutch casualties. In Helmand, some of the militias established a reputation of being fierce fighters, and the Taliban themselves in Nad Ali and Musa Qala feared them. However, similar to the tribal regiments of the 1980s, all these militias had important drawbacks. They were undisciplined and strongly inclined to abuse the civilian population. They tended not to distinguish between personal enemies and actual insurgents. They were apt to err on the side of caution when confronted with suspect insurgents, physically eliminating individuals on the basis of the vaguest proof. One British journalist related an anecdote in which Koka, a leading militia commander in the Musa Qala area of Helmand, executed a young motorcycle driver on sight, on the assumption that he was likely to be a Talib.[20]

The limitations of ad hoc auxiliaries and their obvious unsuitability for a number of tasks, such as guarding U.S. bases and escorting U.S. patrols, led to an early decision to form a permanent force of auxiliaries that U.S. forces would completely control. Known as the Afghan Security Forces, their recruitment and training began in 2001, mostly among the ranks of anti-Taliban militias. The ASF recruits appear to have been paid around $125 to $150 a month, significantly more than the ANA troops or the Afghan National Police (ANP).[21] They would normally be deployed in numbers varying between 100 and 150 at U.S. firebases and forward operating bases, where they would take care of external security and be available to accompany U.S. troops in patrols and on combat missions. The total number of ASF militiamen was not disclosed, but it must have been in the low thousands (two thousand to three thousand men).

The rationale for creating the ASF was manyfold. First, the members would act as intermediaries between U.S. troops and the local population. Since they were recruited locally, they were expected to be acquainted with local customs and mores. They were also thought to be more acceptable to local populations when searching villages and houses and carrying out arrests. The second reason was to limit U.S. casualties. The force members would be deployed at the head and back of every U.S. convoy, and in battle they would approach the enemy ahead of U.S. troops. The U.S. military is not required to disclose information about ASF casualties, so no statistics are available. The ability to withhold information about casualties could be a third rationale for creating the ASF. Judging from anecdotal information concerning ANA troops serving in similar roles from 2004 and from the limited information about ASF casualties,[22] their "screens" appear to have saved quite a few American lives but at the cost of some of their own. Their combat performance was judged satisfactory, but their record in terms of disciplined behavior and brutality was more controversial.[23]

A major problem related to the ASF's existence was political in nature. The direct and unaccountable recruitment of Afghans who served under the orders of U.S. officials was a source of some embarrassment for the Afghan government, particularly as ANA units were becoming available for deployment.[24] A gradually intensifying insurgency from 2003 onward compounded the problem, and the ASF appeared undersized for its task. Although the Afghan Security Forces were hardly ever mentioned in the documents of the Afghan government, the United Nations, or Kabul's diplomatic community, expanding the group's size would have increased the danger of the ASF turning into a political issue. As a result, it was decided to disband the ASF gradually from 2005, and its members were provided incentives to join the ANA or the ANP.[25] Thus, ANA units partially replaced the ASF in the role of auxiliaries.

Most foreign contingents in Afghanistan continued to use directly recruited or loaned auxiliary militias, usually in small groups of ten to twenty men, even after the completion of the disarmament, demobilization, and reintegration program in 2005. The Italians, for example, borrowed militiamen from Herat's strongman Ismail Khan. The Americans also employed similar formations but no longer called them the Afghan Security Force. The formations were instead called the Afghan Security Guards (ASG) to reflect their more limited tasks, such as securing the outer perimeter of the bases or escorting supply convoys. The large majority of the ASG were initially former ASF, but a number of the latter joined the Afghan police and army or dispersed. During 2007 it became common practice for the U.S. Army to hire the ASG ad hoc to guard the increasingly insecure supply convoys, without, however, providing the men any training.[26] The total number of ASG and other militias that the foreign armies in Afghanistan directly recruited is probably some thousands of men. Using these types of local mercenaries was never controversial, given their modest numbers and limited role.

From 2001 to 2008 the foreign contingents' demand for auxiliary troops always exceeded available forces, not least because the insurgency expanded faster than the International Security Assistance Force (ISAF), Enduring Freedom, or the ASF could cope. As a result, some flirted with the idea of using community militias to fill the gap. In general, the consensus was that the arbakai (a type of community militia) of southeastern Afghanistan had contributed significantly to containing the insurgency in Khost and Paktia. They are not known to have directly cooperated with the Americans, although some arbakai received police training from U.S. forces. Pseudo-arbakai imitations are a different story, though. Some governors launched initiatives to create village militias along the lines of the arbakai. Such an attempt seems to have achieved some degree of success in Kunar, where the militias cooperated strictly with U.S. forces, the ANA, the police, and the provincial administration. Although it is questionable whether these militias can be strictly described as arbakai, they had a connection to local communities. In Kapisa too the local pseudo-arbakai cooperated with the Americans, but here the experiment was far less successful and the military impact negligible. For sure they had virtually nothing to do with the local communities, and the provincial authorities individually recruited members reportedly on the basis of their political affiliation.[27]

Apart from the experiments with the pseudo-arbakai, which could only be limited in scale, from 2005 the ISAF started considering the possibility of sponsoring the formation of official militias throughout Afghanistan that could fill the power vacuum in the villages, which clearly had favored the Taliban. The British drove the elaboration of a new approach and, in fact, had already begun experimenting with unofficial militias on the ground.[28] For political reasons, the various plans to create militias tended to incorporate the following elements:

1. A widespread network, covering many of the most vulnerable areas across several provinces (with the military's priority on the areas immediately surrounding the main highway);
2. A community base, or at least something that could be presentable as such; and

3. An established system of accountability and supervision, under which the new militias would have to operate.

The British claimed they had taken their inspiration from the arbakai, but initially others evaluated their views skeptically. U.S. defense secretary Robert Gates was presented a draft plan when he visited Afghanistan in December 2007, but Gen. Dan McNeill attacked the British and claimed the arbakai model could not work in southern Afghanistan, where tribes have disintegrated and have no universally accepted tribal leadership. The final plan featured the recruitment of up to 250 militiamen per district, who would be screened by local leaders and then receive a short training course. This number, of course, would not provide a presence in every village (there are on average about a hundred villages per district); thus, the militias probably would be concentrated along the roads and around the district centers. Minority opposition and wariness continued to exist even within the U.S. Department of Defense.[29] Among those troops fighting in the south, the Canadians remained the most critical of the plan, because they feared that contrary to the conditions in the southeast, the insurgency in the south was too deeply embedded with local society. The lack of alternatives, however, decided in favor of the plan. It bears witness to the need for irregular forces in counterinsurgency warfare that the Canadians were changing their minds by 2009 and ended up accepting militias in their area of operation under certain conditions.[30]

Although the primary task of these militias was supposed to be protecting communities, it was obvious from the beginning that they would have to interact with the foreign military and ASF. Such a structure could only survive and work if well integrated with the much greater firepower of regular armed forces, both Afghan and international. Otherwise, one by one, the insurgents could crush or intimidate the small militias into submission. Only in areas where the insurgency was weak or in its infant phase could the community guards play a significant role on their own, but the plan was actually to prioritize areas where the insurgency had already taken root. Considering that the Afghan government and the international militaries still had problems coordinating with each other (hence, the repeated incidents of shootings between police and foreign military) and that direct cooperation between the ANP and ANA was pretty bad or even nonexistent, the problem of building an effectively integrated system was not simply resolved. The hope that provincial councils of local notables would be able to do so was quite naive, particularly in areas where tribal structures had disintegrated. Where integration existed (Kunar), it was because the U.S. military managed the whole system.[31]

As discussed in the case of other militias, the inevitable role of foreign troops proved to be divisive. Karzai's Afghan government saw it in part as a way to protect whatever supporters it still had left and as a potential source of patronage and influence. Kabul claimed to want militias that would be "relatively formal bodies more akin to a locally recruited police force."[32] Motivated by the desire to reduce its own casualties, the foreign military wanted to create outer rings of defense and release the ANP and ANA for a more aggressive pursuit of the insurgents. When in March 2008 both the Afghan government and the Americans, who were to pay for it, accepted the plan, it more resembled an unwieldy compromise than the achievement of a real consensus on a workable strategy. The resulting Afghan Social Outreach Program (ASOP) would sponsor the Independent Directorate of Local Governance as it established new village councils and would be in charge of paying them (with donors' cash). The councils, in turn, would recruit the "protection force." President Karzai, who had vetoed the plan's earlier drafts either because they were too similar to the strongmen's militias or because the foreign armies had too much control over them, agreed to the revised plan. A good example of the compromises at the root of the agreement was the decision that no new weapons would be issued to the protection force, and its men would use only their personal weapons. They would be issued only communications and other nonlethal equipment.

In practice the unworkable plan faltered quickly. The Ministry of Interior rescued it and assumed responsibility for arming the protection force. As the plan approached implementation, little of the original, unworkable plan was left standing. The pilot project planned for early 2009 in Wardak Province had to be postponed because of problems in obtaining suitable volunteers. Rather than the elders, the National Security Directorate supplied the lists of potential members; however, they were judged as being too factionally biased. The Americans rejected them, delaying the whole project.[33]

In the minds of some of the project's Afghan partners, the risk was that plans that look relatively sound on paper can take on a whole life of their own once implemented. Indeed, the fact that the local police forces controlled the new militias raised more than one question. The project increasingly resembled that of the notoriously failed Auxiliary Police, except for the greater and more direct involvement of foreign actors and, in particular, of the Americans, who were funding the new militias. This development was an additional reason for believing that to avoid the risk of "shifting loyalties" and "local deals," keeping foreign forces away from the militias would probably turn out to be impossible.

Perhaps more worrisome to policymakers in Kabul, and to numerous foreign embassies, is that there is an appetite for creating more strongmen's militias in much of Afghanistan. The protection force plan could have acted as the launching board for them. The possibility that the protection force could drift in the direction of something more akin to strongmen's militias is implicit in the contradiction between the weak military component of the ASOP plan and the major military threat represented by the Taliban, who will no doubt have a strong incentive to target the guards. As the police force itself has been in many districts, the protection force was also likely going to be forced to make some tough decisions. It could start making local deals with the Taliban or shy away from fighting, making the whole exercise a waste of time and money. Alternatively, the protection force would have to acquire the characteristics required to take on the real fight. In semi-regular or irregular formations, the leader's charisma (or lack thereof) usually determines the unit's fighting spirit. Already people wanted to form militias in the eastern and southern districts of Kandahar, for example, where some communities actively cooperated with the police to keep the insurgents at bay. Their leaders were probably eager to be rewarded for their efforts. Being able to form or reform their militias would have allowed them to reestablish some degree of control over the villages and take on the Taliban more effectively. A pro-Karzai notable from the Noorzai tribe in Kandahar jumped at the prospect of forming militias and offered a thousand of his unemployed tribesmen (former militiamen) for the task of cleaning up Helmand and Kandahar.[34]

Considering how all grandiose plans that the international community had put forward in the past had been compromised, it was not too far fetched to fear that if the protection force drifted toward strongmen militias, at least in part it could soon turn into something more malignant. Charismatic commanders are always going to be difficult to restrain, and the experience of the 1980s and 1990s in Afghanistan was that they rapidly took control from the elders who had initially sponsored them. It is one thing to repel a one-off foray from the Taliban and an altogether different one to resist their constant pressure. Where the Afghan police had been disintegrating under the Taliban's relentless attacks—Zabul, Uruzgan, Kandahar, Helmand, Farah, Paktika—the protection force was unlikely to survive long in its original shape.

An unbalanced recruitment process, which was becoming reality as the NDS supplied its lists of candidates, might actually invigorate tensions between elders or communities. As one American colonel in charge of training the ANP argued, "When you enhance the capability of one tribe over another, you open up the possibility for conflict, if not now, possibly later. . . . You're better off to . . . create a new tribe, the tribe of the border police."[35]

Conclusion

Using irregular forces in Afghanistan yielded mixed results. It certainly proved a cheap way to field forces that had local knowledge and could fight energetically against insurgents and opposition. However, throughout the post-1978 period, irregular forces proved difficult to control and discipline. Over time, the recruitment of "untainted" irregular forces became more and more difficult, as the gradual merging of interests among organized criminal syndicates, illegal armed groups, and armed opposition groups contributed to blur the lines between friends and enemies. If criminal elements and illegal armed groups had penetrated state structures at all levels, the chances that irregular forces would remain clean were never high. The option of intensifying the training of irregular forces is either unproductive or defeats the purpose: in the absence of a dedicated officer corps, irregular forces can absorb only a limited amount of training and investment in human resources. If they were to develop a proper command structure, they would lose their character of irregular forces and become as expensive and as limited in counterinsurgency tasks as the regular army was. A professional officer corps would limit the ability of the newly trained force to operate permanently in remote locations. Further, it would be antieconomic to invest many resources in upgrading local irregular forces, which, because of their own nature, cannot be used profitably elsewhere.

The trend since the 1980s has been to invest little in irregular forces and to try instead to create an infrastructure that can control, restrain, and supervise them. This effort has proved difficult, and success has mostly been highly localized. Much of the irregular forces' fighting ability derives exactly from their freedom and ability to act arbitrarily. Once restrained by a supervising structure, their value is reduced to that of mere scouts, whose knowledge of the local terrain facilitates the task of regular forces. Examples of local success were difficult to maintain in the long run, because they were based on good personal relations between the commander of the irregular force and the commander of the foreign troops; the latter, of course, would be rotated out in a matter of months. The dilemma, therefore, cannot be easily resolved.

Surrogate Agents
Private Military and Security Operators in an Unstable World

KEVIN A. O'BRIEN

Since the rise of the great trading companies of the early modern era, the outsourcing of state military and security interests has been a constant. Exploration, exploitation, and conflict have gone hand in hand—whether in Africa, Latin America, the Middle East, or Asia—and private warriors have been the key tools that empire builders have deployed. In the eighteenth and nineteenth centuries, such activities were aimed significantly at extending the trade and resource exploitation bounds of the European empires across the colonized world. In the latter half of the twentieth century such outsourcing, particularly by the United States, France, Portugal, and the United Kingdom, took on another guise, that of either shoring up crumbling colonial relationships or extending the reach of armed forces in regional conflicts (such as in Vietnam, Rhodesia, Sierra Leone, the Belgian Congo, or the Philippines). Mercenaries—hired soldiers thrown up by the decolonization conflicts—were the primary tools used to halt the collapse of colonial possessions or to shore up clients in the developing world. By the 1970s, corporate military resources were contracted increasingly to engage in the latter activity, whether in training and supporting indigenous tribespeople involved in counterinsurgency warfare or in antismuggling and antipoaching operations aimed at securing natural resources.

By the 1990s, this paradigm shifted once again, to the point where multinational corporations (MNCs) engaged in high-risk, high-return extraction operations in the developing world, where the writ of the state was weak at best, increasingly were hiring such private military and security companies (PMSCs). Although this focus on PMSC activities—such as those of the South African PMSC Executive Outcomes or the British company Sandline

International—provided the media and academia a most sensational topic for analysis, the reality of PMSC involvement in both security operations in the developing world and peace-support operations worldwide was more complex.

From the late 1960s—beginning largely in Vietnam and Sierra Leone and continuing through Oman, Zimbabwe, and the Philippines—Western governments (particularly those of the United States and the United Kingdom) contracted increasingly with PMSCs to support counterinsurgency, peacekeeping, peacemaking, and related interventions across the developing world and the professionalization of the newly independent militaries and security forces of former colonies. At the same time, the international community—through the United Nations (UN), the Organization of African Unity, the Organization for Security and Cooperation in Europe (OSCE), and other regional bodies—was also contracting out support to peace-support operations, as Western militaries decreased their contributions to such operations. By the twenty-first century, PMSCs, along with individual security advisers, were involved in peace-support, security sector reform, counternarcotics, counterterrorism, and professionalization and security cooperation initiatives across the spectrum of operations, including in frontline activities.

This work was the key focus of PMSC activities (and contracts) prior to 2002, but everything was perceived to have changed with the launching of the Afghan and Iraqi campaigns following the September 2001 attacks in the United States. Since then, the PMSCs' activities in Iraq and, to a slightly lesser degree, in Afghanistan largely have driven the focus of media, academic, and policy interest concerning these companies. This focus is understandable given the quantity of operations that PMSCs have undertaken in these conflicts, but qualitatively little has changed with this upswing in their activities. Despite the fact that PMSC involvement in Iraq and Afghanistan has concentrated on protecting civilian contractors involved in infrastructure reconstruction and service delivery, the only difference with those operations and similar protective security activities that PMSCs conduct in other parts of the world—today and in the past—is the intensity of the threat they face from insurgents and terrorists in each theater. Otherwise, the PMSCs' enterprises reflect those that they have traditionally supported: protection, military and police training and professionalization, security advisory services, and support to military operations.

PMSCs represent the ultimate corporatization, both commercially and politically, of state proxies in the security field and far more so than similar outsourcing of security concerns and activities to regional or international bodies, let alone to client militias and insurgencies across the developing world. PMSCs, especially in their post–Cold War form, are an altogether different type of proxy for states. This chapter will explore the evolution of this proxyization of military and security functions from the public to the private sector over the last fifty years.[1] It will examine the different boxes into which such activities fell, the reasons that governments (largely but not entirely Western) chose to outsource such activities and operations, and the impact that outsourcing has had on both the environments in which they occurred and on the respective governments involved. It will assess how PMSCs, especially as "battlefield contractors" today, have become ubiquitous in the military operations of all Western militaries as an acknowledged core component of war fighting. It will consider these issues in light of more recent developments in both Iraq and Afghanistan and in other crucial theaters (such as Africa and Southeast Asia) in the so-called war on terrorism. Finally, it will provide an assessment of where such activities may evolve in the future and whether PMSCs are now, alongside humanitarian and nongovernmental aid organizations, an inherent element in any regional conflict or upheaval. Although the topic is vast, including many central ideas and concepts that bear in-depth examination in their own rights,[2] many of these themes will be explored only in passing in order to understand the issues central to this discussion better.[3]

Defining Terms: Proxyization, Outsourcing, Contracting

The proxyization of such security activities is not new. Indeed, its origins can be traced to classical times when rulers preferred to hire mercenaries—ideally, trusted foreigners—to fight their wars and avoid significant losses to national forces. In Europe, this arrangement evolved over the course of the Middle Ages, around the development of both the feudal system of loyalties and fealties and the independent "free companies" of knights and other warriors who sold their services to political and military leaders across the continent for various reasons: to provide security services to that leader, to support their conflicts with each other, and to carry out their expeditionary operations into the Middle East—around the Crusades—and, later, further afield. This evolution continued into the charters granted to both privateers and the great exploration companies of the early modern age, a process that continued well into the twentieth century as the great European empires consolidated their colonies. Although the focus in the decolonization period after 1945 centered on the mercenaries' role in those conflicts, it too often dwelled on the part that white European mercenaries played and not sufficiently on that of the indigenous nationals who sold their military services to the highest bidder in decolonization conflicts in Africa, Southeast Asia, and the Middle East. In truth such groups continued in their quieter, lower-profile roles of supporting Western statutory forces on deployed operations overseas: for example, the United States in Vietnam and Laos; the British in Kenya, the Gulf of Aden, and Oman; or the French in Francophone Africa.

Today, as the nature of warfare has changed, conventional organized warfare in many ways, at least, has been superseded by low-intensity conflict (LIC) in the developing world. Individuals such as Martin van Creveld, Ralph Peters, and Steven Metz heralded this evolution.[4] Van Creveld warned,

> If states are decreasingly able to fight each other, then the concept of intermingling already points to the rise of low-intensity conflict as an alternative. The very essence of such conflict consists in that it circumvents and undermines the trinitarian structure of the modern state, which is why that state in many ways is singularly ill-suited for dealing with this kind of war . . . throughout the Third World, numerous new states have never been able to establish themselves *vis-à-vis* other kinds of social entities, including ethnic tribes in particular. In the face of their quarrels, the distinction between government, army and people began to fall apart before it had even been properly established.[5]

The state arose following the end of the wars of the sixteenth and seventeenth centuries in which principalities and cities made war on each other; the state system that arose in Europe attempted to regulate the provision of needs to the citizens of these allied principalities and cities. Previously, princes and rulers hired independent professional warriors, in addition to their feudal levies, to form the backbones of their armies; witness the Free Companies or condottieri of the Middle Ages and the Renaissance. With first the establishment of the Westphalian state system and later the emergence of national armies during the period of the Napoleonic Wars, citizen-soldiers (and thus citizen-armies) became the accepted norm, and military service came to be associated with nationalism. It was only under Louis XIV in the seventeenth century that an organized national standing army came about, a concept later perfected by Frederick II of Prussia. Finally, the introduction of conscription during the French Revolutionary Wars set in motion the development of modern mass armies built around a professional nucleus and organized into specialized units for combat and support.[6] Thus, warfare became the pure domain of the nation-state in order to regulate its activities. Private soldiery (which was generally classified as "mercenary") was frowned upon (with the exceptions of foreign contingents, such as the German legions of the Georgian British Army or, later, such groups as the Gurkha regiments of the British Army) and later condemned outright in the latter half of the twentieth century.[7]

As Sam Roggeveen points out,

> The idea that soldiery (indeed war itself) was acceptable only if it was invested with a moral purpose has retained its currency. . . . As there can only be one true universal "way of life", there can be no room for compromise in a contest between them. . . . It follows that if system A is the true way of life, then system B must not only be untrue but evil, inspiring much greater ferocity in the fight than would be likely if one were simply fighting for the limited aim of increasing a king's power or prestige.[8]

This state of affairs, however, has begun to change once again. The increasing influence and strength of multinational corporations (whose economic power sometimes exceeds that of many small states), and the termination of great powers' support to proxy or client-states in the developing world with the end of the Cold War, resulted in many of these states being unable, or sometimes unwilling, to provide for their own national security and defense, particularly in situations of guerrilla conflict. The use of private

security or military elements has filled the void, thus becoming more common once again. According to Roggeveen,

> We would like to believe that those young men and women who enrol
> in our defence forces do so as much out of a sense of duty as for personal
> gain, but you will note that Defence Force recruitment campaigns con-
> centrate *exclusively* [original emphasis] on the career opportunities avail-
> able in the armed forces . . . [thus] the volunteer soldier who chooses
> to fight for a private company ought to be regarded as the moral equiv-
> alent of the volunteer who chooses [to fight] for his country.[9]

From this position, it is clear that under circumstances in which the state
is not strong enough or established enough to provide for its citizens, it
must find someone else to do so. This conceptualization of warfare as being
part of societal interaction clashes with the more traditionally distinct concept of warfare being primarily the state's domain. As LIC becomes the dominant nature of warfare in the twenty-first century (witness such recent
conflicts as those in Tajikistan, Sudan, the Philippines, Colombia, Nagorno-
Karabakh, or Chechnya), the nature of war fighting also continues to evolve.

The PMSC has stepped into this gap in society, slowly replacing the mercenary in his previous guise. By privatizing security and the use of violence
and by removing it from the state's domain and deferring it to private interests,
the state in these instances is being both strengthened and disassembled.
While PMSCs are attempting to reconstruct the state to ensure stability and
establish sufficient security for economic activities, they are also removing
the state's right to control violence and war.

PMSCs as Proxies in Today's Global Security Environment

Mercenaries, PMSCs, and Other Non-Statutory Actors

In his 1994 study "The New Warrior Class,"[10] Ralph Peters outlined four
groups that compose this "class." The first is the *mercenary*, a soldier willing
to sell his military skills to the highest bidder, no matter what the cause.

Such activities have continued unabated from the postcolonial period to today, but they have gradually evolved from the type of mercenary activity witnessed following decolonization in Africa during the 1960s (for example, the interventions in the Belgian Congo by Jean "Black Jacques" Schramme or the exploits of "Mad Mike" Hoare or Col. Bob Denard) to a more controlled involvement. In these conflicts, such people become involved not merely for the monetary compensation but also out of their interest in the nature of the specific conflict (exemplified by the involvement of patrio-religious mercenaries in the wars of the former Yugoslavia) and their self-awareness that it is the only lifestyle that they could have, all of which contribute to the creation of this "warrior class." During the 1996–1997 conflict in Zaire, the emergence of the "White Legion"—three hundred multinational mercenaries raised by French and Serbian soldiers fighting for Mobuto Sese Seko—was exemplary of the continued existence of this class of combatant that fought both out of monetary motivation and a continued attraction to the warrior lifestyle.[11] Evidence that former U.S. Special Forces and intelligence personnel provided military advice and operational support to various Mexican drug cartels since the late 1990s similarly highlights a growing post–Cold War trend in which former elite members of the U.S. security establishment support the very elements against which they had operated for years.[12]

The second category of this warrior class is that of the *religiously motivated combatant*. Often fighting only out of religious conviction in a struggle, these combatants have demonstrated a remarkable ability to move throughout the world in recent years. Since the late 1980s nowhere has this been more notable than in the global movement of mujahidin and the wider jihadist nebula. This campaign emerged during the Soviet-Afghan War, in which so-called International Brigades of Islamist soldiers—formed, for example, by either elements of the Muslim Brotherhood or the Pakistani Inter-Services Intelligence Directorate—moved into Afghanistan to fight the Soviet invaders.[13] These forces, later broadly referred to as the "Afghan Arabs" who mixed with the Afghan mujahidin, slowly coalesced around Abdullah Azzam and his lieutenant, Osama bin Laden, in the Afghan Services Bureau (later to become al-Qai'da, or "The Base"). As the Soviet-Afghan War ended, many of these individuals moved around the world, fighting in conflicts in such diverse areas as Bosnia and Kosovo, Mindanao in the Philippines, Somalia, Yemen, Indonesia, across the Middle East and North Africa, Chechnya, Kashmir, and, of course, Afghanistan again since 2001 and in Iraq since 2003. Veterans of these conflicts have also formed the basis for jihadist terrorist cells active around the world since the early 1990s.

The wars in Bosnia and Herzegovina, in which religiously motivated combatants from throughout the Islamic and Christian worlds flooded to fight the religiously aligned combatant rivals, provide some of the best examples of this type of warrior.[14] Many Islamic countries used the mujahidin as proxies for their own involvement in these conflicts. For example, Bosnian Muslim forces included members of an Iranian Revolutionary Guards brigade, and Turkish "guest workers" from Germany joined the war following training in Turkey.[15] The Croatian Army also used mercenaries. Early in the conflict between Croatia and Serbia, Croat president Franjo Tudjman allegedly used foreign mercenaries to fill out the ranks and capabilities of his army. This was partly blamed for the army's early defeat in Croatia. Ultimately, it is believed that more than forty thousand Islamist mercenaries fought in the conflicts in the former Yugoslavia, compared with fifteen thousand in Chechnya.[16]

The third type of new warrior making its mark on regional conflict is the *child soldier*. In many parts of Africa, Asia, and (to a lesser degree) South America, children younger than eighteen years old who have lived in war zones throughout their lives have been pulled into the fighting. A good example was the 1996–1997 rebel alliance of Laurent Kabila's in Zaire, 70 percent of whose personal forces were younger than age eighteen. They faced a group of Mai-Mai primarily comprised teenagers who were grouped into units from their home villages and who strongly believed in a magic that made them invincible in battle.[17] Many of these warriors have been fighting since a young age—before they were ten years old—and grew up knowing only combat. Confronting such a problem is beyond the abilities of the international community: these children see their only future as soldiers in such wars as leverage in anarchic societies.

Finally, the fourth type of new warrior is the *PMSC and its employees*, with its origins in two types of more common participants—the mercenary and the private (corporate) security official. Prior to the mid-1990s, this category generally comprised individuals tasked primarily with personal and installation protection. With the withdrawal of first the colonial powers and then the superpowers from the developing world, this class of combatants grew in numbers, strength, organization, and motivation—as the supply of personnel and resources for their activities grew in parallel with the demands for their services—to the point that many private military and security companies now include capabilities in transport, intelligence, combat firepower, and paramedical skills. Although they are most often accused of being mercenary forces engaged in "criminal activities and violations of human rights" (as was noted consistently in the reports of the UN High Commissioner for Refugees [UNHCR] on the "Use of Mercenaries as a Means of Violating Human Rights and Impeding the Exercise of the Right of Peoples to Self-Determination" from 1995 onward),[18] a clear distinction emerges between the more traditional mercenary forces and those engaged in high-profile, high-risk private security operations, especially in Africa, Latin America, Southeast Asia, and the former Soviet Union.

All four categories of the new warrior have been fueled by the change in global security dynamics since 1990. Security forces around the world continued to shrink following the end of the Cold War, resulting in an outflux of trained and, more often than not, battle-hardened combatants and former intelligence officers into the civilian sector, particularly in South Africa and the former Soviet Bloc, and from downsized Western militaries. In addition, similar problems have been a constant in many militaries in the developing world, where changing regimes and security sector reform (SSR) and disarmament, demobilization, and reintegration (DDR) activities have also "forced" many soldiers—some with little professional training—into their local or regional conflict markets. Although a number of countries instituted programs to assist with this demobilization and the transition from warrior to effective member of civil society (such as the National Service Corps, which supported the postapartheid transition in South Africa), the success in implementing such programs has been the exception rather than the rule. In many developing countries, as well as those of the former Soviet Bloc, this transition has failed for a number of reasons, including the state's inability to provide basic sustenance and living conditions, education, and training programs for these former combatants. Sometimes the sheer numbers of those being demobilized has led directly to the emergence on the international security scene of tens of thousands of demobilized combatants whose only livelihood has been war. Thus, many have chosen to return to that life, realizing either they do not fit into civil society or they simply prefer the warrior "lifestyle," both of which are key points when considering motivational issues (which too often focus on the monetary aspect). Some became mercenaries, some joined PMSCs, and others existed in that murky in-between world of service as advisers to governments, international and non-governmental organizations, criminal consortia, and MNCs operating across the developing world and in newly emerging democracies.

For these reasons, mercenarism remains, but PMSCs are of a different ilk to mercenaries. Organized along corporate lines, with all the bureaucracy and corporate governance mechanisms that that structure implies, those PMSCs operating from Western countries at least provide support to clients whose aims and profiles are in line with Western foreign and security policy objectives. They are members of trade associations and lobby governments, as any industry does, around issues relating to regulation, corporate law, and policy concerns. They have boards of directors, shareholders, annual reports, and, crucially, legal teams. Frequently and increasingly Western governments—such as those of the United States, Great Britain, Canada, Germany, Australia, and others—contract them to support their statutory military operations overseas. They also work extensively for the United Nations and its various bodies worldwide, the World Bank, various NGOs, and humanitarian assistance organizations to provide security to their operations in regions of armed conflict—security that national armed forces previously provided. Can the ultimate evolution of this assistance, where private firms actually conduct peace-support operations on behalf of the UN or other multilateral security organizations, be far away? Indeed, it is already upon us.

In short, PMSCs are distinct from the mercenaries who previously operated in the postcolonial world and those who continue to operate today. As will be discussed further, however, all PMSCs should not be seen through the same lens. Those private security companies originating and operating in many conflicts in the developing world lack the corporate structures and transparency—indeed, they are virtually nonexistent in many cases—found in Western PMSCs.

Private Military and Security Companies Today

Considerable effort, driven somewhat by a desire to separate them into those providing private security versus those providing public security, has been made to distinguish the types of actors in the PMSC field. James Cockayne most usefully summarizes these groups as being international (externally contracted) PMSCs that provide both security and military services; local, formal, and informal security service providers; and "moonlighting" state security forces.[19] To this list can be added mercenaries, private armies, militias, and warlords (which include those statutory forces *not* delivering public security). However, such separations are artificial in most instances and do not graft accurately or easily to the reality on the ground.[20]

In spite of this caution against making separations, this qualitative distinction is most useful—given that it provides a focus on the origin of the PMSC actor, which *does* demonstrate differences in approach, activity, and outcome—and should be kept in mind when considering the different forms that PMSCs can take. However, no single strategy or solution will be applicable to all three groups, and each must be assessed according to its characteristics. Although this chapter concentrates on foreign-based PMSCs, the other actors, especially those originating locally to a conflict, must also be acknowledged. The similarities in *outcome* can be appreciated when assessing the impact of privatized security activities on local security environments.

Alongside the preceding categories, consideration must also be given to *individual contractors* or small groups of contractors provided through the official support activities by one government to another (for example, by the British government through its overseas security sector reform and counterterrorism training programs or by the U.S. government through its State Department–led International Military Education and Training Program). In many instances, these individuals are retired government personnel and are not part of a "company" as it could be construed. Although they fulfill many of the same roles that the other categories of actors do, they are often overlooked when considering the place and role of PMSCs, especially when compared with "mercenaries," by dint of their official status with the supporting government, and they often provide services parallel to those statutory contributions from the supporting government. Examples include the Security Sector Development Advisory Team (SSDAT) of the UK Department for International Development (DFID),[21] the CANADEM contracting mechanism, or the U.S. Department of Justice's International Criminal Investigative Training Assistance Program (ICITAP).[22]

This interaction raises another complicating point, that is, the contracting of PMSCs to support Western militaries on deployed operations. The notion of contractors on the battlefield has long been a mainstay of military deployments (across the environmental range of military activities—land, sea, and air), but since the late 1990s, the role of PMSCs and other private actors (such as administrative and accommodation companies) in supporting such operations has increased dramatically.[23] Both lawmakers and policymakers note a clear distinction between these services and more stereotypical notions of PMSC activities and how they are contracted:[24]

- services contracted by governments to support Western military deployments and diplomatic missions (e.g., ArmorGroup's provision of security for many British government personnel in Afghanistan, and the U.S. Navy's dependence on extensive private technical support to run combat and firing systems);
- services contracted by Western governments to support others (e.g., the deployment of DFID SSDAT advisers or academic experts working on Global Opportunities Fund projects to support African and Southeast Asian governments in SSR; the U.S. government's contracting of DynCorp and L-3 MPRI to support Liberian and African Union peace-support, SSR, and DDR activities);
- services contracted by external actors on interventions (e.g., the United Nations' contracting of PMSCs to provide refugee protection, logistics and airlift, de-mining, and peace-support operations; the contracting of PMSCs to provide protection to NGOs and humanitarian aid delivery in the field);
- services contracted by internal, or host nation, actors (e.g., the hiring of Executive Outcomes by the Angolan and Sierra Leonean governments; the hiring of MPRI by the Croatian military in 1994–1995 prior to Operation Storm); and

■ services contracted by multinational corporations (e.g., the use of PMSCs to provide security to commercial extraction and infrastructure operations in Iraq and in African countries).

The point of making these distinctions is that the line between mercenaries, militias, private security companies (PSCs), and private military companies (PMCs) are often blurred all three ways: individuals who previously engaged in what could be defined as "mercenary" activity (i.e., selling their skills on the open military market without a corporate affiliation) then could go to work for either a PMC or PSC. Also, PSCs involved in defensive physical guarding operations could cross the line into offensive military operations. It is thus extremely difficult, if not impossible, to make clear distinctions among different categories of actors when it comes to assessing the services they offer (especially where one company can offer many different services).[25] For this reason, this chapter places a stronger emphasis on delineating and assessing the *activities* or *services* that different actors provide—as proxies for their host nations or contracting parties—as the starting point for developing policy and governance mechanisms surrounding PMSCs.

The Operational Environment for PMSCs Today

Since the early1990s, PMSC (and "battlefield contractor") activities have grown dramatically, most particularly in supporting governments in the developing world and in aiding Western governments and international organizations (IOs), NGOs, or MNCs in their interventions in those countries. Their services include the protection of strategic resources globally, the provision of military assistance training teams to developing world governments, their involvement in de-mining and other noncombat services, and their advisory roles to governments engaging in security sector reform and disarmament, demobilization, and reintegration programs in post-conflict states. Although such services had significantly spiked long before the "bubble" of PMSC involvement in Iraq and Afghanistan began in 2002–2003—most particularly in terms of combat services (witness, for example, Executive Outcomes' operations in Africa in the 1990s) and the intensity of the environment (or "space") that PMSCs encounter today (compare DynCorp's operations in Colombia with those in the Balkans, Afghanistan, and Liberia)—companies today that look (or, indeed, are) remarkably similar to those that were operating in the 1960s, 1970s, and 1980s ultimately offer the same services. As had been the case, though largely unremarked, in previous conflicts, PMSCs in the twenty-first century became intimately involved in the wars in Afghanistan and Iraq and operated directly alongside the Coalition and allied forces in those conflicts. Moreover, they became absolutely essential to those intervention efforts, providing support ranging from protection for reconstruction and development to drug crop eradication and close-protection services for the new leaders in those countries. At the same time, throughout the world, PMSCs have extended their support for and involvement in peace-support and humanitarian operations,[26] operating alongside member-state militaries and protecting aid delivery and related support activities in the field. Finally, security, military, and intelligence contractors are now an inherent part of any security force in the Western world and provide technical, advisory, and other support services to the military on a daily basis.

The UN peace-support missions in Sierra Leone, Liberia, Côte d'Ivoire, and the Democratic Republic of the Congo also have outsourced their supply and logistical needs to private security companies. Throughout Sierra Leone's civil war, Executive Outcomes, and later Sandline International, provided operational and combat support to the Sierra Leonean and British armed forces at various points. Most recently, the UN Mission in Ethiopia and Eritrea contracted a commercial de-mining team to replace the Slovak military de-mining group and reduced its mission costs. Another contemporary example is the recent pledge from the United States, the largest aid donor to Sudan, to support the African Union's peace-support mission there with private contracts awarded to DynCorp and Pacific Architects and Engineers (PAE). Understandably, the presence of such proxies in Africa has raised questions related to the accountability and democratic oversight of this industry; the extent to which governments, the United Nations, and relief agencies are outsourcing key state functions; and the influence that these companies gain in the process.

Surveying the Landscape of PMSC Operations

It is a difficult task to review and assess accurately the historical and comparative nature of PMSC activities, whether they are war fighting, peacekeeping, peace-support operations, or advisory services. Although a great deal of anecdotal evidence exists, a significant portion of which is negative, determining the reality of such involvement (outside of some well-documented cases) is challenging. In addition, establishing how to classify PMSC activities in order to bound this assessment is equally difficult. For example, should only those PMSC activities providing armed or otherwise direct support to combat forces, such as policing support or military airlift, be included in an assessment of proxyization? Or should all supporting activities that have a direct impact on military operations—such as SSR-related intelligence advice, DDR-related training activities, and so on—be included? Indeed, some previous PMSC operations, such as parts of Executive Outcomes' and Sandline International's activities in Sierra Leone and Angola, today could come under the banner of DDR and SSR. Therefore, such operations can also provide lessons in understanding the complex relationship between the mission and the actor, especially in situations where one PMSC actor may move from war fighting to post-conflict DDR and SSR and back again to war fighting, all the while supporting and otherwise interacting with one or more peace-support forces. The Sierra Leonean case, for example, involved PMSCs supporting those operations of the Economic Community of West African States Monitoring Group (ECOMOG), the British military, and the post-settlement International Military Assistance Training Team.

For this reason, PMSC activities should be differentiated between conflict operations and post-conflict missions. In so doing, when considering the more active services—military, military support, security, and logistics— examples of PMSCs (or companies that can provide PMSC services) providing logistical, welfare, administrative, or other types of rear-area support to statutory interventions that do not have an immediate and tangible impact on the abilities of the intervention to carry out the duties will be excluded. Similarly, when considering the more passive services—SSR and DDR, training, and advising, for example—those services that are geared toward administration, management, and other rear-area activities that do not have an immediate and tangible impact on the security environment of the mission will be excluded. This metric—that is, the manner in which PMSC activities have a direct impact on the strategic environment in which they operate—is the best means of assessing whether national objectives are being proxyized through the use of such companies.

PMSCs as Proxies in Conflict Operations

This section will analyze the role of PMSCs in combat operations and peace-support operations writ large. The first example is monitoring and other conflict prevention mechanisms. During the three OSCE monitoring missions in Kosovo conducted in the late 1990s, twenty employees from DynCorp were contracted (for both observation and direct support on logistics and maintenance issues) to support the Kosovo Diplomatic Observer Mission (KDOM) in fulfillment of the U.S. government's commitment to the sixty-person mission (alongside Canada, the United Kingdom, France, Russia, and the European Union). When the KDOM was replaced in November 1998 by the Kosovo Verification Mission, DynCorp employees again fulfilled the U.S. government's commitment. The mission was withdrawn in March 1999, however, owing to the growing violence in Kosovo. Following the North Atlantic Treaty Organization's war with Serbia, the OSCE Mission in Kosovo (OMIK) was established in July 1999 in direct support to the UN Interim Administration Mission in Kosovo (UNMIK). Once again, the approximately five hundred American members of the UNMIK Police, which the OMIK supported, were DynCorp employees under contract from the U.S. State Department.

The "Plan Colombia" provides another example. As part of the U.S. government's "war on drugs," begun in the late 1980s, it began using PMSCs to assist in training Colombian government forces in antidrug interdiction operations, as well as to support those operations. Their activities included contracting DynCorp to fly eradication missions, supported by helicopter gunships, to defoliate coca fields; employing MPRI and DynCorp to professionalize the Colombian military to combat the Revolutionary Armed Forces of Colombia and narco-guerrillas; and hiring PMSCs to conduct aerial surveillance of enemy troop movements and locations and to generate actionable intelligence.

Looking at the broad range of peacemaking and peace enforcement operations yields a number of notable examples. The first is the role of PMSCs in Croatia and Bosnia during the Balkan conflicts that were used to support Western (particularly U.S.) objectives to resolve the conflicts and prevent other ones from erupting. In Bosnia alone, 5,900 civilian contractors supported 6,000 U.S. Army personnel, close to a one-to-one ratio.[27] The British PMSC Defence Systems Limited (later ArmorGroup) was contracted to provide, among other logistics and support skills, UN military observers as part of the United Nations' commitment to its Protection Force (UNPROFOR) from 1992 to 1996, as well as personnel at the command and operational levels. The American PMSC MPRI was (infamously) contracted to provide military professionalization advice and general staff-level training of the Croat Ministry of Defense (and the Bosnian Muslim army), prior to the Croatians' retaking of the Krajina region in August 1995. DynCorp also provided the U.S. contribution to the International Police Task Force (IPTF) in Bosnia (as well as the wider Implementation Force/Stabilization Force) beginning in 1996–1997. Six years after IPTF began, the U.S. State Department's inspector general investigated and determined that the quality of both DynCorp's training services and the recruits whom the company screened and hired into the IPTF programs were very high. The State Department criticized DynCorp, however, for improper contracting procedures (not the least of which involved a rise in the contract's value from $4.5 million to $270 million without entering into any competitive procurement process).[28] The company was also embroiled in a human-trafficking and sex slavery scandal in its Bosnian operation that had a significant negative impact on its public profile.[29]

During Sierra Leone's civil war, several PMSCs were active in a wide variety of operations. Most noteworthy, Executive Outcomes was contracted for a number of tasks: to combat and defeat the Revolutionary United Front (RUF) and its Armed Forces Revolutionary Council confederates; to secure the country's strategic resources from RUF and confederate hands; to train a local militia (the Kamajors) to form the backbone of a new Sierra Leonean military; to restructure the government's security policies, policing, and intelligence dispensation; and to undertake a limited security sector reform contract with the Republic of Sierra Leone Armed Forces. Executive Outcomes and two of its affiliates, Lifeguard Services and Sandline International—along with other smaller PMSCs such as Southern Cross Security Services—also provided strategic and tactical support to ECOMOG peace-support operations in Sierra Leone and neighboring Liberia and Burkina Faso. Executive Outcomes provided similar services in Angola as well as in other African and Southeast Asian countries.

In Iraq and Afghanistan, PMSCs have been used extensively across a range of peacemaking (in the case of Iraq) and peace enforcement (in the case of Afghanistan) operations. In Iraq, initially with the Coalition Provisional Authority (CPA) and subsequently with the Iraqi Ministry of Interior, the U.S. government contracted PMSCs to provide all the security for reconstruction and infrastructure-building programs. In Afghanistan, PMSCs were also contracted for the same purpose by donor governments involved in Afghanistan and by the Afghan Ministries of the Interior and Defense. PMSCs have also provided security services to donor government representation in Iraq and Afghanistan. For example, the UK Foreign Office contracted ArmorGroup to provide all static and mobile security for its government representatives in Iraq and Afghanistan. PMSCs have developed, along with external security advisers, the national security policy of both Iraq and Afghanistan. For example, the CPA in Baghdad, and subsequently the U.S. State Department, hired the Rand Corporation to write, monitor, and help guide the implementation of the national security policies of Iraq.[30] PMSCs have also conducted professionalization training for the Iraqi and Afghan military and police forces—MPRI and Vinnell Corporation were contracted to train the new Iraqi and Afghan militaries, and DynCorp did the same for the Iraqi and Afghan police—as well as counternarcotic forces in Afghanistan.[31] Finally, in Baghdad, the British PMSC Aegis Defence Services also ran the Reconstruction Operations Center and the parallel Logistics Movement Coordination Center,[32] responsible for coordination and information sharing between the Multinational Force and the PMSCs active in Iraq. Although a formal equivalent did not exist in Afghanistan at the time of writing, an informal equivalent was achieved through the collocation of British PMSC personnel in the British Provisional Reconstruction

Team's headquarters in Kandahar. The similar cultures and backgrounds of the British statutory and PMSC personnel helped immensely in establishing informal cooperation and information sharing.[33]

Protecting humanitarian aid delivery, personnel, and refugees in conflict zones—sometimes but not always under a UN mandate and banner—is one of the most challenging security problems in conflict environments. As humanitarian aid delivery NGOs increasingly become targets in such conflicts, the traditional mantle of protection given these NGOs—that is, their neutrality and noncombatant status—has increasingly little relevance to these actors' security.[34] Further, after attacks against UN diplomatic and other high-profile individuals in such conflicts as Iraq, Lebanon, and Afghanistan, many NGOs—including even those organizations such as the International Committee of the Red Cross or Médecins sans frontières (Doctors without Borders) that previously foreswore any protection to ensure their neutrality—have turned more and more to PMSCs to provide their security. They have done so for several reasons: to ensure their own protection, to safeguard those refugees and internally displaced persons they take responsibility for, and to distinguish refugees from combatants.

The local security environment and mission requirements usually determine the PMSC security services needed, and they can involve armed protective services, unarmed protective services, and security advice to the NGOs and IOs. For example, in the aftermath of the Rwandan genocide in Eastern Zaire, the UNHCR hired local "moonlighting" Zairian police to ensure the refugees' security in the camps in Kivu.[35] With the UNPROFOR in Bosnia, the British PMSC Defence Systems Limited provided drivers and security to UN aid convoys and to the aid agencies and NGOs operating under the UN banner as well as those operating separately from the United Nations. And, in 2005, the U.S. State Department jointly awarded the American PMSCs Blackwater, Triple Canopy, and DynCorp the five-year Worldwide Personal Protective Service contract, worth $1 billion. In return, the PMSCs supplied all such services to those personnel the U.S. government so designated, including foreign government, NGO, and IO officials. The State Department made extensive use of this contract in Iraq largely owing to the fact that, as was noted in the award, the department itself was "unable to provide protective services on a long-term basis."[36]

These areas may be some of the biggest in which (Western) states have proxyized their roles and contributions to private companies, for they do not want to intervene militarily in many of these conflicts, even if it is to help secure aid distribution and refugees' security. PMSCs have filled this gap increasingly but not without controversy or difficulty. As Cockayne and others have noted, the problem of maintaining security cannot be allowed to create, intentionally or unintentionally, a barrier between the local population receiving aid and protection and those individuals responsible for providing them. In the case of most NGOs that deliver aid, this scenario is less of a problem than it is in the case of deployed civilian personnel, whose protection (largely owing to the combatants in the conflict perceiving them as legitimate targets) often overrides the interests of the local population. This ability to distinguish is, of course, easier said than done.[37]

Post-Conflict Operations and PMSCs

In the broad humanitarian post-conflict space, PMSCs have played many roles in supporting national and international objectives that statutory forces normally filled, not the least of which is peacekeeping activities. In Bosnia, the U.S. Army contracted with ITT Industries (under a $100 million-plus contract) in July 2002 to provide force protection services to U.S. Army Europe Task Force Eagle located in Tuzla, Bosnia-Herzegovina. Under this contract, ITT provided installation security and force protection at numerous Task Force Eagle base camps.[38] Liberia has also witnessed successive PMSC contracts. During the 1990s, the U.S. State Department contracted with International Charter Incorporated (ICI) of Oregon, a helicopter transport company, and Pacific Architects and Engineers (PAE), an American company that provides logistical support, to assist the deployment of ECOMOG's Nigerian-led peacekeeping force into Liberia. Because Nigeria remained under embargo and ostracized owing to Sani Abacha's dictatorship, official government-to-government support was not possible; thus, the proxyized role of ICI and PAE was crucial. Although the contracts focused on providing logistical and airlift support to ECOMOG, when fighting intensified around the U.S. Embassy, ICI defended the embassy from the air until U.S. Special Forces arrived to relieve them. Similarly, in Sierra

Leone, during the post-1999 peacekeeping component of Sierra Leone's conflict-ridden history, a wide number of PMSCs—Sandline International, Southern Cross Security Services, Lifeguard Services, and others—interacted with the Sierra Leonean government, with the UN Assistance Mission in Sierra Leone, with the British military intervention, and subsequently with the UK-led International Military Advisory and Transition Team, which is still active today in Sierra Leone.

Outside of peacekeeping, another significant area for PMSC support is, broadly, security sector reform and disarmament, demobilization, and reintegration. With the conclusion of the peace agreement and the election of a new government in Liberia, the U.S. and Liberian governments agreed to contract MPRI to reform the Liberian national security structures and policies, and DynCorp was hired to transform and retrain the Liberian military and police in February 2005. In Iraq, the wider peacemaking efforts of, first, the CPA and Coalition forces and, subsequently, of the Iraqi Ministries of Interior and Defense alongside the Multinational Force have involved significant SSR and DDR activities. These efforts included reforming the security forces (military and police), security structures (Ministries of Defense and Interior, primarily, along with the new National Security Council and the intelligence services), and security policies and strategies.[39] As noted earlier, MPRI and the Vinnell Corporation were tasked with training the new Iraqi Army, and DynCorp was contracted to train the new Iraqi police.

In Afghanistan, SSR has occurred differently than it did in Iraq; Afghanistan was a somewhat less frenetic environment, allowing for a somewhat more orderly process. MPRI was tasked with developing Afghanistan's national defense, including creating an action plan outlining a new national defense strategy and structure; forming and reorganizing a Ministry of Defense and its General Staff; reworking management systems with an emphasis on personnel, logistics, acquisitions, operational command and control, and resource management and budgeting systems; and forming and training both a National Army with a border security element and a National Air Force. Similarly, as already noted, DynCorp was contracted to train the new Afghan National Police and counternarcotics police, and ArmorGroup was contracted to provide police-mentoring and prison reform programs along with mine clearance and disarmament services.

From 1999 to 2002, MPRI also provided retraining and restructuring support to the Nigerian Ministry of Defense under the Nigerian Democratization Program. Paid for jointly by the U.S. government—initially by the U.S. Agency for International Development and subsequently by the State Department—and the Nigerian MOD and Office of Transition Initiatives, the program included efforts to restore greater civilian control over the military. U.S. Special Forces conducted a separate military training program that was designed for peacekeeping duty in Sierra Leone (Operation Focus Relief). It involved training and equipping five Nigerian battalions, as well as one Ghanaian and one Senegalese battalion. Their training was reportedly aimed at enhancing combat skills and strengthening command and control, and it included a human rights component. The program was criticized for its lack of an effective monitoring and accountability component, a serious shortcoming given the Nigerian military's history of human rights abuses.[40]

Security and intelligence advisory services also provide innumerable examples of government outsourcing to PMSCs. These cases cover a wide range of activities, including supporting intelligence enterprise reform as part of SSR, providing intelligence services directly to a client, developing intelligence policies and dispensation, advising clients on strategic and tactical security matters, developing or reforming specific intelligence elements (e.g., police, military, fishers, national, antipoaching, and so on), and assisting with numerous other aspects of intelligence training activities (for example, on Western intelligence analytic techniques or on the management of the intelligence enterprise). Providing these security and intelligence advisory services are an equally differentiated number of PMSCs, including large PMSCs, such as Executive Outcomes and the ArmorGroup; specialist PMSCs, such as MPRI; or most notably, security and intelligence advisers that donor governments contract to support developing world capabilities through SSR and bilateral or multilateral assistance programs. The various bodies of the United Nations also frequently hire security advisers to support their requirements both at headquarters and in the field. Examples of these arrangements include the following:

- Executive Outcomes, Sandline, and Southern Cross Security Services, at different times, developed a fisheries intelligence capability in Sierra Leone;

- Geolink and the French PMSC Secrets provided tactical intelligence advice to Zaire's Mobutu during his fall from power in 1996;
- The UK Department for International Development contracted British security and intelligence advisers as part of wider SSR activities to reform Sierra Leonean, Ethiopian, and Indonesian intelligence enterprises;
- A British PMSC's intelligence specialists were collocated with British forces in Afghanistan under the International Security Assistance Force; and
- Numerous British, Canadian, American, Australian, and other nationals helped transform South Africa's security and intelligence structures at the end of apartheid, with PMSCs—Kroll, the highest among them—providing long-term support to South Africa's post-apartheid intelligence services.

Key Policy, Strategy, and Operational Issues

The PMSC industry has grown exponentially from its upswing in the 1990s. Although this expansion has been most significantly a result of the Iraq and Afghanistan "bubbles," it masks increases in the overall industry worldwide. In 1999 it was estimated that "projected total revenues for the security services market world-wide for the year 2000 is expected to grow to US$61.8 million and continue to US$87.9 million by the year 2005. This increased demand for more private security and military business service-related activities is due to growing economic activity in developing countries. Overall, the private security sector generates more than US$50 billion world-wide annually, including arms sales and services."[41]

In reality, individual contracts for the work done in Iraq and Afghanistan alone broke the $250 million, $500 million, or $1 billion thresholds, with more than $30 billion of the estimated $87 billion spent on the wars in Iraq and Afghanistan in 2003 spent on private companies, across a range of services including security.[42] As of the end of 2005, the U.S. Government Accountability Office (GAO) estimated that $60 billion had been allocated "for security, governance, and reconstruction efforts in Iraq," of which it estimated that "costs to obtain private security services and security-related equipment . . . ranged from 10 to 36 percent of project costs."[43] The GAO's mid-2006 assessment also found that more than 48,000 contractors working for 181 PMSCs were active in Iraq (although this figure likely includes the broad range of PMSC employees and not only those carrying weapons).[44] This group dwarfed the British military presence and reduced the ratio between contractors and statutory military forces to less than one in five (as compared with one in a hundred during the 1991 Gulf War).

At the same time, it is not only the overseas (foreign) PMSC market that has grown. The domestic market has also expanded dramatically since 1991, perhaps to a larger degree than its overseas counterpart. For example, in 2005–2006, the South African Police Service spent R100 million on private security support. With estimates of more than 125,000 personnel,[45] the industry in South Africa had grown 150 percent from 1997 to 2005 and its earnings went from R1.2 billion in 1990 to R13 billion in 2000.[46] Since 2001, the domestic U.S. homeland security market has thrived considerably, and several PMSCs that were active in Iraq, such as Blackwater (later renamed XE, then Academi) or Triple Canopy, positioned themselves to provide support to U.S. homeland security, emergency management, and counterterrorism requirements into the future. This "market" could be as large—if not larger—than that witnessed in Iraq over the last decade in both financial and operational terms. In some sense, this domestic arrangement is given similar justifications to using PMSCs overseas, that is, to relieve statutory military forces from support activities, in a climate of restricted resources, and allow them to concentrate on core military functions.

As the industry has grown—and its reach has increased, both geographically and in terms of the services it offers to clients—a number of governments globally have started to develop policies for regulating domestically based PMSCs. Some governments, such as that of the United States, see their role as essential to the operations of American security forces, whereas others, such as that of South Africa, have banned many PMSC activities and attempted to regulate those activities that are allowed. Still other governments, such as that of the United Kingdom, have long cooperated (indeed, contracted) with PMSCs to support British foreign policy objectives (such as the aforementioned Military Assistance Training Teams overseas) without a clear policy in place to govern such activities. And other governments, such as that of France, view a number of these "companies" as being an integral part of their Ministries of Defense and use them extensively to support overseas military sales and offer advisory services.

Meanwhile, the international community has continued to struggle with the issue of regulating these companies' activities, partly in an attempt to ban mercenary operations globally and partly to clarify the legal standing of such players in regional conflicts under international law (most particularly the laws of armed conflict and international humanitarian law). This effort relates largely and directly to continuing politico-ethical quandaries surrounding the legitimacy of such companies: Are they simply corporate bands of mercenaries? Or are they—touching upon the oft-quoted "monopoly of violence"—a direct offshoot of the privatization (and proxyization) of many other state functions? These questions remain deeply contentious. Some regional organizations, such as the African Union, have implemented laws against mercenarism (which does not get to the heart of this issue), whereas others, such as NATO or the European Union, have introduced regulations governing only some of the relevant areas, such as contracting with PMSCs or allowing them to provide military advisory services as a subset of strategic exports. The major intergovernmental organizations with an interest in these questions, primarily the United Nations, the International Committee of the Red Cross, and the Red Crescent, have continued to struggle with the complexities of this issue.

Whatever the perceived success or utility of using PMSCs, the oversight of such proxyization remains in question, especially where covert activities are at play (e.g., Plan Colombia). Employing PMSCs in such situations allows governments to bypass public debate on the private contractors being deployed in support of national objectives, particularly as (at least until the Iraq War refocused the spotlight) both their casualties and their wrongdoings were not subject to the same public scrutiny as were those of statutory forces. This avoidance of the "body bags" issue is especially relevant because the public's perception of PMSC activities is, at best, about individuals who are selling their services and therefore are accepting the risks—which somehow remains distinct from those joining the military, given its "national" charter. In such circumstances, determining the PMSCs' accountability for both the maintenance of international law and breaches thereof is difficult—if not impossible—to determine, let alone bring to account. The same issue is applicable to those local (indigenous) forces that PMSCs train and support, and it raises the question of what safeguards are in place (if any) to ensure private contractors will instill the same ethical and moral principles in their training programs in these circumstances as would be expected of them by the international community.

To this point, existing oversight and accountability processes have proved to be insufficient in the face of such large volumes of contracts and personnel on the ground and worldwide (especially in both Iraq and Afghanistan). They have failed to halt villainy and criminality, to prevent improper or unskilled labor from entering the PMSC market, to maintain oversight and surveillance of PMSC activities, and to disabuse some PMSCs of a sense of immunity early in each operation (made more notable in Iraq with the CPA's initial, infamous Memorandum 17, which granted immunity from prosecution to employees "associated with the CPA").

A related point is the ability of PMSCs to judge, assess, and differentiate the backgrounds of those local individuals being (re)trained through SSR and DDR initiatives, with a particular eye to exorcising human rights violators and criminals. In many of the cases noted—for example, in Iraq, Nigeria, Afghanistan, Sierra Leone—questions arose regarding the effectiveness of the PMSCs' own accountability mechanisms, especially in comparison with equivalent donor-government teams and their military, security, law enforcement, judiciary, and investigative expertise, which could be more adept at weeding out such violators.

Conclusion

PMSCs are fundamental players in the global military and security scene today and will continue to be so. Many countries—not the least of which, the United States—will continue to contract PMSCs to undertake missions and activities that, for various reasons, their governments are unable or unwilling to do themselves. This proxyization must be considered from two perspectives: First, how contracting with such corporations will allow many governments to contribute to regional peace and security, in a manner that they would otherwise be unable to (for reasons of resources, politics, or popular opinion). The second consideration, however, has to be how such companies—rather than pursuing wide-ranging international peace and security objectives through their support of developing world governments—may be the covert tool of Western governments' foreign policies and employed to avoid public scrutiny and transparency. In some senses, and regardless of whether they carry themselves according to all norms of international humanitarian and human rights law, this perceived inscrutability is the nub of concern over how Western governments use PMSCs across the developing world. The development of strict and enforceable oversight and regulatory regimes surrounding PMSC activities internationally is the only way in which the role and activities of such companies, as contracted by Western governments in proxy, can be synched with a wider international peace and security agenda.

Other significant policy and operational issues remain unresolved when considering how PMSCs serve as proxies for national governments and their strategic objectives. Dominant among them is the broad proxyization of foreign policy objectives and mechanisms. From an ultra-Realist perspective, the use of PMSCs, either unilaterally or in support of a wider intervention, can force a resolution to a conflict. These examples, particularly the Sierra Leonean, Croatian, and Bosnian cases, demonstrate how a relatively small number of former Western professional soldiers can dramatically improve the fighting ability of relatively disorganized and unprofessional non-Western forces. They also show—once again, from an ultra-Realist perspective—how PMSCs could be used to advance a nation's policies abroad without directly involving its own military forces. This subcontracting is the case in many other kinds of peace-support missions, where given the overstretch of (Western) military contingents in such operations, the statutory forces retain core military functions whereas secondary or support forces (such as static and mobile guarding) are contracted to PMSCs. The spin-up or surge capability such proxyization represents cannot be discounted, especially for national governments looking to support benevolent overseas objectives—such as security assistance or professionalization to developing world governments—when national statutory resources are overstretched. Indeed, the potential use of PMSCs to support national objectives in the United Nations and regional security organizations has long been an issue for the United Nations' Department of Peacekeeping Operations as well as other UN bodies such as the Office for Projects Services, the Development Program, and others.

This situation does not mean, however, that PMSCs provide any kind of solution to those foreign policy objectives. PMSCs are only capable of providing short-term security and stability in a conflict or post-conflict environment. Long-term security and stability must come from an international peace-support force. Equally, their use may send an unintended political message: the American government's use of a PMSC in Kosovo may have signaled a lack of commitment and resolve to that conflict's stakeholders (in this example, the Serb leadership). In strategic terms, that move sends the wrong message, often leading to war. The flip side of this concern is that PMSCs can provide additional support to (Western) governments' foreign assistance programs without direct statutory military involvement. This participation is often viewed as provocative and escalatory, or as a supplement to such statutory involvement for overstretched and resource-limited Western governments that still seek to support regional peace and stability promotion. The use of PMSCs as direct proxies for achieving foreign policy objectives thus remains a complex, multifaceted issue.

Multinational Corporations
Potential Proxies for Counterinsurgency?

WILLIAM ROSENAU AND PETER CHALK

A different version of this chapter was published as William Rosenau, Peter Chalk, Rennie McPherson, Austin Long, and Michelle Parker, Corporations and Counterinsurgency, OP-259 (Santa Monica, CA: Rand Corporation, 2009). Used by permission of the Rand Corporation.

The insurgencies, civil wars, and humanitarian interventions of the 1990s introduced U.S. military planners, strategists, and analysts to the important roles unofficial entities such as nongovernmental organizations (NGOs) and private military companies (PMCs) play in internal conflicts.[1] Today in countries as diverse as Colombia, Papua New Guinea, and Nigeria, multinational corporations (MNCs) are helping to shape zones of conflict in significant ways. However, although academic specialists have noted the growing governance and security roles of MNCs, U.S. strategy and policy have been slow to acknowledge the significance of these corporate actors and the importance of private forms of governance more generally.[2] *The U.S. Army–Marine Corps Counterinsurgency Field Manual* (FM 3-24), for example, notes only in passing that MNCs "engage in reconstruction, economic development, and governance activities,"[3] while failing to capture the range, nature, and consequences of the MNCs' presence in conflicted areas.

Across the global south, MNCs frequently dwarf indigenous governments in terms of capabilities, resources, and presence. Yet U.S. counterinsurgency policy (and, indeed, national security policy more generally) remains heavily state-centric in its orientation.[4] (Re)building a strong, legitimate polity lies at the heart of the American approach to counterinsurgency, which sees a robust, centralized state as the essential guarantor of indigenous security. Putting aside the question of whether this position is always and everywhere feasible or even desirable, the American approach overlooks the "real and existing" providers of security outside the state, such as religious sodalities, customary police and courts, militias, and in some instances, MNCs.[5] As mentioned, the real or potential contributions of NGOs and PMCs are acknowledged, but the inputs of another critically important non-state actor, the MNC, essentially are ignored.

The role of MNCs in conflict environments is a relatively new subject for scholarly and policy-oriented inquiry.[6] The small body of research that does exist approaches the issue from corporate social responsibility, human rights, and environmental policy perspectives. This chapter, in contrast, considers MNCs from a security studies viewpoint and examines MNCs as actors in conflict systems. The focus here is on firms in the oil, gas, and mining industries, or the so-called extractive sector. (One subset of MNCs, namely, PMCs, is considered in another chapter.) Multinational corporations affect, and are affected by, the violent environments in which they do business. This chapter pays particular attention to the efforts certain firms take to promote stability through social development and security measures—in other words, conflict mitigation, conflict transformation, or, more bluntly, "corporate counterinsurgency."

To provide context for the subsequent analysis, this chapter begins by considering some of the general themes surrounding the conduct of business in zones of conflict. This overview is followed by a case study of Shell Nigeria, which for decades has faced serious violent opposition to its activities in the Niger Delta. Although every conflict is unique and situation specific, the scale of violence in the region where Shell Nigeria operates—and the complexity of the physical, social, and political environment—is probably greater than what similar firms experience elsewhere in the world. However, Shell Nigeria is representative of the kinds of challenges large multinational firms confront as they conduct natural-resource extraction operations in war-torn environments. As with other MNCs, Shell Nigeria is an actor in a conflict system, and it has labored to forestall, contain, and mitigate conflict by shaping its violent operating environment.

The chapter concludes with some policy considerations. Specifically, it will offer a preliminary assessment of the costs and benefits of engaging MNCs in counterinsurgency operations. Such engagement would be problematical for the U.S. government and even more so for private sector firms. Rather than seek to harness MNCs as explicit components of a counterinsurgency campaign, policymakers should instead invest more heavily in developing an understanding of all the actors in conflict environments where the United States might have an interest. If the Americans' approach to counterinsurgency is excessively state-centric, it is also misguidedly binary, focusing almost exclusively on incumbent-insurgent dynamics while overlooking the critical role of other non-state actors.

Doing Business in Conflict Zones

For most multinational firms, a highly violent operating environment—and, with it, the prospect of the death or injury of employees and the destruction of corporate infrastructure—is a powerful incentive to depart or, indeed, not to enter a region in the first place. Advocacy groups and the international community frequently demand that MNCs in conflict zones halt their operations and remove themselves from the affected country, arguing that the continued presence of these firms helps maintain a "war economy" that sustains combatants.[7] Service firms and manufacturers with comparatively modest investments either do not face these obstacles and issues or have assets that are mobile; thus, relocating in the face of political instability is their usual reaction.[8]

For some MNCs, however, financial and other considerations create strong incentives for them to stay. Firms that decide to do so are most often those involved in oil, gas, and mining operations. For firms in these extractive sectors, relocation is rarely an option. They are compelled to remain where natural resources are to be found ("asset specificity," in the language of economics). Moreover, long production cycles and expected returns on extensive capital investment frequently outweigh the costs of continuing to operate in a conflict-ridden area.[9] Equally, the terms of concession agreements with host governments typically carry time frames measured in decades, which necessarily precludes the option of early divestment. Many firms in the extractive sector, therefore, must learn to adapt to conditions of violent instability.

Some MNCs choose to do little beyond enhancing the physical security of their enterprises. At the basic level, this process involves providing safe havens for employees and their families during periods of acute conflict, as Firestone Natural Rubber Company did for thousands of its workers and their families during the Liberian civil wars of the 1980s and 1990s.[10] In other instances, MNCs work to shape their operating environment in more strategic ways. One tact that has been common to many companies is an emphasis on social investment and community development initiatives. These approaches generally take the form of building houses, schools, hospitals, roads, and sanitation systems; supplying electricity and other services; and providing micro-credit programs to support economic diversification activities and business and employment opportunities, with NGOs typically playing a significant collaborative role.[11] Several corporate enterprises' policy is to channel assistance through tripartite partnerships made with community representatives and government officials. These arrangements are designed to enable collaboration toward mutually agreed objectives and to mitigate the danger of reinforcing perceptions that central authorities are either unwilling or unable to provide basic services (which is often a major source of substate tension).

Certain firms have also worked to improve the performance of local civil servants by providing training aimed at promoting institutional transparency and accountability. A number of businesses have expanded these practices into what can be best termed "state-building." In Papua New Guinea, for example, Placer Dome Inc. (now Barrick Gold) created a local police force to provide public safety services to local residents, while in Colombia's oil-rich Casanare region, British Petroleum (BP) has sought to strengthen the judicial system by supporting a "Justices of the Peace" program aimed at developing "legitimate ways for resolving daily conflicts which would take months in the formal legal arena."[12] Corporate support for local institutions can take less benign forms as well. As discussed in the later case study, Royal Dutch Shell reportedly hired armed contractors and government security forces to protect the company's infrastructure, many of which have been subsequently held responsible for widespread brutality and abuse.

The Bottom Line: Risk Reduction

The goal of corporate actions in terms of risk reduction is not a charitable one; rather, its goal is to create an acceptable operating environment that will ultimately foster shareholder value.[13] Although they acknowledge that the conflicts that threaten their enterprises often have deep social and political roots, MNCs typically do not attempt to address their underlying causes. In the view of many corporate officials, such a role is both beyond the capacity of private businesses and remains the ultimate responsibility of governments, international organizations, and NGOs. Moreover, the monetary value of engaging in conflict mitigation is extremely difficult to quantify and, hence, may not resonate as particularly relevant to the firm's bottom line. A lack of hard data on the actual relationship between political stability and a corporation's earnings can exacerbate this perception, not least because it precludes a straightforward cost-benefit analysis. Moreover, most companies conceive a favorable or at least tolerable operating environment as one that is *predictable* rather than *peaceful* and where risk has been reduced to a manageable level.[14] As such they may simply not see the need to engage in concerted conflict management practices over the long term.[15]

Firms that operate in turbulent areas undoubtedly are also sensitive to the negative effects that can result from conflict containment and mitigation strategies. "Hard" measures, such as using government security forces to protect corporate infrastructure, can lead to human rights abuses, court cases, and negative publicity. In the words of economist Philip Swanson, "Government security forces using force to suppress local protesters against the operations of extractive industry corporations is the commonest form of violence associated with the presence of these corporations in developing countries today."[16] "Softer" techniques, such as community development, carry their own dangers as they can inadvertently exacerbate local ethnic and political tensions by appearing to favor one group over another. As Mary Anderson and Luc Zandvliet conclude, "Building schools and clinics, working with local leaders, promoting local economic activities can all feed conflict, rather than reduce it, if there is no analysis of how choices made with regard to these programs will play into the conflicts in the broader society."[17]

This problem is especially likely to occur if the benefits that flow from a mine or drilling site (in terms of access to housing, jobs, and clinics) favor one particular group or the population in the immediate vicinity of the project. Under such circumstances wealth gaps can either be created or entrenched, serving to foster or heighten divisions between "haves and have-nots."[18] Moreover, precisely because of the significant opportunities that the establishment of a mine or drilling site affords, these projects tend to act as "migratory magnets." Ensuing influxes of outsiders can quickly upset local demographic balances and, in turn, generate communal hostility and tension.

All that said, there is little question that a concerted "hearts and minds" strategy can serve important corporate interests. MNCs that do decide to remain in zones of conflict can face damaging "name and shame" campaigns by concerned NGOs, and an erosion of brand reputation, if they fail to take effective action to reduce conflict. In addition, taking social measures is becoming increasingly necessary to access political risk insurance from major underwriters as Lloyd's of London and the World Bank's Multilateral Investment Guarantee Agency.[19] Just as importantly, most MNCs are now required to demonstrate visibly to their shareholders that they are having a positive impact on the communities with which they interact, both in terms of ensuring the sanctity of fundamental freedoms and stimulating progress for overall local development.[20] Equally, emerging legal precedents in the United States have widened the definition of "complicity" in human rights violations, potentially exposing companies to legal sanction if they fail to take active measures to counter abuses that they know of (or could have known of) and from which they have benefited.[21]

To give greater context to the actual or potential role MNCs can play in counterinsurgency (COIN), the following section details a case study that illustrates several of the corporate risk reduction approaches already discussed, including community development, state-building, and hard security, and highlights the manifold challenges and pitfalls associated with such approaches. In the words of Kenneth Omeje, it became imperative for Royal Dutch Shell, the major multinational firm involved, to "manage the grievances of the local people and to dissuade them from disruptive violence."[22] However, as the case makes clear, corporate attempts to quell conflict, no matter how well intentioned, had the inadvertent effect of aggravating communal tensions and fueling violence. As will be seen, the potential of MNCs to serve as conflict accelerants makes them problematical counterinsurgency partners.

Shell in the Niger Delta: Doing Business in a "Zone of Insurrection"

Nigeria is Africa's top oil producer (behind Angola), the seventh-biggest producer of petroleum within the Organization of Petroleum Exporting Countries (OPEC), and currently accounts for some 15 percent of non-Gulf oil exports to the United States (a proportion that is expected to rise to 25 percent by 2020 as Washington seeks to lessen its dependence on traditional Middle Eastern suppliers).[23] The petroleum sector is the backbone of the Nigerian economy and is the state's financial mainstay, providing 80 percent of the country's gross domestic product and 95 percent of its foreign exchange earnings.[24] The Niger River Delta, an area of some seventy thousand square miles in the country's south,[25] is the nation's oil heartland. ExxonMobil, Chevron, Total Fina Elf, and other large multinational oil companies operate in the region, but the most significant corporate actor is Royal Dutch Shell, whose Nigerian subsidiaries (known collectively as Shell Nigeria)[26] produce nearly half of the country's average daily total.[27] The scale of Shell Nigeria's physical presence and operations is considerable, covering some thirty thousand square kilometers and including six thousand kilometers of pipeline, ninety oil fields, seventy-three flow stations, and two oil export terminals. The company employs 4,500 people directly, and another twenty thousand work for Shell Nigeria contractors.[28]

In Nigeria, as in many countries where petroleum is found, oil extraction takes place in a fractious and highly complex operating environment. With a population of 27 million people in five thousand communities and fifty ethnic groups speaking a total of 250 dialects,[29] the Niger Delta is often bewildering in its economic, social, political, and topographical complexity.[30] The region is also one of widespread armed militancy, fueled by gross economic and political equality, conflicts between and among communities for land and other resources, and chronic neglect. As the U.S. State Department has noted, the country's federal and state governments have failed to use the oil revenues to promote regional development.[31] Indeed, with the exception of the security forces, the government has no presence in the delta. In the words of one oil company executive, "You won't find police stations, court houses or primary schools for vast stretches. There are no post offices. There is no presence of the government for miles."[32]

For decades, the delta has been a "zone of insurrection," with oil at the heart of the region's turbulence, not least by feeding popular expectations that associated revenue flow would dramatically improve the life for local indigenes.[33] However, despite the fact that oil has generated an estimated $500 billion for Nigeria, the delta remains the country's least developed region.[34] Unemployment is high, and ethnic groups such as the Ijaw, Ogoni, Ekwere, and Itsekiri continue to live in extreme poverty, with some 70 percent of the population subsisting on less than one U.S. dollar a day.[35] For many young men (characterized by one author as a "reserve army" of discontent),[36] violent criminality—aided by the ready availability of illicit small arms and light weapons (including AK-47 rifles, rocket launchers, and rocket-propelled grenades) and the absence of effective policing—remains an attractive (and perhaps the only) career prospect. Petroleum exploration and production has ushered in what one scholar has termed "excruciating environmental conditions . . . often aggravated by oil spills, gas flaring, the discharge of waste into communal lands and waters, and other fallout of poor oilfield management by the multinational oil companies."[37] Delays in compensation from oil companies for environmental damage have exacerbated these conditions, sparking further conflict. Compounding the situation is a lack of transparency over ownership for land marked for oil exploration in the region. In and around the city of Warri, for example, the Ijaw, Itsekiri, and Urhobo ethnic groups have clashed over the distribution of crude revenues, jobs, and contracts and over other issues such as the control of the local government.[38] Finally, the petroleum companies themselves act as major magnets for violent criminal predators. The illegal siphoning and acquisition of oil (known as bunkering) and the kidnapping of MNC workers for ransom serve as significant illicit revenue streams, fostering a climate of insecurity. Oil-related violence conservatively is estimated to cost the lives of a thousand people a year as well as an annual revenue shortfall of at least $1.1 billion.[39]

Adding to the complexity of this environment is a rich array of militias, gangs, armed youth groups, vigilantes, cults (a type of criminal gang with origins in Nigeria's university population), and insurgents. Indeed, the conflict in the Niger Delta is difficult to characterize as an insurgency in any traditional sense, given the layered and highly variegated nature of the region's militancy. It is impossible to categorize any group as purely criminal or purely political or to attribute "greed" or "grievance" as the primary motivation for taking up arms.[40] Militants tend to exist along a spectrum, with some inclining toward the purely criminal and others more purely political in their orientation. Some groups that appear to be largely criminal have political, social, and even environmental agendas, whereas other ostensibly ideological organizations engage in extensive criminality.

A notable example of the latter is the Movement for the Emancipation of the Niger Delta (MEND), which with its flair for publicity (such as its attack on two Shell pipelines in April 2008 to "welcome" a U.S. warship that was transiting the Gulf of Guinea[41]) has emerged as the violent group with the most prominent international reputation. MEND portrays itself as a defender of minority rights against brutal and rapacious government authorities. In so doing, the movement taps into a deep strain of popular resistance to the economic, environmental, and political maladies that emerged following the discovery of oil.[42] To give expression to its rhetorical agenda, MEND has attacked oil pipelines, and other facilities are a prominent feature of its violent repertoire. Together with other militants, the organization carried out 106 attacks on pipelines, pumping stations, and other oil-related infrastructure between 2006 and April 2008.[43] Shell has estimated that such actions cost the company at least 169,000 barrels per day at a cost of some $61 million.[44] Oil workers, both Nigerian and expatriate, are also a favored target for MEND and other armed groups, and more than two hundred people were kidnapped in 2007, according to the U.S. State Department.[45] At the same time, the movement engages in more narrowly defined (but highly lucrative) criminal activity to a degree that makes it difficult to characterize the organization as a strictly political entity.[46]

Delineating sharp distinctions between state and non-state violence is also difficult. Politicians, drawing on funds generated by corrupt practices, have employed gangs such as the Niger People's Volunteer Force and the Niger Delta Vigilante to help rig their own elections. As Human Rights Watch notes, once in office "they either abandon the well-armed gangs to their own devices or continue using them to intimidate their opponents" and engage in lucrative crimes such as bunkering.[47] Gangs are also available for hire, and local communities use these freelance vigilantes to settle grievances against corporations, groups, or individuals.[48]

Nigeria's government has responded to unrest in the delta with a heavy, repressive hand. The federal government has militarized the delta, with army, navy, and the feared paramilitary Mobile Police, widely deployed both to protect the oil facilities and to suppress popular protests. Although the central administration has taken steps to redress grievances through measures such as the creation of the Niger Delta Development Corporation,[49] most of these initiatives have been criticized as halfhearted and are generally perceived as cynical attempts to dampen local demand for a larger allocation of oil revenues. The application of force remains Abuja's preferred approach to dealing with everything from demonstrations and strikes to the occupation of oil facilities. Indeed, because it lacks both the means and the will to mediate disputes, the state acts, in essence, as a source of violence and an instigator of conflict. As one scholar has noted, the Nigerian polity "is prepared to have recourse to repressive violence, not because it has much chance of succeeding, but because its own inherent weaknesses prevent recourse to less violent means."[50] In the Niger Delta, this repression includes summary executions, assaults, and the destruction of entire villages.

Shell Nigeria's Conflict Mitigation Strategy

The region's chronic violence and instability have driven some multinational corporations out of the Niger Delta. Perhaps the most vivid example occurred when in 2006 Willbros, one of the world's largest service suppliers to the oil and gas industry, left the delta after operating nearly forty-five years in Nigeria and announced that dangers in the region exceeded "acceptable risk levels."[51] But for Shell, this turbulent environment has proved simply too lucrative to abandon. As one analyst has ventured, although the environment is "highly complex, threatening, and generally explosive," the delta's petroleum deposits are "too rich for Shell to walk away from, or for that matter too tempting not to further explore and commercialize."[52] Moreover, as with other firms in the extractive sector, the

resources necessary for corporate survival and success are fixed geographically, meaning that relocating out of Nigeria to a more salubrious environment is simply not a reasonable option for Shell.

Until the late 1990s, the company's response to its violent operating environment focused largely on providing security for its personnel and facilities.
Although for decades Shell had funded scholarships, agricultural extension
programs, and other social development activities, these efforts were relatively modest.[53] The firm's preferred approach paralleled that of the Nigerian
state. Indeed, the corporation and the federal government became deeply
intertwined in the politics of the delta. Shell, for example, paid the salaries
of Nigerian police responsible for protecting corporate operations (the so-
called supernumerary police)[54] and permitted the armed forces to use its
landing strips and other corporate facilities.[55] The company also enjoyed a
notably close and at times even symbiotic relationship with the dictatorship
of Gen. Sani Abacha, who ruled Nigeria between 1993 and 1998. During
this period, accusations were rife that Shell was complicit in government
corruption and human rights abuses, which greatly harmed the company's
reputation inside and outside the country. This collusion became particularly evident following the imprisonment and subsequent execution in 1995
of Ken Saro-Wiwa, a prominent author, political activist, and outspoken
Shell critic from the oil-rich Ogoni region.[56]

For much of the 1990s, many critics depicted Shell as an environmental,
social, economic, and political outlaw; as a "Gulliver on the rampage, waging an ecological war wherever it sets down its oil rig";[57] and as an "enemy
of the Nigerian people."[58] For the residents of the oil-producing region, the
use of military forces to defend oil company personnel and installations
linked Shell with a corrupt and brutal Nigerian state, further exacerbating
tensions with local communities.[59] Internationally, the firm's ties with the
Abacha regime soiled the corporation's reputation at a time when it (and
other large multinationals around the world) was coming under increasing
pressure from activist NGOs to maintain higher standards of ecological and
corporate social responsibility.[60]

Primarily as a result of this negative publicity and exposure, Shell instituted a different approach to doing business in the delta during the late
1990s. The new mode of operation, best termed as a hearts and minds

strategy, aimed at addressing and managing local grievances and dissuading populations from engaging in oil-related violence. In words that echo those of the NGOs that previously criticized the company's practices in the region, Shell explicitly acknowledged the need for a comprehensive, multidimensional solution to managing oil-related violence in the delta: "We believe that the situation needs to be addressed through dialogue, alongside immediate infrastructure development and providing employment. We continue to work with the communities, the federal, state and local governments, and other agencies in an effort to help restore peace in the Niger Delta."[61]

Today, Shell Nigeria's activities include community investment, support to micro-enterprises, and the provision of health care, education, and agricultural services. In 2005 the corporation began negotiating long-term agreements, known as global memorandums of understanding (GMOUs), with host communities to provide "planned and integrated activities that will hopefully encourage sustainable development for communities." Indigenous villages and townships are encouraged to direct and manage their own long-term development by taking responsibility for identifying projects and determining who should implement them. Shell spent $71.4 million in support of these locally led efforts in 2010, the last year for which figures are available.[62]

It needs to be stressed, however, that Shell has not abandoned the harder aspects of security. A corps of the supernumerary constabulary continues to be deployed across the delta and provides protection for the company's personnel and installations.[63] Although higher management does not say so publicly, it is widely suspected that these officers are paid for directly out of corporate accounts.[64] Shell has also been in discussions with Nigerian authorities over how the company might benefit from the Joint Task Force (JTF), an army-navy-police organization that the federal government deployed to patrol the creeks, inlets, and mangrove swamps that make up the Niger Delta. Although the company has offered to provide human rights training to the JTF, the unit continues to have a well-earned reputation for brutality. In early 2005, for example, the JTF, responding to an attack on government officials near Odioma, killed seventeen residents and burned the town to the ground.[65]

Assessing Shell Nigeria's Response

Despite its good intentions from the late 1990s onward, it would appear that Shell has been largely unable to positively sway the operating environment in the Delta. Oil-related violence—within and between communities, against the government, and directed at Shell—does not appear to have diminished.[66] Indeed, given the deeply fractious nature of the operating environment, the pathologies of the Nigerian government, including far-reaching corruption, and the sheer scale of the instability, actual conflict mitigation may be beyond the power of Shell or any other corporate entity. Moreover, the presence of crude and the wealth it represents helps to destabilize oil-bearing communities and sustain a political economy of violence. Because of its potential for generating revenue and the vulnerability of its personnel and associated infrastructure, petroleum in the delta has proved to be a tempting target for predation by armed groups and a major factor driving ethno-communal conflict over competing claims to oil-bearing lands (as demonstrated by the internecine violence among the Ijaw, Urhobo, and Itsekiri in Warri).[67]

Just as significant, although Shell may have no vested interest in promoting instability as such, corporate actions may have unintentionally contributed to a cycle of conflict. As noted, oil companies frequently prepare social development GMOUs in response to demonstrations, shutdowns, or oil spills, some of which stem from sabotage. Such activism, some of which may turn violent,[68] therefore becomes validated as a means for seeking the redress of popular grievances. Equally, as Shell itself has acknowledged, its failure to meet community expectations (some of which are unrealistically high) at times has led to violent protest. The subsequent police and military repression has further incited, radicalized, and alienated delta communities.[69]

As even critics concede, firms like Shell are trapped in a difficult, if not impossible, situation. "They cannot meet the expectations of the communities in which they operate. At the same time, you have a government unwilling to do anything about the delta," according to one human rights activist.[70] With the exception of the security forces, the Nigerian government is essentially absent in the region. MNCs provide public goods, to the extent that they exist at all. Problematically, neither Shell nor any other company reasonably can be expected to replace the state, and they generally do not wish to assume that role. Like other oil multinationals, Shell is well aware that social development activities could foster a "dependency mentality" among aid recipients and, in so doing, further undermine the already limited legitimacy and capacity of the government.[71] In the view of senior corporate officials, it is ultimately the central Nigerian administration's responsibility to promote peace and development in the region: "What the military could not do, the democratic government [should] have done through the proper policy and [by] ploughing money made into development."[72]

Conclusion

Since the end of the Cold War, overseas development assistance to the global south has stagnated, whereas foreign direct investment has grown dramatically. For many governments, NGOs, and multilateral organizations, this shift opened the opportunity (and the need) to engage the private sector as a partner in international development.[73] Of more direct salience, at least for the purposes of this chapter, it also engendered the question of whether engaging MNCs for less gentle purposes—namely, counterinsurgency, stability operations, and related activities—equally makes sense. As Albrecht Schnabel has observed, the transnational nature of most contemporary insurgencies means that "the nation-state alone cannot and should not manage an insurgency."[74]

   The crippling financial costs associated with the war in Iraq and ongoing operations in Afghanistan, combined with a protracted domestic economic crisis, suggest that U.S. civilian and military planners might be wise to consider off-loading at least some aspects of counterinsurgency to the private sector. There are certainly indications that senior officials may now be thinking along these lines, at least in a general way. Although it provides few specifics, recent U.S. Army doctrine on stability operations—a broad set of noncombat missions, many of which overlap with COIN—explicitly stresses the need to engage private sector actors as a source of what the military terms "soft power."[75] On the one hand, such an approach offers a number of potential benefits to Washington, at least theoretically. To the extent that an MNC in a given conflict zone provides useful social and economic blandishments to the local population, the U.S. government and the host nation receiving its assistance would not be required to do so, thereby freeing their resources for other purposes. Moreover, given the high financial stakes and the long-term commitments that MNCs typically make to a country or region, private sector initiatives in some circumstances may be more effective and targeted than what could otherwise be provided. Finally, the intimate on-ground knowledge of local conditions, actors, and dynamics that corporate employees possess would serve as an undoubtedly invaluable source of knowledge and intelligence, acting as a highly useful "force multiplier" for government counterinsurgents and analysts.

On the other hand, corporate counterinsurgency is problematical both for the United States and the host nation(s) it supports. On the most basic level is the issue of command and control. The interests of large-scale transnational firms and the state will not always converge, and unlike government contractors or civil servants, MNCs simply cannot be ordered to do a task. Inevitably, questions of accountability would also arise, particularly regarding who should be held liable for human rights abuses and other misdeeds that corporate counterinsurgency "partners" might perpetrate. Underscoring all these factors are questions connected with national sovereignty. As mentioned earlier, current U.S. counterinsurgency doctrine and policy, rightly or wrongly, is heavily state-centric, with much emphasis placed on building the host country's legitimacy. As Mary Anderson concludes, however, "Corporations that substitute for governments undermine local confidence in their legal structures and weaken even those capacities that do exist among local civil servants."[76] Any heavy reliance on MNCs would therefore conflict with traditional American approaches to COIN.

From the perspective of the U.S. government and its clients, corporate counterinsurgency is a mixed bag of positives and negatives. From the point of view of the MNCs, though, costs clearly outweigh any benefits. Indeed, any potential rewards are difficult to discern. Both the state and the corporation want "stability," but they naturally define this goal in different ways. Whereas American COIN planners equate stability with *regime* security, large firms in the extractive sector are generally not concerned about the attendant success or failure of any given government. Indeed, given the predatory nature of state policy in a country like Nigeria, the central administration is frequently one of the primary sources of instability. True, U.S. counterinsurgency assistance could contribute to greater state capacity, which might in turn relieve MNCs of at least some of the burdens associated with providing for their own site and communal hearts and minds campaigns. However, as counterinsurgency "free riders," corporations run the risk of becoming ensnared in a U.S.-sponsored COIN campaign, which if aimed at shoring up a widely despised regime, could very well make an MNC an even larger target for local resistance and for opposition from international NGOs. Further, attempting to engage MNCs by appealing to their patriotic instincts is likely to go unheeded, for these organizations are examples of what James Rosenau termed "sovereignty-free actors"[77] with no fixed national allegiances. In theory, host countries could pressure firms to join their side by threatening to eliminate corporate concessions. In reality, however, governments that are heavily dependent on revenues that extraction generates are loathe to drive out firms, not least because these entities play an integral role in keeping the state in power. In sum, MNCs have little or no incentive to join in government counterinsurgency ventures, nor do governments appear to have the means to encourage (or compel) unwilling corporations to participate in them.

For all these reasons, relying on multinational firms as potential counterinsurgency proxies appears to make little sense. However, as this chapter has suggested, policymakers would be wise to commit more resources to understanding the role of MNCs in strategically significant regions of the world and how their actions might add or detract from wider COIN efforts. Unfortunately the state-centric bias of U.S. policy has led to a binary focus that has centered on incumbent regimes and the insurgents who oppose them. This position is to the detriment of additional actors who quite clearly populate and, in some cases, definitively shape zones of conflict, such as security contractors, customary institutions, and MNCs. In further developing American counterinsurgency doctrine, it would seem logical, if not encumbent, to address this analytical lacuna as a matter of both practical and academic concern.

Notes

Preface

1 Frank Hoffman, *Conflict in the 21st Century: The Rise of Hybrid Wars* (Washington, DC: Potomac Institute, 2007), 8.

2 See, for example, Antoine Bousquet, *The Scientific Way of Warfare: Order and Chaos on the Battlefields of Modernity* (London: Hurst, 2009).

3 Personal correspondence with Tim Stevens, associate fellow, International Centre for the Study of Radicalization and Political Violence, July and August 2009.

4 For these observations, I am indebted to the participants of a virtual symposium of the Complex Terrain Laboratory on Peter Singer's book *Wired for War: The Robotics Revolution and Conflict in the 21st Century* (New York: Penguin Press, 2009), held March 29 through April 6, 2009.

Chapter 1. Terrorists as State "Proxies": Separating Fact from Fiction

1 "Woolsey: Iran and State-Sponsored Terrorism," Voice of America editorial, April 29, 1993, http://www.globalsecurity.org/intell/library/news/1993/14191772-14194893.htm. Woolsey was then director of the Central Intelligence Agency. Since his retirement he has suggested that Iraq may have sponsored both the 1993 World Trade Center attacks and the *Bacillus anthracis* letter mailings in the United States.

2 Quoted from Michael A. Ledeen, *The War against the Terror Masters: Why It Happened, Where We Are Now, How We'll Win* (New York: St. Martin's Press, 2002), 9. On the same page, he identifies the post-Soviet "terror masters" as the "radical regimes of Iran, [Saddam Hussein's] Iraq, Saudi Arabia, Libya, Syria, and Sudan." Other conservatives have also adopted the cartoonish phrase "terror masters." See Kenneth R. Timmerman, *Countdown to Crisis: The Coming Nuclear Showdown with Iran* (New York: Three Rivers Press, 2006), 242.

3 Bruce Hoffman, *Inside Terrorism* (New York: Columbia University Press, 2006), 263.

4 Martin van Creveld, "In Wake of Terrorism, Modern Armies Prove to Be Dinosaurs of Defense," *New Perspectives Quarterly* 13, no. 4 (Fall 1996): 58.

5 Quoted from Ghada Hashem Talhami, "Muslims, Islamists, and the Cold War," in *Grand Strategy in the War against Terrorism*, ed. Thomas R. Mockaitis and Paul B. Rich (London: Frank Cass, 2003), 114. Compare Stephen Segaller, *Invisible Armies: Terrorism into the 1990s* (London: Sphere Books, 1987), 154. Although I agree with Talhami's view that non-state

terrorism would still constitute a significant security problem in the absence of state sponsorship, I do not subscribe to her argument (on the same page) that it is necessarily an "outgrowth of the perceptions and actions of disadvantaged communities," which, under pressure, "resort to violence against groups that oppose and oppress them." By "terrorism" I am referring to the use or threatened use of violence, usually directed against victims selected for their symbolic or representative value, as a means of instilling anxiety in, transmitting one or more messages to, and thereby manipulating the perceptions and behavior of wider target audiences. Since terrorism is therefore nothing more than a violent technique of psychological manipulation, there is no reason to suppose that one has to be "disadvantaged" to employ it. Note, also, in the interests of terminological precision, that the term "terror" refers to a psychological state marked by fear and anxiety and must therefore be distinguished from "terrorism." There is no such thing as a "terror network," only a "terrorist network."

6   For another recent attempt to categorize different types and levels of state support for terrorism, see Daniel Byman, *Deadly Connections: States That Sponsor Terrorism* (New York: Cambridge University Press, 2005), chapters 1–3.

7   For a recent criticism of realist-oriented IR theories on this basis, see Scott M. Thomas, *The Global Resurgence of Religion and the Transformation of International Relations: The Struggle for the Soul of the Twenty-First Century* (New York: Palgrave Macmillan, 2005), 55–56. Thomas rightly notes (see page 56) that "the impact of non-state actors, including the role of religious actors, is marginalized from the core of this approach to international relations."

8   Unfortunately, many self-styled "terrorism experts" have themselves never seriously studied extremist milieus and terrorist organizations, since they have typically failed to carry out in-depth research on these topics and have not systematically and comprehensively examined the available primary sources. See, e.g., the critical judgments leveled by Andrew Silke, "An Introduction to Terrorism Research," in *Research on Terrorism: Trends, Achievements and Failures*, ed. Andrew Silke (London: Frank Cass, 2004), 9–12; and John Horgan, "The Case for Firsthand Research," in ibid., 30. I made similarly harsh criticisms of both the lax scholarship and the political biases in the terrorism field back in the early 1990s. See Jeffrey M. Bale, "The 'Black' Terrorist International: Neo-Fascist Paramilitary Networks and the 'Strategy of Tension' in Italy, 1968–1974" (PhD diss., University of California at Berkeley, 1994), 26–33. Sadly, these long-standing shortcomings in the field have become even more pronounced in the wake of the terrorist attacks on the United States on September 11, 2001.

9   Indeed, most governments have formulated official definitions of terrorism that intentionally restrict the term to the violent actions carried out by non-state actors, thereby trying to make it impossible for others to label or characterize their governments as terrorists. In short, they have simultaneously sought to exclude their own regimes from the category of terrorism, by definitional fiat, while also frequently accusing rival states of sponsoring terrorism. On the basis of this inconsistent and indeed contradictory conceptual logic, states can apparently never be terrorists themselves, but only sponsors of terrorism carried out by non-state entities. For the state-centric biases inherent in what he labels "orthodox terrorism theory," see Jason Franks, *Rethinking the Roots of Terrorism* (New York: Palgrave Macmillan, 2006), especially 46.

10   For the Cold War era, see especially Edward Herman and Gerry O'Sullivan, *The "Terrorism" Industry: The Experts and Institutions That Shape Our View of Terror* (New York: Pantheon Books, 1989); Alexander George, "The Discipline of Terrorology," in *Western State Terrorism*, ed. Alexander George (New York: Routledge, 1991), 76–101; and Philip Paull, "International Terrorism: The Propaganda War" (master's thesis, San Francisco State

University, 1982), 59–94. For the post-9/11 era, see John Mueller, *Overblown: How Politicians and the Terrorism Industry Inflate National Security Threats, and Why We Believe Them* (New York: Free Press, 2006), 6–7, 33–47; George Kassimeris, "The Terrorism Industry: The Profits of Doom," in *Playing Politics with Terrorism: A User's Guide*, ed. George Kassimeris (New York: Columbia University Press, 2008), 301–20; Sam Raphael, "In the Service of Power: Terrorism Studies and U.S. Intervention in the Global South," in *Critical Terrorism Studies: A New Research Agenda*, ed. Richard Jackson, Marie Breen Smyth, and Jeroen Gunning (New York: Routledge, 2009), 49–65; David Miller and Tom Mills, *The Politics of Terrorism Expertise: Knowledge, Power and the Media* (New York: Routledge, 2011); and Maximilian Forte, "Minerva and the Terrorism Industry: 'The Rule of Experts as a Means to Covert Imperial Rule,'" *Zero Anthropology*, October 24, 2008, posted by academicians critical of prospective collaboration between scholars and military funders, http://openanthropology.wordpress.com/2008/10/24/minerva-and-the-terrorism-industry-the-rule-of-experts-as-a-means-to-covert-imperial-rule/. Note, however, that Mueller defines the term "terrorism industry" more broadly than Herman and O'Sullivan originally did and ascribes material rather than ideological motives to it. Likewise, Ian S. Lustick has emphasized that many different types of interest groups have sought to exploit the war on terrorism for their own political or financial purposes. See his *Trapped in the War on Terror* (Philadelphia: University of Pennsylvania Press, 2006), chapter 5.

11 See, e.g., Noam Chomsky, *Pirates and Emperors: International Terrorism in the Real World* (Cambridge, MA: South End Press, 2002); Noam Chomsky, *9-11* (New York: Open Media/Seven Stories Press, 2001); Noam Chomsky and Edward S. Herman, *The Washington Connection and Third World Fascism*, vol. 1, *The Political Economy of Human Rights* (Boston: South End Press, 1999), especially chapters 3–4; Edward S. Herman, *The Real Terror Network: Terrorism in Fact and Propaganda* (Boston: South End Press, 1982); George, *Western State Terrorism*; and Frederick H. Gareau, *State Terrorism and the United States: From Counterinsurgency to the War on Terrorism* (Atlanta: Clarity Press, 2004), chapters 1–7. Similar sorts of antiestablishment, left-wing perspectives have recently made a resurgence in the form of "critical terrorism studies," as reflected in Jackson, Smyth, and Gunning, *Critical Terrorism Studies*; and the journal *Critical Studies on Terrorism*, which Jackson edits. The blatant antistate and anti-Western biases of this new current are well illustrated in Scott Poynting and David Whyte, eds., *Counter-Terrorism and State Political Violence: The "War on Terror" as Terror* (New York: Routledge, 2012).

12 Chomsky and Herman, *Washington Connection and Third World Fascism*, 6–7, 85–95. Elsewhere, Herman contrasts what he calls "lesser" (insurgent non-state) and "mythical" (Soviet-backed) terrorist networks with retail right-wing terrorism and especially with U.S. sponsorship of national security states that rely on wholesale terrorism. See Herman, *Real Terror Network*, 47–82, 110–37.

13 Other left-leaning critics of the official line on terrorism have instead adopted different arguments: that the threat of terrorism is minor or inconsequential, that there is no non-state or state-sponsored Islamic terrorist threat, and that the official Western discourses about terrorism since 9/11 are essentially false. See, e.g., Mueller, *Overblown*; Emran Qureshi and Michael A. Sells, eds., *The New Crusades: Constructing the Muslim Enemy* (New York: Columbia University Press, 2003); Richard Jackson, *Writing the War on Terrorism: Language, Politics and Counter-Terrorism* (Manchester, UK: Manchester University Press, 2005), especially chapter 4; and Adam Hodges and Chad Nilep, eds., *Discourse, War and Terrorism* (Philadelphia: John Benjamins, 2007). However, it is one thing to say that governments or other political interests have oftentimes exaggerated and instrumentally

exploited the terrorist threat, which is perfectly true, and another thing altogether to insist that there is no significant terrorist threat, a claim that is manifestly absurd during an era in which terrorists kill dozens or more people in various parts of the world every single month. For a generally less partisan treatment of the political exploitation of terrorism in different countries, see Kassimeris, *Playing Politics with Terrorism*.

14   Bale, "'Black' Terrorist International," 28–31.

15   Roberta Goren, *The Soviet Union and Terrorism* (London: Allen & Unwin, 1984), 6.

16   Ray S. Cline and Yonah Alexander, *Terrorism as State-Sponsored Covert Warfare* (Fairfax, VA: Hero Books, 1986), 32. Cf. the state-centric definition of "international terrorism" by Israeli hard-liner Benjamin Netanyahu: "the use of terrorist violence against a given nation *by another state*, which uses the terrorists to fight a proxy war as an alternative to conventional war." See his *Fighting Terrorism: How Democracies Can Defeat the International Terrorist Network* (New York: Farrar, Straus and Giroux, 2001), 52 (italics in original). Note that Cline was a high-ranking CIA officer and former station chief in Taiwan, where some have suggested that he personally played a covert role in the creation of the World Anti-Communist League, an international private network that eventually encompassed many right-wing terrorist groups. See Scott Anderson and Jon Lee Anderson, *Inside the League: The Shocking Exposé of How Terrorists, Nazis and Latin American Death Squads Have Infiltrated the World Anti-Communist League* (New York: Dodd Mead, 1986), 55–56.

17   For a recent overview, see Odd Arne Westad, *The Global Cold War: Third World Interventions and the Making of Our Times* (New York: Cambridge University Press, 2007). Former East German spy chief Markus Wolf himself emphasized that "many of these unholy alliances" between the two superpowers and repressive regimes and violent non-state groups in the third world were "the tragic product of the Cold War." See his memoir *Man Without a Face: The Autobiography of Communism's Greatest Spymaster*, with Anne McElvoy (New York: Times Books, 1997), 249.

18   An even more simplistic and ludicrous notion peddled in some extreme right circles was that all the world's terrorist groups were ideologically left wing. See, e.g., Robert D. Chapman and M. Lester Chapman, *The Crimson Web of Terror* (Boulder, CO: Paladin Press, 1980), 99, who argued that terrorists everywhere are "very much alike," including being "Marxist-Leninist." No doubt that last assertion will come as a great surprise to victims of right-wing paramilitary squads and violent jihadists in various parts of the world.

19   This sort of literature is voluminous. See, e.g., Stefan T. Possony and L. Francis Bouchey, *International Terrorism: The Communist Connection* (Washington, DC: American Council for World Freedom, 1978), 21–40; Robert Moss, "Terrorism: A Soviet Export," *New York Times Magazine*, November 2, 1980, 42–58; Samuel T. Francis, *The Soviet Strategy of Terror* (Washington, DC: Heritage Foundation, 1981), especially 5–25; Claire Sterling, *The Terror Network: The Secret War of International Terrorism* (New York: Berkeley Books, 1982); Edouard Sablier, *Le fil rouge: Histoire secrète du terrorisme international* (Paris: Plon, 1983); Goren, *The Soviet Union and Terrorism*; Ray S. Cline and Yonah Alexander, *Terrorism: The Soviet Connection* (New York: Crane Russak, 1984); Jillian Becker, *The Soviet Connection: State Sponsorship of Terrorism* (London: Institute for European Defense and Strategic Studies, 1985); and Michael Ledeen, "Soviet Sponsorship: The Will to Disbelieve," in *Terrorism: How the West Can Win*, ed. Benjamin Netanyahu (New York: Farrar, Straus and Giroux, 1986), 88–92.

20   Cited by Sterling, *Terror Network*, 286. This claim was made at a 1979 conference held in Jerusalem under the auspices of the Jonathan Institute, which others have identified as an

important institutional component in the terrorism industry. See Paull, "International Terrorism," 8–31; and Herman and O'Sullivan, *"Terrorism" Industry*, 104–6.

21 Cline and Alexander, *Terrorism: The Soviet Connection*, 55–60.

22 Sterling, *Terror Network*, 16. The absurdity of this all-encompassing blanket statement should be self-evident. To be fair, to preserve their own credibility, these authors sometimes expressed caveats about whether the Soviets were centrally directing international terrorism. See ibid., 291–92; Possony and Bouchey, *International Terrorism*, 1; and Francis, *Soviet Strategy of Terror*, 40. Yet they nonetheless made every effort to create that very impression.

23 For the non-European state sponsors of terrorism linked to the Soviets, see, e.g., Roger Fontaine, *Terrorism: The Cuban Connection* (New York: Crane Russak, 1988); Joseph S. Bermudez, *Terrorism: The North Korean Connection* (New York: Crane Russak, 1990); and Uri Ra'anan et al., eds., *Hydra of Carnage: The International Linkages of Terrorism and Other Low-Intensity Operations: The Witnesses Speak* (Lexington, MA: Lexington Books, 1986).

24 For the so-called KGB-Bulgarian connection to the 1980 papal assassination plot, see Ray S. Cline, "Soviet Footprints in Saint Peter's Square," *Terrorism* 7, no. 1 (1984): 53–55; Claire Sterling, *The Time of the Assassins: Anatomy of an Investigation* (New York: Holt, Rinehart & Winston, 1985); and Paul Henze, *The Plot to Kill the Pope* (New York: Scribner's, 1985). Henze was formerly a CIA station chief in Turkey. For substantive critiques of this thesis, see William Hood, "Unlikely Conspiracy," *Problems of Communism* 33 (March–April 1984): 67–70; Edward S. Herman and Frank Brodhead, *The Rise and Fall of the Bulgarian Connection* (New York: Sheridan Square, 1986); and Jeffrey M. Bale, "The Ultranationalist Right in Turkey and the Attempted Assassination of Pope John Paul II," *Turkish Studies Association Bulletin* 15, no. 1 (March 1991): 1–63.

25 Among the most unreliable of those oft-cited defectors, at least with respect to terrorism, are former Czech intelligence officer Jan Šejna and former Romanian intelligence officer Ion Mihai Pacepa. See, e.g., Jan Šejna, *We Will Bury You* (London: Sidgwick & Jackson, 1985); and Ion Mihai Pacepa, *Programmed to Kill: Lee Harvey Oswald, the Soviet KGB, and the Kennedy Assassination* (Chicago: Ivan R. Dee, 2007).

26 See, e.g., Harry Rositzke, "If There Were No KGB, Would the Scale and Intensity of Terrorism Be Diminished?" *New York Times*, July 20, 1981, A17 (a question to which he responded in the negative); Brian Jenkins, "World Terrorism—the Truth and Nothing but the Truth," *Manchester Guardian Weekly*, May 24, 1981; Richard E. Rubenstein, *Alchemists of Revolution: Terrorism in the Modern World* (New York: Basic Books, 1987), 51–59; Segaller, *Invisible Armies*, 124–48; and Grant Wardlaw, *Political Terrorism: Theory, Tactics, and Counter-Measures*, 2nd ed. (New York: Cambridge University Press, 1989), 55–57, 175–86.

27 See, e.g., Christopher Andrew and Vasili Mitrokhin, *The World Was Going Our Way: The KGB and the Battle for the Third World* (New York: Basic Books, 2006).

28 For examples of this type of Soviet and communist propaganda, see Boris Svetov et al., *International Terrorism and the CIA: Documents, Eyewitness Reports, Facts* (Moscow: Progress Publishers, 1983); and Vitaly Chernyavsky, *The CIA in the Dock: Soviet Journalists on International Terrorism* (Moscow: Progress Publishers, 1983).

29 See Soviet propagandist Valentin K. Mashkin, *Operación Cóndor: Su rastro sangriento* (Buenos Aires: Cartago, 1985), 15–22 passim. Cf. Stella Calloni, *Los años del lobo: Operación Cóndor* (Buenos Aires: Continente, 1999), 17. It is also one of several theories mentioned by Gerardo Irusta Medrano, *Espionaje y servicios secretos en Bolivia, 1930–1980: "Operación*

Cóndor" en acción (La Paz: self-published, 1995), 279–88. It is now clear, however, that the Chilean secret service first proposed this scheme in early 1974. Although U.S. intelligence agencies apparently facilitated the development of some of its precursors, provided those services with advanced communications equipment, soon became aware of Condor itself, and sometimes appear to have supported its activities tacitly, there is no clear evidence as yet that they actually instigated them. For more, cf. J. Patrice McSherry, *Predatory States: Operation Condor and Covert War in Latin America* (Lanham, MD: Rowman & Littlefield, 2005), 53–58, 78–83, who arguably attributes too much influence to the CIA and the U.S. Defense Department; and Mark J. Osiel, "Constructing Subversion in Argentina's Dirty War," *Representations* 75, no. 1 (August 2001): 119–58, who rightly gives due weight to the indigenous sources of Southern Cone countersubversion and state terrorism, such as the Catholic integralist ideologies associated with groups such as Tacuara and the military's so-called Doctrine of National Security. For more, see Daniel Gutman, *Tacuara: Historia de la primera guerrilla urbana argentina* (Buenos Aires: Ediciones B, 2003); and José Comblin, "The National Security Doctrine," in *The Repressive State: The Brazilian "National Security Doctrine" and Latin America*, ed. Jean-Louis Weil, Joseph Comblin, and Judge Senese (Toronto: Brazilian Studies, 1978).

30   See, e.g., Viktor V. Vitiuk, *Leftist Terrorism*, trans. Andrei Zur and Galina Glagoleva (Moscow: Progress Publishers, 1985), 196–211. Note that Vitiuk was one of the more sophisticated and intelligent of the Soviet propagandists who wrote on the subject of terrorism.

31   See Iona Andronov, *On the Wolf's Track* (Sofia, Bulgaria: Sofia Press, 1983); Iona Andronov, *The Triple Plot* (Sofia: Sofia Press, 1984); Eduard Kovalev and Igor Sedykh, *"Bulgarian Connection": CIA & Co. on the Outcome of the Antonov Trial* (Moscow: Novosti, 1986); and Ivan Palchev, *The Assassination Attempt against the Pope and the Roots of Terrorism* (Sofia: Sofia Press, 1985).

32   See, in general, Michael McClintock, *Instruments of Statecraft: U.S. Guerrilla Warfare, Counterinsurgency, and Counter-Terrorism, 1940–1990* (New York: Pantheon Books, 1992); and Cecilia Menjívar and Néstor Rodríguez, eds., *When States Kill: Latin America, the U.S., and Technologies of Terror* (Austin: University of Texas Press, 2005).

33   The literature on these topics is large and often polemical. For the baleful role of U.S. security agencies in Salvadoran and Guatemalan state terrorism, see Michael McClintock, *The American Connection*, vol. 1, *State Terror and Popular Resistance in El Salvador* (London: Zed Books, 1985); and Michael McClintock, *The American Connection*, vol. 2, *State Terror and Popular Resistance in Guatemala* (London: Zed Books, 1985). More generally, see Lesley Gill, *The School of the Americas: Military Training and Political Violence in the Americas* (Durham, NC: Duke University Press, 2004). For the antidemocratic activities of various "stay-behind" networks in postwar Europe, see the analysis of the European literature by Daniele Ganser, *NATO's Secret Armies: Operation Gladio and Terrorism in Western Europe* (London: Frank Cass, 2005). For U.S. support for diverse anticommunist insurgents who relied heavily on terrorism, cf. Christopher Simpson, *Blowback: America's Recruitment of Nazis and Its Effects on the Cold War* (New York: Weidenfeld & Nicolson, 1988); Jeffrey Burds, *The Early Cold War in Soviet West Ukraine, 1944–1948* (Pittsburgh: Center for Russian and European Studies, University of Pittsburgh, 2001); Maj. D. H. Berger, "The Use of Covert Paramilitary Activity as a Policy Tool: An Analysis of the Operations Conducted by the U.S. Central Intelligence Agency, 1949–1951" (unpublished thesis, Marine Corps Staff and Command College, Decatur, Georgia, 1995); Anderson and Anderson, *Inside the League*; Don Bohning, *The Castro Obsession: U.S. Covert Operations in Cuba, 1959–1965* (Washington, DC: Potomac Books, 2006); Warren Hinckle and William W. Turner, *The Fish Is Red: The Story of the Secret*

War against Castro (New York: Harper & Row, 1981); Sam Dillon, *Commandos: The CIA and Nicaragua's Contra Rebels* (New York: Henry Holt, 1991); Glenn Garvin, *Everybody Had His Own Gringo: The CIA and the Contras* (Washington, DC: Brassey's, Inc., 1992); Jonathan Marshall, Peter Dale Scott, and Jane Hunter, *The Iran-Contra Connection: Secret Teams and Covert Operations in the Reagan Era* (Boston: South End Press, 1987).

34 To cite only two examples, one may note the eye-opening information about covert state-sponsored terrorism found in the archives of the Portuguese secret police and the Paraguayan security forces following the collapse, respectively, of the dictatorial Caetano and Stroessner regimes. See Frédéric Laurent, *L'orchestre noir* (Paris: Stock, 1978), 117–65; and Fabrizio Calvi and Frédéric Laurent, *Piazza Fontana: La verità su una strage* (Milan: Mondadori, 1997), 60–81, for the former; and Alfredo Boccia Paz, Myrian Angélica González, and Rosa Palau Aguilar, *Es mi informe: Los archivios secretos de la Policía de Stroessner* (Asunción: Centro de Documentación y Estudios, 1994); and Gladys Meilinger de Sannemann, *Paraguay y la "Operación Cóndor en los "Archivios del Terror"* (Asunción: no publisher, 1994), for the latter. Similarly, information from the East German and Iraqi archives, as will become clear below, has also shed much more light on covert secret service activities related to terrorism.

35 Indeed, some proponents of this notion, such as Ledeen, had earlier been promoters of the "Soviet terrorist network" thesis. Two other neoconservatives who exerted a significant influence on the Bush administration's post-9/11 counterterrorism policies, Douglas Feith and David Wurmser, had both previously contributed to Ra'anan et al., *Hydra of Carnage*.

36 Ledeen, *War Against the Terror Masters*, 45.

37 Wurmser's remarks are cited in Barton Gellman, *Angler: The Cheney Vice Presidency* (New York: Penguin Press, 2008), 224–25.

38 See Ledeen, *War Against the Terror Masters*, especially 9–28, 45–52; and David Frum and Richard Perle, *An End to Evil: How to Win the War on Terror* (New York: Random House, 2003), especially chapter 3. They remained convinced, e.g., that "a bunch of ragtag terrorists in Afghanistan" could not have carried out the 9/11 attacks without a state sponsor. See Michael Isikoff and David Corn, *Hubris: The Inside Story of Spin, Scandal, and the Selling of the Iraq War* (New York: Three Rivers Press, 2007), 108.

39 See, e.g., Ronen Bergman, *The Secret War with Iran: The 30-Year Clandestine Struggle against the World's Most Dangerous Terrorist Power*, trans. Ronnie Hope (New York: Free Press, 2008), especially part 3; Doron Zimmermann, *Tangled Skein or Gordion Knot? Iran and Syria as State Supporters of Political Violence Movements in Lebanon and in the Palestinian Territories* (Zurich: ETH Zürich, 2004), 7, 15–22, 71–111; Matthew Levitt, *Targeting Terror: U.S. Policy toward Middle Eastern State Sponsors and Terrorist Organizations, Post-September 11* (Washington, DC: Washington Institute for Near East Policy, 2002), chapters 6–7; Con Coughlin, *Saddam: King of Terror* (New York: Ecco, 2002), chapter 6; and Stephen F. Hayes, *The Connection: How al Qaeda's Collaboration with Saddam Hussein Has Endangered America* (New York: HarperCollins, 2004).

40 Laurent Murawiec, *Princes of Darkness: The Saudi Assault on the West* (Lanham, MD: Rowman & Littlefield, 2005); Steven Schwartz, *The Two Faces of Islam: Saudi Fundamentalism and Its Role in Terrorism* (New York: Knopf, 2003); and Arnaud de Borchgrave, "Pakistan's Terror Inc.," *Washington Times*, January 14, 2008.

41 See, e.g., Robert Dreyfuss, *Devil's Game: How the United States Helped Unleash Fundamentalist Islam* (New York: Henry Holt, 2005); John Cooley, *Unholy Wars: Afghanistan, America, and International Terrorism* (London: Pluto Press, 2002); and Peter Dale Scott, *The Road to 9/11:*

Wealth, Empire, and the Future of America (Berkeley: University of California Press, 2008), chapters 7–10.

42   See, e.g., Richard Labévière, *Dollars for Terror: The United States and Islam*, trans. Martin DeMers (New York: Algora Publishing, 2000); Alexandre del Valle, *Islamisme et États-Unis: Une alliance contre l'Europe* (Lausanne: L'Age d'Homme, 1999); Jürgen Elsässer, *Wie der Dschihad nach Europa kam: Gotteskrieger und Geheimdienste auf dem Balkan* (Berlin: Homilius, 2008); and Maloy Krishna Dhar, *Fulcrum of Evil: ISI—CIA—Al Qaeda Nexus* (New Delhi: Manas, 2006).

43   This is certainly the implication in German conspiracy theorist Elsässer's remarks. See Silvia Cattori, "Jürgen Elsässer: 'The CIA Recruited and Trained the Jihadists,'" Réseau Voltaire website, August 14, 2006, http://www.voltairenet.org/article143050.html.

44   To put it another way, a state would have to find suitable non-state puppets if it hoped to function as their puppet master.

45   For illustrative examples from diverse extremist milieus, cf. Jeffrey M. Bale, "'National Revolutionary' Groupuscules and the Resurgence of 'Left-Wing' Fascism: The Case of France's Nouvelle Résistance," *Patterns of Prejudice* 36, no. 3 (July 2002): 24–49; Goldie Shabad and Francisco José Lleras Ramo, "Political Violence in a Democratic State: Basque Terrorism in Spain," in *Terrorism in Context*, ed. Martha Crenshaw (University Park: Pennsylvania State University, 1995), 402–69; and Fawaz A. Gerges, *The Far Enemy: Why Jihad Went Global* (New York: Cambridge University Press, 2005).

46   Note, e.g., that many leading scholars have characterized even the structure of the totalitarian Nazi regime as polycentric. See Martin Broszat, *The Hitler State: The Foundation and Development of the Internal Structure of the Third Reich* (London: Longman, 1981), conclusion.

47   For examples of just how convoluted this situation can be, see Bale, "'Black' Terrorist International," chapters 2–3.

48   Cf. Byman, *Deadly Connections*, 14.

49   Indeed, Alex P. Schmid and Albert J. Jongman refer to such notions as "conspiracy theories of terrorism" in their classic work *Political Terrorism: A New Guide to Actors, Authors, Concepts, Data Bases, Theories, and Literature*, rev. ed. (New Brunswick, NJ: Transaction Books, 2004), 101–8. However, the authors make no effort therein to distinguish between conspiracy theories proper and real-world covert and clandestine politics. For that discussion, see Jeffrey M. Bale, "Political Paranoia v. Political Realism: On Distinguishing between Bogus Conspiracy Theories and Genuine Conspiratorial Politics," *Patterns of Prejudice* 41, no. 1 (2007): 45–60.

50   Bale, "Political Paranoia v. Political Realism," *Patterns of Prejudice*, 58.

51   For the view that extremism is a distinct phenomenon with recognizable characteristics, cf. John George and Laird Wilcox, *American Extremists: Militias, Supremacists, Klansmen, Communists, and Others* (Amherst, NY: Prometheus Books, 1996), 54–62; Gian Mario Bravo, *L'estremismo in Italia* (Rome: Riuniti, 1982), 7–18; Neil J. Smelser, *The Faces of Terrorism: Social and Psychological Dimensions* (Princeton, NJ: Princeton University Press, 2007), especially 58–80; and Eric Hoffer, *The True Believer: Thoughts on the Nature of Mass Movements* (New York: Perennial, 2002), though "true believers" are even more common within sectarian vanguard parties than the mass movements they aspire to lead. Cf. also Maxwell Taylor, *The Fanatics: A Behavioural Approach to Political Violence* (London: Brassey's,

1991), especially chapter 2, wherein "ten features of fanaticism" are listed that are analogous to several of the characteristics associated with extremism.

52 See, e.g., Daniel Byman et al., *Trends in Outside Support for Insurgent Movements* (Santa Monica, CA: RAND, 2001), 23–40. In their opinion, "states are primarily motivated [to support insurgencies] by geopolitics rather than ideology, ethnic affinity, or religious sentiment."

53 Karl-Wilhelm Fricke, *MfS intern: Macht, Strukturen, Auflösung der DDR-Staatssicherheit. Analyse und Dokumentation* (Cologne: Wissenschaft und Politik, 1991), 57; and Tobias Wunschik, *Baader-Meinhofs Kinder: Die zweite Generation der RAF* (Opladen, Germany: Westdeutscher, 1997), 389–93.

54 Wunschik, *Baader-Meinhofs Kinder*, 393–95; Butz Peters, *Tödlicher Irrtum: Die Geschichte der RAF* (Berlin: Argon, 2004), 539–53, 556–76; and Michael Müller and Andreas Kanonenberg, *Die RAF-STASI Connection* (Berlin: Rowohlt, 1992), 67–103, 140–71, 208–18. For the general activities and organization of Hauptabteilung XXII, see Tobias Wunschik, *Die Hauptabteilung XXII: "Terrorabwehr"* (Berlin: Bundesbeauftragte für die Unterlagen des Staatssicherheitsdienstes der ehemaligen Deutschen Demokratischen Republik [BstU], 1996); and Roland Wiedmann, *Die Organisationsstruktur des Ministeriums für Staatssicherheit 1989* (Berlin: BstU, 1995), 264–77.

55 Peters, *Tödlicher Irrtum*, 578–80; Müller and Kanonenberg, *RAF-STASI Connection*, 171–89; Wunschik, *Baader-Meinhofs Kinder*, 396–97; and John Koehler, *STASI: The Untold Story of the East German Secret Police* (Boulder, CO: Westview Press, 1999), 387–401. Some have argued that MfS chief Erich Mielke may have fantasized that, in the event of an armed conflict between West and East Germany, some RAF terrorists could have been mobilized to serve as auxiliaries for the Nationale Volksarmee's professional "partisan units" from the Arbeitsgruppe des Ministers/Sonderfragen (AGM/S, Minister's Working Group/Special Questions).

56 Koehler, *STASI*, 359–86. However, apparently neither the Soviets nor the East Germans trusted Carlos, who they claim to have regarded as an unreliable and decadent adventurer, narcissist, and troublemaker. The MfS kept him under constant surveillance, fearing that he might engage in actions harmful to East Germany.

57 Cf. Peter Siebenmorgen, *"Staatssicherheit" der DDR: Der Westen im Fadenkreutz der Stasi* (Bonn: Bouvier, 1993), 225–35; Wunschik, *Baader-Meinhofs Kinder*, 390–93, 398–401; Wunschik, *Hauptabteilung XXII*, 44–45; Peters, *Tödlicher Irrtum*, 576–77; John C. Schmeidel, *Stasi: Shield and Sword of the Party* (New York: Routledge, 2008), 154, 156. Some have even suggested that the MfS secretly alerted the West German authorities about the location of the RAF's arms depot outside Frankfurt, where information was discovered that soon led to the arrest of virtually the entire "second generation." See Schmeidel, *Stasi*, 159.

58 In Wunschik's opinion, e.g., the "unholy cooperation" between the MfS and the RAF had little actual impact or significance. See *Baader-Meinhofs Kinder*, 402. One caveat should nonetheless be made. The federal German commission responsible for handling the MfS archives has sealed vast quantities of former MfS records presumably because much embarrassing information could be found therein, not only about the Stasi, but also about the covert activities of the Bundesnachrichtendienst (BND, Federal Intelligence Service) and other Western secret services. Hence it likewise remains possible that much more evidence exists of MfS involvement in terrorism than is now in the public domain.

59 Jillian Becker, preface to Goren, *Soviet Union and Terrorism*, ix. Cline and Alexander refer to the PLO, with more justification, as the "transmission belt" for disseminating Soviet funds,

weapons, and training to other terrorist groups. See *Terrorism: The Soviet Connection*, 31–54. Cf. Yonah Alexander and Joshua Sinai, *Terrorism: The PLO Connection* (New York: Crane Russak, 1989), 186–91.

60   Goren, *Soviet Union and Terrorism*, ix.

61   Galia Golan, *The Soviet Union and the Palestine Liberation Organization: An Uneasy Alliance* (New York: Praeger, 1980), 250.

62   For the structural complexity, factional infighting, bitter personal rivalries, and underlying processes of organizational fission and fusion that have always characterized the PLO, see the detailed accounts in John W. Amos II, *Palestinian Resistance: Organization of a Nationalist Movement* (New York: Pergamon Press, 1980), chapters 3–6; Yezid Sayigh, *Armed Struggle and the Search for State: The Palestinian National Movement, 1949–1993* (New York: Oxford University Press, 2000), passim; and Helena Cobban, *The Palestine Liberation Organization: People, Power and Politics* (Cambridge, UK: Cambridge University Press, 1984), parts 1–2.

63   Cobban, *The Palestine Liberation Organization*, chapters 9–10; and James Adams, *The Financing of Terror: How the Groups That Are Terrorizing the World Get the Money to Do It* (New York: Simon & Schuster, 1986), 39–43. Hence, one can only wonder which, if any, of these multiple paymasters constituted the PLO's real "terror master."

64   Adams, *Financing of Terror*, chapters 4–5; and Loretta Napoleoni, *Terror Incorporated: Tracing the Dollars behind the Terror Networks* (New York: Seven Stories Press, 2005), chapter 3.

65   For their "uneasy alliance," see Adams, *Financing of Terror*, 43–49; Golan, *Soviet Union and the Palestine Liberation Organization*, passim; Roland Dannreuther, *The Soviet Union and the PLO* (New York: Palgrave Macmillan, 1998); and Cobban, *Palestine Liberation Organization*, 221–28. The Mitrokhin documents confirm that neither the Soviet leadership nor the KGB trusted Arafat, in part because he was a manipulator who distorted information and stubbornly maintained good relations with both "reactionary Arab regimes" and the communist dictator of Romania, Nicolae Ceaușescu, whom the Soviets also did not trust. See Andrew and Mitrokhin, *World Was Going Our Way*, 251.

66   Golan, *Soviet Union and the Palestine Liberation Organization*, 211.

67   See, e.g., Bard O'Neill, *Armed Struggle in Palestine: A Political-Military Analysis* (Boulder, CO: Westview Press/National Defense University, 1978), 197–98.

68   Andrew and Mitrokhin, *World Was Going Our Way*, 246–50, 252–55. The KGB had one other agent in the PFLP, Ahmad Mahmud Samman. Both Haddad and Samman died in 1978, after which the KGB was unable to recruit suitable replacements.

69   Although much of the literature on Iran's sponsorship of terrorism is also partisan and tendentious, more than enough reliable evidence exists to justify labeling Iran as a state supporter of terrorist groups.

70   The most detailed journalistic efforts to argue for an Iraqi regime–al-Qa'ida link are those of Hayes, *The Connection*; and Ray Robison, *Both in One Trench: Saddam's Secret Terror Documents* (Charleston, SC: BookSurge, 2007). Unfortunately, their analyses of the available intelligence information is overly alarmist and partisan, and many of the specific claims they refer to as evidence were derived from unreliable sources or subsequently disconfirmed. Interestingly, however, captured Iraqi documents reveal not only that Saddam Hussein's intelligence services provided funds, suicide belts, and other materials to Palestinian rejectionist groups but also that around the time of the Gulf War they established links to Islamist parties in Pakistan (the Jami'yyat 'Ulama-i Islami [Assembly of Islamic Scholars]) as well as to actual jihadist groups in Jordan (the Palestinian Jama'at al-Tajdid wa al-Jihad [Renewal and Jihad

Organization]), Egypt (the Tanzim al-Jihad al-Islami [Islamic Jihad Organization] and the Jama'a al-Islamiyya [Islamic Group]), and Afghanistan (Gulbuddin Hekmatyar's Hizb-i Islami [Islamic Party]). See Institute for Defense Analysis (IDA), Joint Advanced Warfighting Program, *Saddam and Terrorism: Emerging Insights from Captured Iraqi Documents, Volume 1 (Redacted)*, Iraqi Perspectives Project (Alexandria, VA: Institute for Defense Analysis, 2007), 13–21. In the last two cases, the goal was apparently to find local allies who could make trouble for Iran or for Muslim countries that joined the Gulf War Coalition.

71 The most convenient summary of the evidence concerning purported al-Qa'ida links to Saddam Hussein's regime can be found in Select Committee on Intelligence (SSCI), S. Rep. 109-331, at 60–112 (2006). For the reported meetings between Iraqi regime and al-Qa'ida representatives, see 70–73.

72 Ibid., 73–74.

73 Ibid., 85–86, 89.

74 Ibid., 86–88.

75 Ibid., 88–94. Here the key figure was Iraqi intelligence operative and Ansar subleader Abu Wa'il, who functioned either as an inside informant, a liaison between the regime and the Ansar group, an Islamist double agent, or a secret operative and possible provocateur for the Iraqi regime.

76 Cf. Laurie Mylroie, *The War against America: Saddam Hussein and the World Trade Center Attacks: A Study of Revenge* (New York: Harper, 2001), which argues that Saddam Hussein sponsored the 1993 jihadist bombing of the World Trade Center; and Jayna Davis, *The Third Terrorist: The Middle East Connection to the Oklahoma City Bombing* (Nashville, TN: Nelson Current, 2004), which suggests that the Iraqi regime was in part responsible for the 1995 Oklahoma City bombing.

77 CIA, "Iraq and al-Qa'ida: Interpreting a Murky Relationship," June 21, 2002, 1. Note that the authors of this report were told to "lean far forward and do a speculative piece . . . [and] stretch to the maximum the evidence that [they] had." Interview with CIA deputy director of intelligence, cited in SSCI, S. Rep. 109-331, at 61.

78 See George Tenet, *At the Center of the Storm: The CIA during America's Time of Crisis* (New York: Harper Perennial, 2008), 341. On the same page he likewise suggested that at most the two parties were "trying to determine how best to take advantage of the other."

79 Cf. SSCI, S. Rep. 109-331, at 62–68, 92; IDA, *Saddam and Terrorism*, 41–43, 45–46; U.S. Government, National Commission on Terrorist Attacks upon the United States, *Final Report* (Washington, DC: Government Printing Office, 2002), 61, 66, 128, 468n55, 470nn74–76, 502n49, 522–23nn69–70; Richard A. Clarke, *Against All Enemies: Inside America's War on Terror* (New York: Free Press, 2004), 32; and Council on Foreign Relations, "Backgrounder: Iraqi Ties to Terrorism," April 29, 2003, http://www.cfr.org /publication/7702/.

80 See Byman, *Deadly Connections*, 155.

81 This involvement is apparent even if one excludes the generally partisan and often propagandistic Indian literature on the ISI and its alleged direction of Islamist terrorism, e.g., Srikanta Ghosh, *Pakistan's ISI: Network of Terror in India* (New Delhi: A. P. H., 2000); Bhure Lal, *Terrorism Inc.: The Lethal Cocktail of ISI, Taliban and Al-Qaida* (New Delhi: Siddharth, 2002); and Rajeev Sharma, *Pak Proxy War: A Story of ISI, bin Laden, and Kargil* (New Delhi: Kaveri, 1999). See the next note for more sober sources.

82   For the ISI's sponsorship of jihadist terrorist groups in South Asia, see Steve Coll, *Ghost Wars: The Secret History of the CIA, Afghanistan, and Bin Laden, from the Soviet Invasion to September 10, 2001* (New York: Penguin Books, 2004), 67–68, 113, 119–20, 128–29, 131, 157, 165–66, and passim; Bruce Reidel, "Pakistan and Terror: The Eye of the Storm," *Annals of the American Academy of Political and Social Science* 618 (July 2008): 31–45; and Byman, *Deadly Connections*, chapters 6–7. Of course, in response to U.S. pressure and provision of aid in the wake of 9/11, the Pakistani government has adopted a more circumspect but no less deceptive policy toward jihadist terrorists, one that combines helping the Americans capture or kill certain high-profile al-Qaʻida figures and doing little or nothing to interfere with the activities of the Taliban or Kashmiri jihadists. See, e.g., Shaun Gregory, "The ISI and the War on Terrorism," *Studies in Conflict and Terrorism* 30 (2002): 1013–31; Ashley J. Tellis, "Pakistan's Record on Terrorism: Conflicted Goals, Compromised Performance," *Washington Quarterly* 11, no. 2 (Spring 2008): 7–32; and Carlotta Gall, "Pakistani Military Still Cultivates Militant Groups, a Former Fighter Says," *New York Times*, July 3, 2011, http://www.nytimes.com/2011/07/04/world/asia/04pakistan .html?_r=3&pagewanted=1&hp. For information about the main ISI-sponsored jihadist organizations in Pakistan, see Muhammad Amir Rana, *A to Z of Jehadi Organizations in Pakistan* (Lahore: Mashal Books, 2006), 328–42 (Lashkar, a Wahhabi group), 214–57 (Jaysh and Harkat, Deobandi groups), and 459–68 (Badr, a Mawdudist group); and K. Santhanam Sreedhar and Sudhir Saxena Manish, *Jihadis in Jammu and Kashmir: A Portrait Gallery* (New Delhi: Sage Publications, 2003), 224–30 (Lashkar) and 196–201 (Jaysh).

83   For the ISI's reported complicity in the Mumbai attacks, see Jason Burke, "Pakistan Intelligence Services 'Aided Mumbai Terror Attacks,'" *The Guardian*, October 18, 2010 (based primarily upon Indian interrogations of David Headley, a Lashkar operative and onetime U.S. government informant), http://www.guardian.co.uk/world/2010/oct/18 /pakistan-isi-mumbai-terror-attacks; and the series of reports on Pakistan's terror connections on the Pro Publica website, http://www.propublica.org/topic/mumbai-terror -attacks. However, some Pakistani journalists have instead emphasized the role of rogue ISI operatives or pro-jihadist ex-military officers in the Mumbai (and other) attacks. Cf. Imtiaz Gul, *The Most Dangerous Place: Pakistan's Lawless Frontier* (New York: Penguin Books, 2011), 169–74; and Syed Saleem Shahzad, *Inside Al-Qaeda and the Taliban: Beyond Bin Laden and 9/11* (London: Pluto Press, 2011), 68–69, 94–98 (former army majors Harun Ashiq and Abdul Rahman, then collaborating with Brigade 313 and Lashkar). For the location of Osama bin Laden's hideout, the material found therein, and its problematic implications, see Adam Entous, Julian E. Barnes, and Matthew Rosenberg, "Signs Point to Pakistan Link," *Wall Street Journal*, May 4, 2011, http://online.wsj.com/article /SB10001424052748704322804576303553679080310.html; and Carlotta Gall, Pir Zubair Shah, and Eric Schmitt, "Cellphone Offers Clues to Bin Laden's Pakistani Links," *New York Times*, June 23, 2011 (discusses bin Laden's links to the Harkat ul-Mujahidin).

84   See, e.g., Ryan Clarke, *Lashkar-i-Taiba: The Fallacy of Subservient Proxies and the Future of Islamist Terrorism in India* (Carlisle, PA: U.S. Army War College, Strategic Studies Institute, 2010). The most extreme cases of jihadist blowback have involved terrorist attacks directed against the Pakistani military itself.

85   Coll, *Ghost Wars*, 63–68; and Cooley, *Unholy Wars*, 2, 5–7, 10. Perhaps the most reckless example, which President Reagan's national security adviser William Casey instigated in the mid-1980s, was covert American support for terrorist actions carried out inside Soviet Central Asia by some of the CIA's and ISI's Afghan jihadist "allies." Cf. Scott, *Road to 9/11*,

125–27; and Mohammad Yousaf and Mark Adkin, *The Bear Trap: Afghanistan's Untold Story* (London: Leo Cooper, 1992), 25–26, 189.

86 Cf. John Prados, foreword to Ganser, *NATO's Secret Armies*, xiii: "In this age of global concern with terrorism it is especially upsetting to discover that Western Europe and the United States collaborated in creating networks that took up terrorism. In the United States such nations are called 'state sponsors' and are the object of hostility and sanction. Can it be the United States itself, Britain, France, Italy, and others who should be on the list of state sponsors?" Indeed, "what is clear from the examination of state terrorism, mass killings, state repression, and human rights violations is that these actions have been committed by states which are rich and poor, revolutionary and reactionary, expansionist and reclusive, secular and religious, east and west, north and south. In short virtually all types of states have at some time engaged in or promoted behaviors which many neutral observers would characterize as terrorism, either within their own borders or in the wider international system." See Michael Stohl, "The State as Terrorist: Insights and Implications," *Democracy and Security* 2, no. 1 (2006): 5.

87 For these groups, see Amos, *Palestinian Resistance*, 99–110; and Cobban, *Palestine Liberation Organization*, 157–61, 163–64.

88 See, in general, Jeffrey A. Sluka, ed., *Death Squad: The Anthropology of State Terror* (Philadelphia: University of Pennsylvania Press, 1999); and Bruce B. Campbell and Arthur D. Brenner, eds., *Death Squads in Global Perspective: Murder with Deniability* (New York: St. Martin's Press, 2000). There are also several studies of individual death squads. See, e.g., Ignacio González Janzen, *La Triple-A* (Buenos Aires: Contrapunto, 1986), for the Alianza Anticomunista Argentina (AAA, Argentine Anticommunist Alliance); and Melchor Miralles and Ricardo Arques, *Amedo: El estado contra ETA* (Barcelona: Plaza & Janes/Cambio 16, 1989), for the Grupos Antiterroristas de Liberación (GAL, Antiterrorist Liberation Groups) and their precursors in Spain.

89 For more on provocateurs, see Anna Geifman, *Entangled in Terror: The Azef Affair and the Russian Revolution* (Wilmington, DE: Scholarly Resources Books, 2000); and Nurit Schleifman, *Undercover Agents in the Russian Revolutionary Movement: The SR Party, 1902–14* (Basingstoke: St. Antony's/Macmillan, 1988), 113–17 (on provocateurs and terrorism).

90 Gary Marx, "Thoughts on a Neglected Category of Social Movement Participant: The Agent Provocateur and the Informant," *American Journal of Sociology* 80, no. 2 (September 1974): 402–42; and Jean-Paul Brunet, *La police de l'ombre: Indicateurs et provocateurs dans la France contemporaine* (Paris: Seuil, 1990).

91 See, in general, Philip Jenkins, *Images of Terror: What We Can and Can't Know about Terrorism* (New York: Aldine de Gruyter, 2003), chapter 5. Note, however, that nowadays conspiracy theorists of various types claim that virtually every major terrorist incident is a "false flag" operation. Hence one needs to be skeptical of all such claims in the absence of reliable evidence.

92 Gianni Flamini, *Il partito del golpe: Le strategie della tensione e del terrore dal primo centrosinistra organico al sequestro Moro* (Ferrara: Bovolenta, 1981–1985), especially volumes 1–3; Bale, "'Black' Terrorist International," chapters 2–4; Franco Ferraresi, *Threats to Democracy: The Radical Right in Italy after the War* (Princeton, NJ: Princeton University Press, 1996), chapters 4–6; Philip Willan, *Puppetmasters: The Political Use of Terrorism in Italy* (London: Constable, 1991); Vittorio Borraccetti, ed., *Eversione di destra, terrorismo, stragi: I fatti e l'intervento giudiziario* (Milan: Angeli, 1986); and neo-fascist insider Vincenzo Vinciguerra, *Ergastolo per la libertà: Verso la verità sulla strategia della tensione* (Florence: Arnaud, 1989).

93 See Philip Jenkins, "Under Two Flags: Provocation and Deception in European Terrorism," *Terrorism* 11 (1989): 275–89; Gilbert Dupont and Paul Ponsaers, *Les tueurs: Six années d'enquête* (Anvers, Belgium: EPO, 1988); René Haquin, *Des taupes dans l'extrême droite: La Sûreté de l'État et le WNP* (Anvers, Belgium: EPO, n.d.); Walter de Bock et al, *L'Enquête: 20 années de déstabilization en Belgique* (Paris and Brussels: Longue Vue, 1989); and Danny Ilegems, Raf Sauviller, and Jan Willems, *De Bende-Tapes* (Louvain, Belgium: Kritak, 1990).

94 See, respectively, (Brig. Gen.) Frank Kitson, *Gangs and Counter-Gangs* (London: Barrie & Rockliff, 1960), 72–211; Laurent, *L'orchestre noir*, 148–56; and Yoram Peri, *Between Battles and Ballots: Israeli Military in Politics* (Cambridge, UK: Cambridge University Press, 1983), 237–38.

95 Pepe Díaz Herrero et al., "French Connection: El jefe de los terroristas libios es un agente francés," *Cambio 16* 755 (May 19, 1986): 36–39; and Miguel Angel Liso, "París confirma su infiltración en el terrorismo libio," *Cambio 16* 756 (May 26, 1986): 38–39 (incorrect heading). For neo-fascist infiltration of radical leftist groups in Italy, see Flamini, *Partito del golpe*, passim. The most extraordinary examples occurred in connection with a series of neo-fascist infiltrations of anarchist groups and terrorist attacks leading up to the December 1969 Piazza Fontana bombing in Milan. See the detailed recent analysis of Paolo Cucchiarelli, *Il segreto di Piazza Fontana* (Milan: Ponte alle Grazie, 2009). For another possible case, see Jeffrey M. Bale, "The May 1973 Attack on Milan Police Headquarters: Anarchist 'Propaganda of the Deed' or 'False Flag' Provocation?" *Terrorism and Political Violence* 8, no. 1 (Spring 1996): 132–66.

96 See, e.g., Habib Souaïdia, *La sale guerre* (Paris: Gallimard, 2001), especially chapters 5–7; and Mohammed Samraoui, *Chronique des années de sang: Algérie: Comment les services secrets ont manipulé les groupes islamistes* (Paris: Denoël, 2003). The units most often blamed for carrying out terrorist attacks that were attributed to the GIA or for covertly directing GIA terrorist cells were the Département du Renseignement et de la Sécurité (DRS, Intelligence and Security Department) and the Centre de Conduite et de Coordination des Actions de Lutte Anti-Subversive (CCC/ALAS, Center for the Conduct and Coordination of Activities in the Antisubversive Struggle). No one should conclude, however, that most of the horrendous atrocities and massacres attributed to the GIA, an extreme *takfiri* group (i.e., one that labels other, less militant Muslims as "infidels"), were actually false flag operations carried out by state security forces.

97 Hoffman, *Inside Terrorism*, 259–60. See also, respectively, Patrick Seale, *Abu Nidal: A Gun for Hire* (London: Hutchinson, 1992); Yossi Melman, *The Master Terrorist: The Story Behind Abu Nidal* (New York: Adama Books, 1986); Michaël Prazan, *Les fanatiques: Histoire de l'armée rouge japonaise* (Paris: Seuil, 2002), chapters 3–6; William Regis Farrell, *Blood and Rage: The Story of the Japanese Red Army* (Lexington, MA: Lexington Books, 1990); David Yallop, *Tracking the Jackal: The Search for Carlos, the World's Most Wanted Man* (New York: Random House, 1993); and John Follain, *Jackal: The Complete Story of the Legendary Terrorist, Carlos the Jackal* (New York: Arcade Publishing, 1998).

98 See the analysis in Bale, "'Black' Terrorist International," 568–71, in connection with the strategy of tension in Italy.

99 Cf. Lionel Beehner, "America's Useless Terrorism List," *Los Angeles Times*, October 20, 2008; and Daniel L. Byman, "The Changing Nature of State Sponsorship of Terrorism" (Washington, DC: Saban Center Analysis Paper, Brookings Institution, May 2008), http://www.brookings.edu/papers/2008/05_terrorism_byman.aspx. I do not share Beehner's view, however, that the focus should be on the "socioeconomic causes of why terrorism takes root in the first place," since the historical record has not substantiated any of the

structural theories about the so-called root causes of terrorism. There are no root causes that compel states or insurgent groups to adopt particular asymmetric military techniques—e.g., terrorism—anymore than there are root causes that force states to adopt particular conventional operational techniques, such as blitzkrieg tactics.

100 Cf., e.g., Robert Kaplan, *The Coming Anarchy: Shattering the Dreams of the Post Cold War* (New York: Vintage, 2001); Mark Juergensmeyer, *Global Rebellion: Religious Challenges to the Secular State, from Christian Militias to al Qaeda* (Berkeley: University of California Press, 2008); and Carolyn Nordstrom, *Global Outlaws: Crime, Money, and Power in the Contemporary World* (Berkeley: University of California Press, 2007).

Chapter 2. Missing Their Mark: The IRA's Proxy Bomb Campaign

1 "International Association for the Study of Anglo-Irish Literature Bibliography Bulletin," *Irish University Review* (1970).

2 Benedict Kiely, *Proxopera: A Tale of Modern Ireland* (Boston: David R. Godine Publishing, 1987).

3 Robert A. Pape, *Bombing to Win: Air Power and Coercion in War* (Ithaca, NY: Cornell University Press, 1996).

4 "Alternative Theories into the Bombing of Pan Am Flight 103," http://www.martinfrost.ws/htmlfiles/locherbie2.html.

5 Christopher Wain, "Lessons from Lockerbie," *BBC News*, December 21, 1998.

6 Britta Sandberg and Bernhard Zand, "Using the Disabled for Jihad," *Der Spiegel* (International Edition), February 19, 2008.

7 Marc Sageman, interviewed by Mia Bloom, October 2006.

8 Sandberg and Zand, "Using the Disabled for Jihad."

9 J. Bowyer Bell, *IRA Tactics and Targets* (Dublin: Poolbeg, 1990), 28.

10 Sean O'Callaghan, *The Informer* (New York: Bantam, 1998), 308.

11 Oliver MacDonagh, *States of Mind: A Study of Anglo-Irish Conflict, 1780–1980* (London: Allen & Unwin, 1983), chapter 5; and M. L. R. Smith, *Fighting for Ireland?* (London: Routledge, 1995), chapter 2.

12 Eamon Collins, *Killing Rage*, with Mick McGovern (London: Granta, 1997), 210.

13 Ibid., 37.

14 David McKittrick, "IRA's New Tactic Breaches Security Forces' Defences," *The Independent*, October 25, 1990.

15 J. Bowyer Bell, *The Gun in Politics: An Analysis of Irish Political Conflict, 1916–1986* (New Brunswick, NJ: Transaction Books, 1987), 160.

16 Quoted in Mike Davis, *Buda's Wagon: A Brief History of the Car Bomb* (New York: Verso, 2007), 56.

17 John Horgan and Max Taylor, "The Provisional IRA: Command and Functional Structure," *Terrorism and Political Violence* 9, no. 3 (1997): 1–32. As Horgan and Taylor describe, Twomey would also be responsible for the internal restructuring of the IRA in the late 1970s, resulting in the famed cellular structure that came to characterize IRA operations throughout the remainder of its existence.

18 O'Callaghan, *The Informer*, 66.

19 Bell, *IRA Tactics and Targets*, 40.

20 Ed Moloney, *A Secret History of the IRA* (New York: Norton, 2002), 116.

21 Ibid., 116.

22 Ibid.

23 Collins, *Killing Rage*, 8.

24 O'Callaghan, *The Informer*, 102.

25 Collins, *Killing Rage*, 107, 110.

26 O'Callaghan, *The Informer*, 237.

27 Collins, *Killing Rage*, 230.

28 Ibid., 225.

29 Bloom interview of Marc Sageman.

30 Donatella Della Porta, *Social Movements, Political Violence, and the State: A Comparative Analysis of Italy and Germany* (Cambridge, UK: Cambridge University Press, 1995), 109, passim.

31 Tony Geraghty, *The Irish War: The Hidden Conflict between the IRA and British Intelligence* (Baltimore: Johns Hopkins University Press, 2002), 211.

32 John Cooney and Ian Bruce, "IRA Hardliner Takes Control," *The Herald* (Glasgow), February 20, 1996.

33 Associated Press, "IRA Threatens Reprisals against Civilians Working for British Army," October 26, 1990.

34 Tim Pat Coogan, *The Troubles: Ireland's Ordeal and the Search for Peace* (New York: Palgrave Macmillan, 2002), 248.

35 Associated Press, "Police Identify 'Human Bomb' Victim; Irish-British Talks Founder," October 26, 1990.

36 "IRA Threatens Reprisals," 1990.

37 Associated Press, "Police Identify 'Human Bomb' Victim."

38 Jamie Dettmer and Edward Gorman, "Seven Dead in IRA 'Human Bomb' Attacks," *The Times* (London), October 25, 1990.

39 Jamie Dettmer, "IRA 'Held Rehearsals of Checkpoint Bombings,'" *The Times* (London), October 26, 1990.

40 IRA members, interviewed by John Horgan, October 2006–March 2007.

41 Ibid.

42 Collins, *Killing Rage*, 155–56.

43 David Hearst, "Radio Bombs Jolt Ulster Security," *The Guardian* (London), October 27, 1990.

44 "Crown Forces under Severe Pressure," *An Phoblacht*, December 6, 1990.

45 Horgan interviews of IRA members.

46 "IRA Threatens Reprisals." McEvoy's family told the press that they were cutting all contact with security forces after that day. "No service will be provided for troops or police at the service station."

47 Deric Henderson and John von Radowitz, "IRA Bombs Kill Six Soldiers, but Third Attack Fails," Press Association, October 24, 1990.

48 Kevin Cullen, "Faded Passion as Irish Recall Bobby Sands," *Boston Globe*, May 5, 1991; and Horgan interviews of IRA members.

49 Steven Prokesch, "Peace Hopes Dim in Londonderry," *New York Times*, November 4, 1990.

50 Cited in Chris Parkin, John von Radowitz, and Mark Thomas, "Six Face Charges at Anti-Terrorist Court," Press Association, October 25, 1990.

51 Dettmer and Gorman, "Seven Dead in IRA 'Human Bomb' Attacks."

52 McKittrick, "IRA's New Tactic."

53 Glenn Frankel, "IRA Car Bombs Kill 6 British Soldiers, 1 Civilian in Northern Ireland," *Washington Post,* October 25, 1990.

54 Horgan interviews of IRA members.

55 O'Callaghan, *The Informer*, 110–11.

56 James Dalrymple and Liam Clarke, "'Satanic' IRA Men Denounced by Bishop," *The Sunday Times*, October 28, 1990.

57 Prokesch, "Peace Hopes Dim."

58 "IRA Blast 'Shows Empty Words,'" *The Times* (London), February 5, 1991.

59 Owen Bowcott, "Land Where the Watchtower Is a Common Sight: The Everyday Inconvenience of Surveillance in Ulster," *The Guardian* (London), February 9, 1991.

60 Horgan interviews of IRA members.

61 Owen Bowcott, "Driver Escapes Proxy Bombing," *The Guardian* (London), February 5, 1991.

62 Geoff Garvey, "My Gunpoint Ride with Bomb; London Minicab Man Tells of IRA Hijack," *Evening Standard* (London), June 16, 1992.

63 Kieran Cooke and Ralph Atkins, "Station Bombings: Hardliners Steer IRA Back to Attacking Soft Targets." *Financial Times* (London), February 19,1991.

64 O'Callaghan, *The Informer*.

65 "The Battle against the Bombers," *Economist*, November 21, 1992, 67.

66 Cooke and Atkins, "Station Bombings."

67 Parkin, von Radowitz, and Thomas, "Six Face Charges."

68 "High Court Rejects Claim on Right to Silence Offences against the State Act 1939, Ruled Valid under Constitution," *Irish Times*, June 30, 1994.

69 Horgan interviews of IRA members.

70 Moloney, *A Secret History of the IRA*, 389.

71 Henry McDonald, "UK Agents 'Did Have Role in IRA Bomb Atrocities,'" *The Observer,* September 10, 2006.

72 Andrew Kydd and Barbara F. Walter, "Sabotaging the Peace: The Politics of Extremist Violence," *International Organization* 56, no. 2 (April 2002): 263–96.

73 Prokesch, "Peace Hopes Dim," 15.

74 "The Torpor of Terror," *The Guardian,* October 26, 1990.

75 Kieran Cooke and Ralph Atkins, "Extra Troops Sent to Ulster amid Fears of Terrorist Upsurge," *Financial Times* (London), December 1, 1990.

76 Severin Carrell and John O'Farrell, "A Message for Gerry Adams," *The Scotsman*, February 22, 1998.

77 James W. Spain, *Holy Ireland* (Bloomington, IN: Xlibris Corporation, 2001), 154.

78 Stephen Alderman, "Baker Announces Whitehall Security Review," Press Association, February 7, 1991.

79 Donna Carton, "Provos' Most Evil Bomb Hits Streets of Colombia," *Sunday Mirror*, February 9, 2003.

80 Jim Cusack, "Taliban Using IRA Bomb Techniques in Terror War," *Irish Independent*, March 6, 2007.

81 Ibid.

82 U.S. Army source, in interview, Fort Leavenworth, KS, 2006.

83 Bloom interview of Marc Sageman.

84 Member of the British Army, interviewed by John Horgan, 2007.

85 Sandberg and Zand, "Using the Disabled for Jihad."

86 McKittrick, "IRA's New Tactic."

87 Cooney and Bruce, "IRA Hardliner Takes Control."

Chapter 3. Fighting with a Double-Edged Sword?
Proxy Militias in Iraq, Afghanistan, Bosnia, and Chechnya

1 See, for example, Antonio Giustozzi's chapter in this volume, as well as his book, *Koran, Kalashnikov, and Laptop: The Neo-Taliban Insurgency in Afghanistan* (New York; Columbia University Press, 2008), 105, 166–67, 170, and 180.

2 "Al-Qa'eda in Iraq Alienated by Cucumber Laws and Brutality," *Telegraph* (UK), August 11, 2008.

3 Karl Vick, "Insurgent Alliance Is Fraying in Fallujah; Locals, Fearing Invasion, Turn against Foreign Arabs," *Washington Post*, October 13, 2004. For more on the inherent tensions between foreign jihadists with macro-fundamentalist agendas and local fighters, see Brian Glyn Williams, "The Failure of al Qaeda Basing Projects from Afghanistan to Iraq," in *Denial of Sanctuary: Understanding Terrorist Safe Havens*, ed. Michael Innes (London: Praeger, 2007).

4 Greg Bruno, "The Role of the 'Sons of Iraq' in Improving Security," *Council on Foreign Relations,* April 25, 2008.

5 "Iraqi Neighbours Rise Up against Al-Qa'eda," *Telegraph* (UK), April 14, 2008.

6 "With U.S. Backing, Abu Risha Rose from Young Clan Leader to Head of Sunni Fight against Al Qaida," *International Herald Tribune,* September 13, 2007.

7 "Ware: Woodward's Iraq Claims off the Mark," CNN.com, September 9, 2001.

8 Shi'a elements in the government in fact have been linked to Shi'a death squads.

9 Shaun Waterman, "Costs of War: Conceptual Confusion," *International Relations and Security Network ISN Security Watch*, September 16, 2008.

10 See, for example, Hoda Abdel-Hamid, "Diyala 'Awakening Council' Shuts Down in Protest," Al Jazeera English, February 9, 2008, http://www.youtube.com/watch?v=7dA3U6C6e7E&NR=1.

11 Richard A. Oppel Jr., "Iraq Takes Aim at U.S.-Tied Sunni Groups' Leaders," *New York Times*, August 21, 2008.

12 Ibid.

13 Hoda Jasim and Rahma al Salem, "The Awakening Council: Iraq's Anti-al-Qaeda Sunni Militias," *Asharq Alawsat*, December 12, 2007.

14 Erica Goode, "Friction Infiltrates Sunni Patrols on Safer Iraqi Streets," *New York Times*, September 22, 2008.

15 "Securing Baghdad with Militiamen," BBC News, August 27, 2008.

16 Mark Kukis, "Turning Iraq's Tribes against Al-Qaeda," *Time*, December 26, 2006.

17 "The Awakening: Protectors or Predators?" *New York Times*, August 22, 2008.

18 "On Safer Streets of Baghdad, Friction Infiltrates Patrols by Awakening Groups," *New York Times*, September 23, 2008.

19 Bruno, "The Role of the 'Sons of Iraq' in Improving Security."

20 Barnett Rubin, *The Fragmentation of Afghanistan: State Formation and Collapse in the International System* (New Haven, CT: Yale University Press, 1992), 240–42. The Pashtuns played a role similar to that of the dominant Sunnis in Iraq prior to the U.S. invasion. Pashtuns make up roughly 40 percent of Afghanistan's population, followed by Tajiks, 25 percent; Hazaras, 10 percent; and Uzbeks 9 percent.

21 Angelo Rasanayagam, *Afghanistan: A Modern History* (London: I. B. Tauris, 2005), 100; and Antonio Giustozzi and Noor Ullah, "'Tribes' and Warlords in Southern Afghanistan, 1980–2005," Working Paper no. 7, series 2 (London: Crisis States Research Centre, September 2006).

22 Rubin, *The Fragmentation of Afghanistan*, 159.

23 For more on Dostum see Brian Glyn Williams, "Report from the Field. General Dostum and the Mazar i Sharif Campaign: New Light on the Role of Northern Alliance Warlords in Operation Enduring Freedom," *Small Wars and Insurgencies* 21, no. 4 (December 2010), 610–32; and Brian Glyn Williams, *Afghanistan Declassified. A Guide to America's Longest War* (Philadelphia: University of Pennsylvania Press, 2012).

24 For more on the Pashtun repression of Uzbeks, Turkmen, and Hazaras, see John Lee, *The "Ancient Supremacy": Bukhara, Afghanistan & the Battle for Balkh, 1731–1901* (Leiden, the Netherlands: E. J. Brill, 1997).

25 For a tour of Dostum's peaceful realm in the early 1990s, see the BBC's "Dostum the Kingmaker: Afghanistan." Video is available at http://www.youtube.com/watch?v=xkHdrZ4C1TM.

26 General Dostum, interviewed by Brian Glyn Williams, Mazar-i-Sharif, Afghanistan, August 2003.

27 Steven Galster and Jochen Hippler, "Report from Afghanistan," *Middle East Report* 158 (May–June 1989): 40.

28 Gilles Dorronsoro, *Revolution Unending: Afghanistan, 1979 to the Present*, trans. John King (New York: Columbia University, 2005), 213.

29 For more on Dostum, see Brian Glyn Williams, "Writing the Dostumname: Field Research with an Uzbek Warlord in Afghan Turkistan," *Central Eurasian Studies Review* 6, no. 1/2 (Fall 2007), http://www.brianglynwilliams.com.

30 Much of the security of the Communist period continued under Dostum. Women still attended university, Islamic fundamentalist laws were not enforced as they were in mujahidin-controlled areas, and trade with Central Asia made Mazar-i-Sharif prosperous.

31 Dostum, the whiskey-drinking secularist, returned to Afghanistan in April 2001 and subsequently served as a proxy fighter during Operation Enduring Freedom. His horse-mounted fighters fought the Taliban with close air support and helped the U.S. forces take Mazar-i-Sharif.

32 Raymond Bonner, "Bosnian Splinter Group Is Exiled and Unwanted," *New York Times*, August 22, 1995.

33 Murad Al-shishani, "Persuading the Uncertain and Punishing the Recalcitrant: Al-Qaeda Seeks to Absorb Iraq's Awakening Councils," *Terrorism Monitor* 6, no. 21 (November 7, 2008).

34 Khassan Baiev, *The Oath: A Surgeon Under Fire*, with Ruth Daniloff and Nicholas Daniloff (New York: Walker Company, 2003), 213.

35 For an introduction to the Russo-Chechen War, see Brian Glyn Williams, "The Russo-Chechen War: A Threat to Security in Eurasia," *Middle East Policy* 8, no. 1 (March 2001), http://www.brianglynwilliams.com.

36 Anna Politkovskaya, "Anna Politkovskaya's Final Article: Punitive Agreement," *Interlocals.net*, http://therearenosunglasses.wordpress.com/2010/10/14/anna-politkovskayas-last-article/.

37 "The Chechen Republic: Consequences of 'Chechenization' of the Conflict," *Demos Center Joint Report*, http://www.memo.ru/eng/memhrc/texts/6chechen.shtml.

38 "Batal'on 'Vostok' iz Chechni Neset Poteri v Iuzhnoi Osetii," *Kavkaz Uzel*.

39 See, for example, "Pakistan Claims Victory after Battle for Key Taliban and al-Qaeda Stronghold," *The Scotsman*, October 26, 2008.

40 Shaun Waterman, "Costs of War: No to Tribal Militias," *International Relations and Security Network ISN Security Watch*, January 6, 2009.

Chapter 4. Auxiliary Irregular Forces in Afghanistan: 1978–2008

1 Antonio Giustozzi, *War, Politics and Society in Afghanistan, 1978–1992* (London: Hurst, 2000), 198.

2 See ibid.

3 Ibid., 205.

4 Ibid.

5 Personal communications with former police officers, Kabul, 2007–2008; personal communication with former minister of interior S. M. Gulabzoi, Kabul, May 2008; and personal communications with former government officials, Kabul, 2007–2008.

6 Giustozzi, *War, Politics and Society*. On artificial retribalization through patronage, see also Antonio Giustozzi and Noor Ullah, "'Tribes' and Warlords in Southern Afghanistan, 1980–2005," Working Paper no. 7, series 2 (London: Crisis States Research Centre, 2006); Antonio Giustozzi, *Empires of Mud* (London: Hurst, 2009).

7 Giustozzi, *War, Politics and Society*, 198.

8 Former secretary of the Fifty-Third Division, Afghan Army, interviewed by Antonio Giustozzi, London, November 2005.

9 Personal communications with former Taliban commanders and officials, Afghanistan, 2007–2008; personal communications with former mujahidin commanders who cooperated with the Taliban, Kabul, 2007; Niamatullah Ibrahimi, *Divide and Rule: State*

Penetration in jat (Afghanistan) from the Monarchy to the Taliban, Working Paper no. 42 (London: Crisis States Research Centre, 2009).

10 Gary Berntsen and Ralph Pezzullo, *Jawbreaker: The Attack on Bin Laden and Al Qaeda: A Personal Account by the CIA's Key Field Commander* (New York: Three Rivers Press, 2005), 133–34.

11 Ibid.; Henry A. Crumpton, "Intelligence and War: Afghanistan 2001–2002," in *Transforming U.S. Intelligence*, ed. Jennifer Sims and Burton Gerber (Washington, DC: Georgetown University Press, 2005); and Gary C. Schroen, *First In: How Seven CIA Officers Opened the War on Terror in Afghanistan* (New York: Ballantine Books, 2007).

12 Amy Belasco, "Troop Levels in the Afghan and Iraq Wars, FY2001-FY2012: Cost and Other Potential Issues" (Washington, DC: Congressional Research Service, 2009).

13 For a map of militias under the control of the Ministry of Defense and their factional affiliation, see Antonio Giustozzi, "Bureaucratic Façade and Political Realities of Disarmament and Demobilisation in Afghanistan," *Conflict, Security & Development* 8, no. 2 (2008): 169–92.

14 Tim Whewell, "Afghan Warlords Threaten Stability," BBC News, December 1, 2002; Pepe Escobar, "The Roving Eye: Taking a Spin in Tora Bora," *Asia Times Online*, December 7, 2001; Anthony Loyd, "Fear, Vendetta and Treachery: How We Let Bin Laden Get Away," *The Times* (London), December 3, 2002; and personal communication with former militia commanders in Nangarhar, Afghanistan, February 2007.

15 John F. Burns, "A Nation Challenged: Warlords; Fighting Erupts in Afghan City as Warlords Compete for Power," *New York Times*, January 31, 2002; Sultan Aziz Zahid, "Khost in Turmoil," *Afghan Recovery Report* (Institute for War & Peace Reporting), August 2, 2002; and personal communication with UN officials, Kabul, April 2003.

16 Personal communication with UN officials in Kabul, April 2003 and May 2007, and in Khost, October 2008.

17 Martine van Bijlert, "Unruly Commanders and Violent Power Struggles: Taliban Networks in Uruzgan," in *Decoding the New Taliban: Insights from the Afghan Field*, ed. Antonio Giustozzi (London: Hurst, 2009); personal communications with Martine van Bijlert, Kabul, 2007–2008; personal communication with Dutch officials, 2007; and personal communication with Afghan member of parliament from Uruzgan, Kabul, May 2007.

18 Van Bijlert, "Unruly Commanders"; Antonio Giustozzi, *Koran, Kalashnikov, and Laptop: The Neo-Taliban Insurgency in Afghanistan* (London: Hurst, 2008), 56; and personal communications with former members of Hizb-i Islami, Jalalabad, Afghanistan, February 2007.

19 Personal communications with UN official, Kabul, May 2008; and personal communication with Tom Coghlan, Kabul, October 2008.

20 Van Bijlert, 'Unruly Commanders"; personal communication with Coghlan; David Axe, "Afghan Militias Taking On the Taliban," Military.com, June 28, 2007; and David Axe, "Dutch Forces Crush Taliban Offensive," *Aviation Week*, August 20, 2007.

21 S. D. Naylor, "The Waiting Game: A Stronger Taliban Lies Low, Hoping the U.S. Will Leave Afghanistan," *Armed Forces Journal*, February 2006, http://www.armedforcesjournal.com /2006/02/1404902.

22 It is common in Afghanistan to hear complaints about the losses that ANA troops suffered while traveling in pickup trucks and "protecting" U.S. troops traveling in armored vehicles. Personal communications with Afghan notables, Gardez, October 2006; and Susanne Koelbl, "Saving Afghanistan," *Der Spiegel*, September 29, 2006.

23   James D. Campbell, *"Making Riflemen from Mud": Restoring the Army's Culture of Irregular Warfare* (Carlisle, PA: Center for Strategic Leadership, July 2007), 19.

24   Ibid.

25   See Combined Forces Command Afghanistan, "Afghan Security Forces Demobilize, Join ANA, ANP," *Afghan Freedom Watch*, January 23, 2006, 12–13, http://www.cfc-a.centcom.mil/Freedom%20Watch/2006/01-January/Jan%2023.pdf.

26   Darin J. Blatt et al., "Tribal Engagement in Afghanistan," *Special Warfare* 22, no. 1 (January–February 2009); and Sgt. Charles Brice, "Afghan Security Guards Receive Specialized Training," U.S. Army, January 9, 2009, http://www.army.mil/article/15636/Afghan_Security_Guards_receive_specialized_training/.

27   David Kilcullen, *The Accidental Guerrilla: Fighting Small Wars in the Midst of a Big One* (London: Hurst, 2009); and Mohammed Osman Tariq, *Tribal Security System (Arbakai) in Southeast Afghanistan*, Occasional Paper no. 7 (London: Crisis States Research Centre, December 2008).

28   Ann Scott Tyson, "Military Weighs Recruiting Afghan Tribes to Fight Taliban," *Washington Post*, December 4, 2007.

29   See, for example, Dan Green, "Saving Afghanistan: Why the Iraq Strategy Isn't the Answer," *Armed Forces Journal*, November 2008.

30   Personal communication with ISAF official, London, February 2009.

31   Kilcullen, *The Accidental Guerrilla*.

32   Jon Boone, "Top US General Warns on Afghan Defence Plan," *Financial Times*, January 3, 2008.

33   Personal communication with ISAF official; Kathy Gannon, "US Plan to Arm Militias Scares Some in Afghanistan," *Associated Press*, February 4, 2009; and Agence France-Presse, "Afghanistan, US Consider 'Community' Security Forces," December 30, 2008.

34   Jessica Leeder, "Kabul Wants Local Militias to Bolster Security," *Globe and Mail*, October 31, 2008.

35   Ibid.

Chapter 5. Surrogate Agents: Private Military and Security Operators in an Unstable World

1   This chapter is based, in part, on a study conducted for the Canadian government exploring policy and strategy issues relating to the use of PMSCs in contemporary peace-support operations and other military activities in which a set of more than fifty case studies on specific PMSCs, countries, and thematic issues concerning PMSCs was developed. These case studies will not be quoted verbatim here but will be used as the basis for much of the empirical discussions of PMSC activities. As such, sources will be noted for specific aspects where relevant; otherwise, further information on the case studies is available from the author.

2   Examples are the disintegration of Westphalian notions of state sovereignty and its Weberian notions, and the effects that it has had on security and war, the general trend toward globalization and privatization current today internationally, the failures of the international community to respond to each and every massive humanitarian crisis effectively, and so on.

3   The wider policy, strategy, and thematic issues touched on here can be found in the author's writing on PMSCs, for example: "What Future, Privatized Military and Security Activities? The Need for Pragmatic Engagement," *Royal United Services Institute (RUSI) Journal* 152, no. 2 (April 2007), 54–60; "What Should and What Should Not Be Regulated?" in *From Mercenaries to Market: The Rise and Regulation of Private Military Companies*, ed. Simon Chesterman and Chia Lehnardt (Oxford, UK: Oxford University Press, 2007); "Private Military Companies in Africa, 1990–1998," in *Mercenaries: An African Security Dilemma*, ed. Abdel-Fatau Musah and Kayode Fayemi (Sterling, VA: Pluto Books, 1999); Kevin A. O'Brien, "PMCs, Myths and Mercenaries: The Debate on Private Military Companies," *RUSI Journal* 145, no. 1 (February 2000), http://www.globalpolicy.org/nations/sovereign/military /02debate.htm; and "Military Advisory Groups and African Security: Privatised Peacekeeping?" *International Peacekeeping* 5, no. 3 (Autumn 1998), 78–105.

4   Martin van Creveld, *The Transformation of War* (New York: Free Press, 1991), 39–40; Ralph Peters, "The New Warrior Class," *Parameters,* Summer 1994, 16–26; and Steven Metz, *Rethinking Insurgency* (US Army War College, Strategic Studies Institute, June 2007), http://www.strategicstudiesinstitute.army.mil/pdffiles/pub790.pdf.

5   Van Creveld, *Transformation of War*, 194–95.

6   For a good study of mercenaries historically and up to the period of interest for this study, see Anthony Mockler, *Mercenaries* (London: MacDonald, 1969), and its update *The New Mercenaries* (New York: Paragon House, 1987).

7   Sam Roggeveen discusses this point in "The Case for the Mercenary Army," *Australian Defence Force Journal* 126 (September/October 1997): 50–53.

8   Ibid., 50–51.

9   Ibid.

10   Peters, "The New Warrior Class."

11   Agence France-Presse, "French Covert Actions in Zaire on Behalf of Mobutu," May 2, 1997; United Nations Department of Humanitarian Affairs, Integrated Regional Information Network (UNDHA-IRIN), *IRIN Emergency Update No. 74 on the Great Lakes*, January 8, 1997, http://www.reliefweb.net; Robert Block, "Mobutu Calls Up the Dogs of War," *Sunday Times*, January 5, 1997, 18; John Swain, "War-Hungry Serbs Join Mobutu's Army," *Sunday Times*, March 9, 1997, 16; and SAPA-AP, "Fighting Intensifies; Militia Accuses Mercenaries of Joining," June 30, 1997.

12   Christopher Goodwin, "Mexican Drug Barons Sign Up Renegades from Green Berets," *Sunday Times*, August 24, 1997, 14.

13   For a brief study of this occurrence, see Anthony Davis, "Foreign Combatants in Afghanistan," *Jane's Intelligence Review* 5, no. 7 (July 1993): 327–31.

14   See, for example, "Foreign Special Operations: Mujahedin Intensify Operations in Bosnia," *Special Warfare: The Professional Bulletin of the John F. Kennedy Special Warfare Center and School* 8, no. 3 (July 1995). Also see Enrique Bernales Ballesteros, *The Right of Peoples to Self-Determination and Its Application to Peoples under Colonial or Alien Domination or Foreign Occupation: Report on the Question of the Use of Mercenaries as a Means of Violating Human Rights and Impeding the Exercise of the Right of Peoples to Self-Determination* (Geneva: United Nations Commission on Human Rights, January 1996), s16, sIV; and the same report from 1994, 1995, and 1997.

15   "Foreign Special Operations: Mujahedin Intensify Operations in Bosnia," *Special Warfare.*

16   Tom Walker, "US Alarmed as Mujahidin Join Kosovo Rebels," *The Times* (London), November 26, 1998.

17   UNDHA-IRIN, *IRIN Emergency Update No. 74.*

18   Bernales, *The Right of Peoples to Self-Determination,* sA22.

19   James Cockayne, *Commercial Security in Humanitarian and Post-Conflict Settings: An Exploratory Study* (New York: International Peace Academy, 2006), http://www.ipacademy.org/pdfs/COMMERCIAL_SECURITY_FINAL.pdf. Mancini even includes management consultancies, which are involved increasingly in (particularly) security advisory and management services within SSR missions, in his delineation of actors. See Francesco Mancini, *In Good Company? The Role of Business in Security Sector Reform* (London: Demos, 2005), 41, http://www.demos.co.uk/files/Goodcompanyweb.pdf.

20   See O'Brien, "PMCs, Myths and Mercenaries."

21   See Ministry of Defence, Security Sector Development Advisory Team, http://www.mod.uk /DefenceInternet/AboutDefence/WhatWeDo/SecurityandIntelligence/SSDAT/.

22   See U.S. Department of Justice, International Criminal Investigative Training Assistance Program, http://www.usdoj.gov/criminal/icitap/ generally. According to Charles Call, ICITAP serves as "the principal US agency involved in filling the 'institutional gap', restructuring of the entire law enforcement apparatus of countries in transition," which ICITAP views as "the ticket to quick military withdrawal following interventions or peace-support operations." In practice the vast majority of ICITAP's advisers are contracted, drawn heavily from retired American policing, law enforcement, and military backgrounds. ICITAP contractors interact with UN police monitors (UNCIVPOL) and contingent-contributions in peace-support operations and related activities in areas such as Panama, Rwanda, Bosnia, Kazakhstan, Kyrgyzstan, Belarus, Ukraine, Uzbekistan, and the Croatian province of Eastern Slavonia, with new projects set for Brazil, Albania, Belize, and Liberia (as of 2000). See Charles T. Call, "Institutional Learning within ICITAP," in *Policing the New World Disorder: Peace Operations and Public Security*, ed. Robert B. Oakley, Michael J. Dziedzic, and Eliot M. Goldberg (Washington, DC: National Defense University Press, 1998), http://carnegie.org/fileadmin/Media/Publications/PDF/Policing%20the %20New%20World%20Disorder.pdf.

23   Most Western militaries today will state frankly that they would be unable to deploy and conduct operations without the extremely significant levels of support received from private actors, including security and military personnel. The services these militaries provide range from feeding and housing through mechanical and technical to logistical and transport support and even into static and mobile protective security services for military commanders. The flip side to this picture is the Iraq conflict. The Coalition commanders (particularly U.S. commanders) have stated that the Multinational Force-Iraq (MNF-I) is able to concentrate on security and military activities only because of the presence of tens of thousands of PMSC personnel, who are focused on providing security to the reconstruction efforts, including training the Iraqi military and police forces. Without their support, the MNF-I would become overstretched and distracted and unable to carry out its primary mission.

24   Interviews of government (particularly foreign affairs and defense) officials in the United Kingdom, United States, and Canada between 1998 and 2008 made this distinction clear.

25   The UK Diplock Report, written in reaction to the arrest of British nationals tried (and executed in some cases) as mercenaries in Angola in 1975, notes this problem clearly: "Mercenaries, we think, can only be defined by reference to what they do, and not by

reference to why they do it." See Christopher Kinsey, "Challenging International Law: A Dilemma of Private Security Companies," *Conflict Security and Development* 5, no. 3 (December 2005): 281.

26 This "conclusion" remains largely based on anecdote and assumption rather than on hard facts explicitly. Although this analysis does conclude that given the quantitative increase in the roles played by PMSCs in peace-support operations (writ large) as noted throughout, PMSCs are becoming more involved in peacekeeping today, many analysts of the trend note the paucity of hard, verifiable facts to support this conclusion. See Abby Stoddard, Adele Harmer, and Katherine Haver, *Providing Aid in Insecure Environments: Trends in Policy and Operations*, ODI Humanitarian Policy Group Report 23 (London: Overseas Development Group, September 2006), section 5.2.5, http://www.cic.nyu.edu/internationalsecurity /docs/hpgreport23.pdf; Cockayne, *Commercial Security in Humanitarian and Post-Conflict Settings*; and Mancini, *In Good Company?*

27 Lt. Col. Stephen M. Blizzard, "Increasing Reliance on Contractors on the Battlefield: How Do We Keep from Crossing the Line?" *Air Force Journal of Logistics* 28, no. 1 (Spring 2004), http://www.aflma.hq.af.mil/shared/media/document/AFD-100120-044.pdf.

28 See Department of State and the Broadcasting Board of Governors, Office of Inspector General, "Review of U.S. Support to the International Police Task Force in Bosnia (AUD/PPA-02-20)," *Monthly Report of Activities*, March 2002, 3, http://oig.state.gov/documents/organization /10572.pdf. In January 2007, the special inspector general for Iraq reconstruction, Stuart W. Bowen Jr., reported that "he had identified tens of millions of dollars worth of accounting discrepancies, missing weapons and unauthorized billings" by DynCorp, and he accused DynCorp of "lax accounting and monitoring procedures." See Tod Robberson, "DynCorp Faulted for Iraq Spending: Inspector Cites Millions in Discrepancies; Firm Defends Actions," *Dallas Morning News*, January 30, 2007, http://schakowsky.house.gov/index.php?option=com _content&task=view&id=1665&Itemid=17; and Peter H. Stone, "Law, PR Firms Help Contractors Navigate Reconstruction Inquiries," *National Journal*, March 8, 2007, as quoted in *Government Executive*, http://www.govexec.com/story_page.cfm?articleid=36312&sid=21.

29 See Martina E. Vandenberg, "Testimony on Trafficking of Women and Girls to Bosnia and Herzegovina for Forced Prostitution" (Testimony to House Committee on International Relations, Subcommittee on International Operations and Human Rights), Human Rights Watch, April 23, 2002, http://commdocs.house.gov/committees/intlrel/hfa78948.000/hfa78948_0f.htm.

30 See Andrew Rathmell et al., *Developing Iraq's Security Sector: The Coalition Provisional Authority's Experience* (Santa Monica, CA: Rand, 2005), http://www.rand.org/pubs /monographs/2005/RAND_MG365.pdf.

31 MPRI was tasked with developing Afghanistan's national defense, including the development of an action plan that outlined a new national defense strategy and structure: the creation of a national defense planning system; the formation or reorganization of a Ministry of Defense and General Staff; the establishment of management systems with emphasis on personnel, logistics, acquisition, operational command and control, and resource management and budgeting systems; and the formation and training of a national army, including a border security element, and a national air force. See MPRI, "Afghanistan Ministry of Defense Development Program," http://mpri.com/site/int_swasia.html.

32 See Joint Contracting Command–Iraq/Afghanistan, *A User's Guide to Getting Started in Iraq*, http://www.rebuilding-iraq.net/pls/portal/docs/page/pco_content /logistics/shippers_information/a_users_guide.pdf (accessed June 1, 2006).

33   An interview with one British PMSC indicated that it was possible only because of the similar national cultures and backgrounds. Had British PMSCs been operating with American (or perhaps even Canadian) statutory forces, or vice versa, the same informal cooperation may not have developed.

34   See the recent study on this point: Stoddard, Harmer, and Haver, *Providing Aid in Insecure Environments*.

35   Cockayne, *Commercial Security in Humanitarian and Post-Conflict Settings*, 2.

36   Renae Merle, "Embassy Security Firms Chosen: State Department Awards Contracts to Cover High-Risk Offices in 27 Nations," *Washington Post*, June 17, 2005, http://www .washingtonpost.com/wp-dyn/content/article/2005/06/16/AR2005061601675.html.

37   A number of significant papers have commented on this issue, including James Cockayne, *Commercial Security in the Humanitarian Space* (New York: Ralph Bunche Institute, 2006), http://web.gc.cuny.edu/RalphBuncheInstitute/IUCSHA/fellows/Cockayne-paper-final.pdf; and Office for the Coordination of Humanitarian Affairs (OCHA), "Use of Military or Armed Escorts for Humanitarian Convoys: Discussion Paper and Non-Binding Guidelines," September 14, 2001, http://www.who.int/hac/network/interagency /GuidelinesonArmedEscorts_Sept2001.pdf.

38   This sector included Eagle Base, Forward Operating Base (FOB) McGovern, FOB Morgan, FOB Conner, and Hilltop 1326: "US Military Facilities, European Command, Bosnia," GlobalSecurity.org, http://www.globalsecurity.org/military/facility/bosnia.htm. ITT may not have lived up to the terms of the contract. See David Glovin, "ITT Accused in Whistleblower Suit of 'Ghost-Posting' in Bosnia," *Bloomberg*, January 18, 2007, http://www.bloomberg.com /apps/news?pid=newsarchive&sid=aC_T4LKEvhNs&refer=home.

39   One of the best analyses of this process can be found in Andrew Rathmell, "Planning Post-Conflict Reconstruction in Iraq: What Can We Learn?" *International Affairs* 81, no. 5 (2005), 1013–38; and the reprint is available at http://www.rand.org/pubs/reprints/2006/RAND_RP1197.pdf.

40   Human Rights Watch, "Nigeria," in *World Report 2002*, http://www.hrw.org/wr2k2 /africa8.html. An outline of the MPRI contract can be found at http://www.iwatchnews.org /2002/10/28/5678/privatizing-combat-new-world-order.

41   "World Security Services Market," ASIS Security News and Information, http://www.asisonline.org/stat10.html (no longer online).

42   Ian Traynor, "The Privatisation of War," *The Guardian*, December 10, 2003, http://www.guardian.co.uk/international/story/0,3604,1103566,00.html.

43   U.S. Government Accountability Office, *Rebuilding Iraq: Actions Needed to Improve Use of Private Security Providers*, GAO-05-737 (Washington, DC: GAO, July 2005), http://www.gao.gov/new.items/d05737.pdf.

44   GAO, *Rebuilding Iraq: Actions Still Needed to Improve the Use of Private Security Providers*, GAO -06-865T (Washington, DC: GAO, June 2006), http://www.gao.gov/new.items/d06865t.pdf.

45   It should be noted that this figure does not include an additional estimated sixty thousand private security personnel employed as *in-house security* businesses in South Africa. See Jenny Irish, "The South African Private Security Industry," *Policing for Profit: The Future of South Africa's Private Security Industry*, Monograph no. 39 (Pretoria, South Africa: Institute for Security Studies, August 1999), http://www.iss.co.za/Pubs/Monographs/No39/SAPrivSecIndustry.html.

46   Christopher Stone, *Crime, Justice, and Growth in South Africa: Toward a Plausible Contribution from Criminal Justice to Economic Growth*, Center for International Development, Working

Paper no. 131 (Cambridge, MA: Harvard University August 2006), http://www.cid.harvard
.edu/cidwp/pdf/131.pdf; "Report: More than R100m Spent to Guard Cops," *Mail &*
Guardian Online, March 10, 2007, http://mg.co.za/article/2007-03-10-report-more-than
-r100m-spent-to-guard-cops; and Gun Free South Africa, "Oral Submission on the
Firearms Control Amendment Bill [812-2006]," August 16, 2006, http://www.saga.org.za
/GFSA%2016Aug06.htm.

Chapter 6. Multinational Corporations: Potential Proxies for Counterinsurgency?

1   See, for example, Jennifer Morrison Taw, *Interagency Coordination in Military Operations*
    Other than War: Implications for the U.S. Army, MR-825-A (Santa Monica, CA: Rand, 1997);
    James Dobbins et al., *The Beginner's Guide to Nation-Building*, MG-557-SRF (Santa Monica,
    CA: Rand, 2007); David Shearer, *Private Armies and Military Intervention*, Adelphi Papers
    (Oxford, UK: Oxford University Press for the International Institute for Strategic Studies,
    1998); and P. W. Singer, *Corporate Warriors: The Rise of the Privatized Military Industry*
    (Ithaca, NY: Cornell University Press, 2003).

2   See, for example, Mark Duffield, *Global Governance and the New Wars: The Merging of*
    Development and Security (London: Zed Books, 2001), 62–64.

3   U.S. Army and U.S. Marine Corps, *The U.S. Army/U.S. Marine Corps Counterinsurgency Field*
    Manual (Chicago: University of Chicago Press, 2007), 65.

4   For more on what he terms "stateocentrism," see Phil Williams, *From the New Middle Ages to*
    a New Dark Age: The Decline of the State and U.S. Strategy (Carlisle, PA: Strategic Studies
    Institute, U.S. Army War College, June 2008), 4.

5   For a discussion of provision of security by non-state actors in Africa, see Bruce Baker,
    "Protection from Crime: What Is on Offer for Africans?" *Journal of Contemporary African*
    Studies 22, no. 2 (2005): 371–90; and Comfort Ero, "Vigilantes, Civil Defence Forces and
    Militia Groups: The Other Side of the Privatisation of Security in Africa," *Conflict Trends* 1
    (2000): 25–29.

6   Dianna Rienstra, "Assessing the Corporate Sector's Role in Conflict Prevention," in *Conflict*
    Prevention from Rhetoric to Reality, vol. 2, *Opportunities and Innovations*, ed. David Carment
    and Albrecht Schnabel (Lanham, MD: Lexington Books, 2004), 359.

7   Andreas Wenger and Daniel Möckli, *Conflict Prevention: The Untapped Potential of the*
    Business Sector (Boulder, CO: Lynne Rienner, 2003), 129.

8   Aidan Davy, "Companies in Conflict Situations: A Role for Tri-Sector Partnerships,"
    Working Paper 9 (London: Business Partners for Development, Natural Resources Cluster,
    March 2001), 1.

9   Virginia Haufler, "Is There a Role for Business in Conflict Management?" in *Turbulent Peace:*
    The Challenges of Managing International Conflict, ed. Chester A. Crocker, Fen Osler Hampson,
    and Pamela Aall (Washington, DC: United States Institute of Peace Press, 2001), 662.

10 It should be noted that given the significant size of some local workforces, sanctuary often
    benefits large numbers of people other than company employees.

11 Luc Zandvliet, *Opportunities for Synergy: Conflict Transformation and the Corporate Agenda*
    (Berlin: Berghof Research Center for Constructive Conflict Management, February 2005),
    10, http://www.berghof-handbook.net/uploads/download/zandvliet_handbook.pdf.

12　Jenny Pearce, "Beyond the Perimeter Fence: Oil and Armed Conflict in Casanare, Colombia" (London: Centre for the Study of Global Governance, London School of Economics, June 2004), http://www.lse.ac.uk/Depts/global/Publications/DiscussionPapers/DP32_Beyondthe PerimeterFence.pdf; and Luc Zandvliet and David Reyes, "Corporate Engagement Project: Looking at the Principles behind the Practices: BP Operations in Casanare Department, Colombia: Field Visit Colombia: March 1–19, 2004" (Cambridge, MA: Collaborative for Development Action, May 2004), http://www.cdainc.com/publications/cep/fieldvisits /cepVisit10BPCasanare.pdf. BP also took a prominent role in creating a "House of Justice," which brought together under one roof several human rights, social service, and public safety organizations and, in so doing, significantly improved public access to these services.

13　Jonathan Berman, "Boardrooms and Bombs: Strategies of Multinational Corporations in Conflict Areas," *Harvard International Review*, Fall 2000, 31.

14　Zandvliet, *Opportunities for Synergy.*

15　See, for example, David Cortright, ed., *The Price of Peace: Incentives and International Conflict Prevention* (Lanham, MD: Rowman & Littlefield, 1997); and Michael Brown and Richard Rosecrance, "Comparing Costs of Prevention and Costs of Conflict: Toward a New Methodology," in *The Costs of Conflict: Prevention and Cure in the Global Arena*, ed. Michael Brown and Richard Rosecrance (New York: Rowman & Littlefield, 1999).

16　Philip Swanson, "Fuelling Conflict: The Oil Industry and Armed Conflict," Report 378 (Oslo: Fafo, Programme for International Co-operation and Conflict Resolution, March 2002), 27.

17　Mary Anderson and Luc Zandvliet, "Corporate Options for Breaking Cycles of Conflict" (Cambridge, MA: Collaborative for Development Action, May 2001), http://info.worldbank.org/etools/docs/library/57445/CorporateOptionsArticle.pdf.

18　Zandvliet, *Opportunities for Synergy*, 12; and Corporate Engagement Project, "Working in a Changing World: A New Approach to Risk Mitigation in Zones of Conflict" (Cambridge, MA: Collaboration for Development Action, n.d.), 3.

19　See, for example, Andrew Bolger, "Lloyd's to Offer War Cover," *Financial Times*, May 27, 2001.

20　Zandvliet, *Opportunities for Synergy*, 4.

21　International Peace Academy, "Private Sector Actors in Zones of Conflict: Research Challenges and Policy Responses," *IPA Workshop Report*, September 12, 2001, http://www.ipacademy.org /publication/meeting-notes/detail/204-private-sector-actors-in-zones-of-conflict-research -challenges-and-policy-responses.html. In 2004, for example, Unocal agreed to an out-of-court settlement with the victims of human rights abuses that Burmese soldiers committed while guarding a pipeline in which the oil company held a significant stake. For more on this particular point, see Daphne Evitar, "A Big Win for Human Rights," *The Nation*, April 21, 2005, http://www.thenation.com/article/big-win-human-rights; and "Burmese Win Appeal in U.S. Alien Tort Case against Unocal," *Human Constitutional Rights*, October 15, 2002, and updated August 2007, http://www.hrcr.org/hottopics/burmese.html.

22　Kenneth Omeje, "Petrobusiness and Security Threats in the Niger Delta, Nigeria," *Current Sociology* 54 (2006): 479.

23　Organization of Petroleum Exporting Countries (OPEC), *Annual Statistical Bulletin: 2007* (Vienna, Austria: OPEC, 2008), 21; CNN, "Rebels Attack Nigerian Oil Pipeline," July 28, 2008, http://www.cnn.com/2008/WORLD/africa/07/28/nigeria.attack/index.html; Alex Morrison, "Africa and the Global War on Terrorism," testimony before the House International Relations Committee Subcommittee on Africa, November 15, 2001, http://www.yale.edu/lawweb/avalon/sept_11/morrison-001.htm, as of February 15, 2008, 7;

Jean Herskovits, "Nigeria's Rigged Democracy," Foreign Affairs, July–August 2007, 128; Tamara Makarenko, "Terrorist Threat to Energy Infrastructure Increases," *Jane's Intelligence Review*, June 2003, 8–13; and Clive Schofield, "Bakassi Dispute Could Derail West African Peace Processes," *Jane's Intelligence Review*, March 2004, 48.

24 Anonymous sources, in interviews with author, Abuja, Nigeria, September 2008.

25 The Delta region covers some 7.5 percent of Nigeria's landmass.

26 For literary ease, throughout this chapter Shell Nigeria will be referred to as simply Shell.

27 Technically, Shell is the operator of (and 30 percent shareholder in) a joint venture, the Nigerian National Petroleum Corporation, which holds a 55 percent share of the operation, with Elf Petroleum Nigeria and Agip holding 10 and 5 percent stakes, respectively. Twelve percent of all U.S. oil imports are from Nigeria. U.S. Department of State, "Nigeria at a Crossroads: Elections, Legitimacy and a Way Forward," June 7, 2007, http://www.state.gov/p/af/rls/rm/86195.htm (accessed July 29, 2008).

28 Shell Nigeria, *People and the Environment: Shell Nigeria Annual Report 2006* (London: Shell Visual Media Services, 2007), http://narcosphere.narconews.com/userfiles/70/2006 _shell_nigeria_report.pdf (accessed May 2, 2008).

29 David Dafinone, "Roadmap to Peace in Niger Delta," *Insider Weekly* (Lagos), February 18, 2008, 49.

30 Michael Watts, "The Sinister Political Life of Community: Economies of Violence and Governable Spaces in the Niger Delta, Nigeria," Niger Delta Economies of Violence Working Paper no. 3 (Berkeley: Institute of International Studies, University of California, 2004), 13.

31 Phil Carter, director, African Affairs, West Africa, U.S. Department of State, "Remarks on U.S. and International Cooperation in the Niger River Delta," Center for Strategic and International Studies, Washington, DC, March 14, 2007, http://nigeria.usembassy.gov /uploads/images/y48-2DWUQ9ieHn4fi-Svgw/Phil_CSIS_speech_on_Niger_Deltab.pdf (accessed July 30, 2008).

32 Amnesty International, "Nigeria: Ten Years On: Injustice and Violence Haunt the Oil Delta," November 3, 2005, http://www.amnesty.org/en/library/info/AFR44/022/2005.

33 Dimieari Von Kemedi, "Fuelling the Violence: Non-State Armed Actors (Militia, Cults, and Gangs) in the Niger Delta," Niger Delta Economies of Violence Working Paper no. 10 (Berkeley: Institute of International Studies, University of California, 2006),2.

34 Dafinone, "Roadmap to Peace"; and Dorina Bekoe, "Strategies for Peace in the Niger Delta," USI Peace Briefing, December 2005, http://www.usip.org/publications/strategies-peace-niger-delta.

35 Amnesty International, "Nigeria: Ten Years On"; and Isaiah A. Litvak, "Royal Dutch Shell in Nigeria: Operating in a Fragile State," case 906M21 (London, Ontario: Richard Ivey School of Business, University of Western Ontario, 2006), 14.

36 Okechukwu Ibeanu, "Oiling the Friction: Environmental Conflict Management in the Niger Delta, Nigeria," *Environmental Change & Security Project Report* 6 (Summer 2000): 29.

37 Charles Ukeje, "Youths, Violence and the Collapse of Public Order in the Niger Delta of Nigeria," *Africa Development* 26, nos. 1–2 (2001): 346.

38 Anonymous sources, in interviews with author, Abuja, Nigeria, September 2008; Amnesty International, "Nigeria: Ten Years On"; and Minorities at Risk, "Chronology for Ijaw in Nigeria," Center for International Development and Conflict Management, College Park, MD, http://www.cidcm.umd.edu/mar/chronology.asp?groupId=47506.

39 Anonymous sources, in interviews with author, Abuja, Nigeria, September 2008. See also Von Kemedi, "Fuelling the Violence," 2; and Michael Watts, "The Rule of Oil: Petro-Politics and the Anatomy of an Insurgency," paper delivered before the Oil and Politics Conference, Goldsmiths College, University of London, May 10–11, 2007.

40 Anonymous sources, in interviews with author, Abuja, Nigeria, September 2008. For representative positions in the "greed versus grievance" debate, see Paul Collier and Anke Hoeffler, "Greed and Grievance in Civil Wars," *Oxford Economic Papers* 56, no. 4 (2004): 563–95; and Stathis N. Kalyvas, "'New' and 'Old' Civil Wars: A Valid Distinction?" *World Politics* 54, no. 1 (October 2001): 99–118.

41 Kelvin Ebiri, "MEND Attacks Shell's Oil Pipelines in Rivers," *The Guardian* (Lagos), 22 (April 2008).

42 Watts, "The Sinister Political Life of Community," 6.

43 Clara Nwachukwu, "N'Delta Crises: N120m Lost to Pirates in 106 Attacks," *The Punch* (Lagos), April 14, 2008.

44 Agence France-Presse, "Nigeria: Shell Reports 169,000 Barrel per Day Output Loss in Nigeria," April 22, 2008; and Watts, "The Rule of Oil."

45 U.S. Department of State, Bureau of Democracy, Human Rights, and Labor, *Country Reports on Human Rights Practices: Nigeria, 2007*, March 11, 2008, http://www.state.gov/g/drl/rls/hrrpt/2007/100498.htm.

46 Anonymous sources, in interviews with author, Abuja, Nigeria, September 2008.

47 Human Rights Watch, *Politics as War: The Human Rights Impact and Causes of Post-Election Violence in Rivers State, Nigeria* (New York: Human Rights Watch, March 2008), 11.

48 Matthew Skinner, "Delta Blues: Nigeria's Freelance Oil Militants," *Jane's Intelligence Review* 1 (March 2008), online edition, http://jir.janes.com. It should be noted that such communal self-help measures are hardly unique in the African context, given the general absence of state capacity and thus the enduring need to find other sources of security. For more on this point, see Bruce Baker, "Nonstate Providers of Everyday Security in African States," in *Fragile States and Insecure People? Violence, Security, and Statehood in the Twenty-First Century*, ed. Louise Andersen, Bjørn Møller, and Finn Stepputat (London: Palgrave Macmillan, 2007), 123–47.

49 The Niger Delta Development Corporation was established in 2006 with a budget of $15 million and currently has a tenure to 2014. Its primary purpose is to manage community development, livelihood, sustainable natural resource extraction, and small-scale infrastructure provision. Anonymous sources, in interviews with author, Abuja, Nigeria, September 2008.

50 Ukeje, "Youths, Violence, and the Collapse of Public Order," 353–54.

51 Quoted in Jad Mouawad, "Growing Unrest Posing a Threat to Nigerian Oil," *New York Times*, April 21, 2007, 1.

52 Litvak, "Royal Dutch Shell in Nigeria," 14.

53 Anna Zalik, "The Niger Delta: 'Petro Violence' and 'Partnership Development,'" *Review of African Political Economy* 31, 101 (2004): 408.

54 For many delta residents, this mobile force is virtually indistinguishable from Shell and is colloquially referred to as the Shell Police. See "Africa: Whose Energy Future?" *AfricaFocus*, October 3, 2005.

55 Ike Okonta and Oronto Douglas, *Where Vultures Feast: Shell, Human Rights, and Oil in the Niger Delta* (San Francisco: Sierra Club Books, 2001), 59.

56 Litvak, "Royal Dutch Shell in Nigeria," 5.

57 Okonta and Douglas, *Where Vultures Feast*, 45.

58 Litvak, "Royal Dutch Shell in Nigeria," 13.

59 WAC Global Services, "Peace and Security in the Niger Delta: Conflict Expert Group Baseline Report," Working paper, December 2003, http://www.npr.org/documents/2005/aug/shell_wac_report.pdf.

60 Omeje, "Petrobusiness and Security Threats," 493.

61 *Shell Nigeria Annual Report 2006*.

62 Shell, *Sustainability Report 2010*, 19, http://sustainabilityreport.shell.com/2010/servicepages/welcome.html.

63 Ibid. Shell insists that this force strictly adheres to company security guidelines, which reflect international norms, including the United Nations' Code of Conduct for Law Enforcement Officials.

64 Bronwen Manby, "The Price of Oil: Corporate Responsibility and Human Rights Violations in Nigeria's Oil Producing Communities" (New York: Human Rights Watch, January 1999), http://www.hrw.org/reports/1999/nigeria/.

65 Steve Inskeep, "Deadly Oil Skirmish Scars Nigerian Town," National Public Radio, August 25, 2005, http://www.npr.org/templates/story/story.php?storyId=4797925.

66 It is acknowledged that even if the conflict had abated, it would be difficult to attribute this development to any single factor, much less to corporate action alone.

67 Swanson, *Fuelling Conflict*, 20. It should be noted that such violence may actually serve government and corporate interests as it helps to divide groups and communities opposed to state policies. Shell has been the subject of several allegations in this regard, with human rights NGOs claiming that the company has both employed and armed political youth groups for "protection work" at its oil facilities. See, for instance, Ike Okonta, "Behind the Mask: Explaining the Emergence of the MEND Militia in Nigeria's Oil-Bearing Niger Delta," Niger Delta Economies of Violence Working Paper no. 3 (Berkeley: Institute of International Studies, University of California, 2006).

68 In 2003, for instance, interethnic disputes over employment and contracts in the petroleum sector sparked clashes that left thousands of delta residents homeless. See International Crisis Group, *Fuelling the Niger Delta Crisis*, Africa Report no. 118 (Brussels: International Crisis Group, September 28, 2006), 2.

69 Amnesty International, "Nigeria: Ten Years On," 33n125.

70 Quoted in Mouawad, "Growing Unrest," 1.

71 Amnesty International, "Nigeria: Ten Years On," 21.

72 Quoted in "Nigeria: Shell's Critics Unfair, Says Director," *Africa News*, December 24, 2003.

73 Ashley Campbell, "Fuelling Conflict or Financing Peace and Development? Linkages Between MNC Investment, Development and Conflict: A Case Study Analysis of BP Amoco's Social Policies and Practices in Colombia," Country Indicators for Foreign Policy, Carleton University, Ottawa, 2002, http://www.carleton.ca/cifp/app/serve.php/1050.pdf.

74 Albrecht Schnabel, "Insurgencies, Security Governance and the International Community," in *Private Actors and Security Governance*, ed. Alan Bryden and Marina Caparini (Geneva: Geneva Center for the Democratic Control of the Armed Forces, 2006), 68.

75 U.S. Army, Field Manual No. 3-07, *Stability Operations* (Washington, DC: Headquarters, Department of the Army, October 2008).

76 Mary B. Anderson, "Developing Best Practice for Corporate Engagement in Conflict Zones: Lessons Learned from Experience," Internationale Weiterbildung und Entwicklung gGmbH, 2002, updated January 6, 2003, http://www.inwent.org/ef-texte/publicbads /anderson.htm.

77 James N. Rosenau, *Turbulence in World Politics: A Theory of Change and Continuity* (Princeton, NJ: Princeton University Press, 1990), 253.

Index

About the Editor and Contributors

Michael A. Innes is Director of Thesiger & Company (http://www.thesigers .com), an emerging markets research and advisory firm based in London. From 2003 to 2009 he was a civilian staff officer with the North Atlantic Treaty Organization, serving at Supreme Headquarters Allied Powers Europe in Belgium and on operations in Bosnia-Herzegovina, Kosovo, and Afghanistan. In 2006 he was appointed a visiting research fellow in the School of Politics and International Studies, University of Leeds, and in 2007 he was named a research and practice associate of the Institute for National Security and Counterterrorism, Syracuse University. He pursued doctoral research at University College London from 2008 to 2011 and is now a PhD candidate at the School of Oriental and African Studies, University of London. He has published widely in academic and popular outlets and is the editor of two previous books, *Denial of Sanctuary: Understanding Terrorist Safe Havens* (Praeger, 2007) and *Bosnian Security after Dayton: New Perspectives* (Routledge, 2006).

Jeffrey M. Bale is an assistant professor and director of the Monterey Terrorism Research and Education Program at the Monterey Institute for International Studies (MIIS). He also has taught at the University of California at Berkeley, Columbia University, and the University of California at Irvine; was the recipient of postdoctoral fellowships from the Society of Fellows in the Humanities at Columbia, the Office of Scholarly Programs at the Library of Congress, and the Center for German and European Studies at Berkeley; and worked as a senior research associate at the Center for Nonproliferation Studies at MIIS. He has recently published articles in *Patterns of Prejudice*, *Terrorism and Political Violence*, and *Democracy and*

Security. He is currently a member of the editorial advisory board of the journal *Totalitarian Movements and Political Religions* (Routledge) and regularly serves as a consultant for government agencies and private organizations on matters related to terrorism and ideological extremism.

Mia Bloom is an associate professor in International and Women's Studies at the Pennsylvania State University and a fellow at the International Center for the Study of Terrorism. She is the author of *Dying to Kill: The Allure of Suicide Terror* (Columbia University Press, 2005), *Living Together After Ethnic Killing* with Roy Licklider (Routledge, 2007) and *Bombshell: Women and Terrorism* (Penguin and University of Pennsylvania Press, 2011). Bloom is a former member of the Council on Foreign Relations and has held research or teaching appointments at Princeton, Cornell, Harvard, and McGill, with research on ethnic conflicts, political violence, and the mobilization of women and children into terrorist networks. Bloom has a PhD in political science from Columbia University, an MA in Arab studies from Georgetown University, and a BA from McGill University in Russian and Middle East studies. She speaks nine languages.

Peter Chalk is a senior policy analyst with the Rand Corporation in Santa Monica, California. He has worked on a range of projects examining transnational security threats in the Asia-Pacific, Latin America, North America, and sub-Saharan Africa. He is an internationally recognized expert in the field of terrorism, maritime crime, and low-intensity conflict and is author of numerous books, book chapters, and journal articles on these subjects. He has also testified on several occasions before the U.S. Congress and is a regular commentator on mainstream media outlets in the United States, Australia, Canada, and the European Union.

Chalk is an associate editor of *Studies in Conflict Terrorism*—one of the foremost journals in the international security field—and serves as an adjunct professor with the Naval Postgraduate School in Monterey, California, and the Asia Pacific Center for Security Studies in Honolulu, Hawaii. He is also a visiting scholar with the Combating Terrorism Center at the United States Military Academy, West Point, New York, and a specialist correspondent for *Jane's Intelligence Review* and *Oxford Analytica* in London.

Prior to joining Rand, Chalk was an assistant professor of politics at the University of Queensland, Brisbane, and a postdoctoral fellow in the Strategic and Defense Studies Centre of the Australian National University, Canberra.

Apart from his academic posts, Chalk has acted as a research consultant in Britain, Canada, and Australia, and has experience with the UK Armed Forces.

Antonio Giustozzi is an independent researcher associated with IDEAS, a center for the study of international affairs, diplomacy, and grand strategy at the London School of Economics and Political Science. He is the author of several articles and papers on Afghanistan, as well as three books: *War, Politics, and Society in Afghanistan, 1978–1992* (Georgetown University Press, 2000), *Koran, Kalashnikov, and Laptop: the Neo-Taliban Insurgency in Afghanistan 2002–7* (Columbia University Press, 2007), and *Empires of Mud: War and Warlords in Afghanistan* (Columbia University Press, 2007), as well as a volume on the role of coercion and violence in state-building, *The Art of Coercion* (Columbia University Press, 2011). He also edited a volume on the Taliban, *Decoding the New Taliban* (Columbia University Press, 2009), featuring contributions by specialists from different backgrounds. He is currently researching issues of governance in Afghanistan from a wide-ranging perspective, which includes understanding the role of army, police, subnational governance, and intelligence.

John Horgan is director of the International Center for the Study of Terrorism at the Pennsylvania State University, where he is also associate professor of psychology and affiliate professor of international affairs. A leading expert on terrorist psychology, he has published extensively in the area. His books include *The Psychology of Terrorism* (Routledge, 2005), *The Future of Terrorism* (Routledge, 1999, edited with Maxwell Taylor), and *Walking Away from Terrorism: Accounts of Disengagement from Radical and Extremist Movements* (Routledge, 2009). In fall 2012, Oxford University Press will publish his newest book *Divided We Stand: The Strategy and Psychology of Ireland's Dissident Terrorists*. He is a member of the editorial boards of multiple journals, including *Terrorism and Political Violence, Studies in Conflict and Terrorism, Journal of Investigative Psychology and Offender Profiling*, and *Behavioral Science of Terrorism and Political Aggression*. He is associate editor of *Dynamics of Asymmetric Conflict*. Horgan is a member of the Research Advisory Board of the FBI's National Center for the Analysis of Violent Crime. He holds a BA and PhD in applied psychology from University College, Cork.

Kevin A. O'Brien has served as an adviser to Western governments and critical infrastructure sectors on public security matters for more than fifteen years. He has been assessing and commenting on the private military and security industry for most of that period and, among other work, has advised both the UK Foreign Office and the Canadian Department of Foreign Affairs on the question of private military security companies. The author of more than sixty monographs, academic articles, chapters, and trade articles on contemporary security challenges, he serves on the editorial boards of the Taylor and Francis journal *Small Wars and Insurgencies* and the Complex Terrain Laboratory, and has worked previously as a special correspondent for *Jane's Intelligence Review*. His most recent book is *The South African Intelligence Services: From Apartheid to Democracy, 1948–2005* (Routledge, 2011). He has served as the director of Alesia PSI Consultants Ltd., a senior consultant to Innovative Analytics & Training LLC, an associate of the Libra Advisory Group, the deputy director of Rand Europe's Defence and Security Programme, and the deputy director of the International Centre for Security Analysis and fellow in the Department of War Studies, King's College London. He is currently a senior analyst with the government of Canada.

William Rosenau is a senior analyst at CNA Strategic Studies, a federally funded research and development center in Alexandria, Virginia. Before joining CNA, he served in the Rand Corporation's International Security Policy department and as chair of Rand's Insurgency Board; as a policy adviser to the coordinator for counterterrorism, U.S. Department of State; and as a special assistant to the assistant secretary of defense for special operations and low-intensity conflict. He has also been an adjunct professor in the Security Studies Program, Walsh School of Foreign Service, Georgetown University.

His publications include *Acknowledging Limits: Police Advisors and Counterinsurgency in Afghanistan* (Marine Corps University Press, 2011); *US Internal*

Security Assistance to South Vietnam: Insurgency, Subversion, and Public Order (Routledge, 2005); *The Radicalization of Diasporas and Terrorism* (ed., with Doron Zimmermann, Center for Security Studies, ETH Zurich, 2009); *Corporations and Counterinsurgency* (Rand, 2009, with Peter Chalk et al.); *The Evolving Dynamic of Terrorism in Southeast Asia: A Net Assessment* (Rand, 2009, with Peter Chalk and Angel Rabasa); *The Phoenix Program and Contemporary Counterinsurgency* (Rand, 2009, with Austin Long); and *Subversion and Insurgency* (Rand, 2008). His degrees are from Columbia (BA), Cambridge (MA), and King's College London (PhD).

Brian Glyn Williams is a professor of Islamic history at the University of Massachusetts–Dartmouth. He previously taught at the University of London, SOAS. He is author of *Afghanistan Declassified: A Guide to America's Longest War* (University of Pennsylvania Press, 2011). He has considerable fieldwork experience in conflict zones in Eurasia, ranging from Kashmir to Kosovo, and has visited Afghanistan regularly since the overthrow of the Taliban. In Afghanistan his experiences have included living with the warlord General Dostum and working at a NATO base. For his publications, CV, and photos from his fieldwork see his interactive website at http://brianglynwilliams.com.